THE
BISHOP MAKER

WHEN THE BATTLE IS FOR THE SUBCONSCIOUS

A novel by

RHETT STUART

Missage Media

Montpelier, Virginia

THE BISHOP MAKER
By Rhett Stuart

www.bishopmaker.com

Published by
  Missage Media
  P.O. Box 303
  Montpelier, VA 23192
  missagemedia@gmail.com

  ISBN: 978-0-9829547-0-6
  Library of Congress Control Number: 2010935252

Bible passages quoted are from the King James, New King James by Thomas Nelson Inc, or paraphrased. Used by permission.
All rights reserved.

Front Cover design by StudiOh! Copyright © 2010
Back Cover design by Rhett Stuart Copyright © 2010
Printed in the United States of America

Contents

This book was written so my children will know what happened was for their best in the long run.

Many prayers went into the writing of this story, so any praise for anything found of value should go to the Lord.

And, the first being last, to my beloved wife, who has made my life so much more enjoyable.

Foreword

This is the true story of a father's struggle within a close knit, relationship based Christian group whose Assemblies are spread across the USA. The story starts just before the eighty year old fundamental Bible-based group suffers a sudden hostile takeover, as mind control techniques are deployed by a long standing minister who just retired from his mysterious job at a government weapons development center.

It is the most disturbing time of Rhett's life as the group fragments and lifelong relationships are destroyed, but he receives unexpected rewards in his allegiance to Christ. Most of the names are changed, and some conversations and circumstances are consolidated.

Truth is indeed stranger than fiction.

A Bachelor of Science degree in Management and Organizational Behavior from Cal Poly, California led to a career as a white collar crime investigator. His lifetime part in the fundamental group which refused to take any name, and what caused its' dramatic destruction, moved him to tell of it in hopes others might be helped to avoid being exploited by modern and also ancient techniques of deception, and to offer guidance for those already suffering exploitation.

A Religious Sociopath feels justified as he talks fervently about God and expounds on the Bible. Enjoying opportunities to abusively control and exploit humble followers with intimidation and ridicule, he relishes with masked pleasure and delight the fearful illusion his followers have of him as a powerful leader.

1.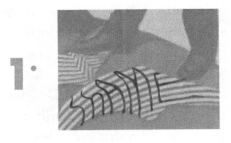

The Devil's Banana Peel

A soft voice deep within Rhett's mind whispered, *Isn't there something a little odd about him? No No! It's wrong to think such a thing! He wants to serve the Lord! He has been a credible minister for twenty-five years, and the Lord is using his highly intelligent mind, vast understanding of the Bible and dynamic speaking ability to minister and counsel us. It is wrong to think evil of a leader like that! Stop it Rhett!*

Rhett's eyes fixated on the large red tie of the tall lean figure in a crisp black suit. Rhythmically articulating his voice and pacing back and forth across the stage at Happy Hill, Deo smoothly moved his hands for emphasis as he intently watched the audience.

It looks like Deo is speaking supernaturally! The mic looks invisible, but I know there's a clear little tube that goes down to his mouth, thought Rhett. He couldn't see Deo's dual flush mounted hearing aids either. Sitting in back with his young children was less distracting to others, and the restroom visits weren't as conspicuous.

Rhett's mind kept wandering as he gazed off to the left side where there were no windows. Deo retired from the Navy a year ago, but nobody knew exactly what Deo's job had been, and Deo couldn't tell anybody, since it was classified. Rhett heard Deo was part of an elite group who conceptualized future military weapons, the current naval smart system for missiles. These lethal and top secret weapon concepts were designed years later, and then built by defense contractors to gain a strategic advantage, such as in the Iraq War.

Rhett discreetly glanced at the time on his cell phone and then looked out the window high up on the right side of the auditorium. It was 12:48 pm on this gorgeous Sunday afternoon late in May, 2005. He sat up straighter to ease the pressure on his low back.

"Okay.... We are nooww on page two of-my-notes," said Deo, now standing behind the podium, "and I have..... four more to-go."

Surely this is another joke to keep up the interest of the audience, thought Rhett.

But it was no joke this time. Rhett and the four hundred or so other people gathered from several local church Assemblies in the heart of Virginia were going to play their part as a captive audience for a bit longer, including about eighty-six children who had been doing their best not to wiggle for the last two hours.

Why do I know so little about Deo? One person said he had an alcoholic father and his mother tried to compensate by being very protective. Must have been rough, growing up playing by himself in that fenced-in back yard, while the neighborhood kids were playing together in the front yards. Kind of unusual I don't know more about him... I know a lot more about almost everybody else here... thought Rhett.

Deo planted himself firmly within the Fredericksburg Virginia Assembly in the mid 1970's. Not one to just watch the corn grow, within a few years he gained the confidence of James Stark. This endorsement from James, the main leader, helped Deo advance in his public speaking and private counseling since 1980 in Virginia.

Deo started ministering on Orderly Following during the next few years, calling it 'Authority, Responsibility and Accountability' at the September retreat in 1985, saying during his lecture, "The only authority we can have is what God gives us. If we have authority, it's because God gave it to us. Does ministry 'just want to have it their way?' No, of course not! We don't feel that way!"

Deo started calling it 'Orderly Following' in 1990.

Rhett watched Deo pacing the stage, "I believe some of you think you'd lose self esteem if you walked in something you can't prove for yourself. I believe that's the Devil's banana peel and the very essence of sectarianism, the things that cause splits for Christian groups. Little innuendos like, 'brothers who can't think for themselves follow ministry and are just mindless man followers'."

Deo's talking about those people who throw dust in the air to conceal their carnal desire for tearing down leadership. I know Deo wants us to read the Bible because he encourages us to take notes of his lectures and go over them later with our Bibles, to make the things the leaders preach our own. Deo just said two months ago all we need is the Bible. We do need to prove all things we believe in the Bible because I have heard that encouraged since my childhood in the California Assemblies, thought Rhett.

Deo continued, "The Devil really encourages things like that, like being independent. It's called P-R-I-D-E. Some men study the Bible for their identity; they say they need to study for themselves. Well, they are just taking glory in their flesh, — and — that — makes — me – SICK! They think ministers walking together are such pansies... I guess! They accuse Orderly Followers of being mindless man followers. 'Show me the chapter and verse!' they say! —That's pride, that's all it is."

Too bad some people feel like they have to sow discord among us like that. It's the young people that suffer from all consequences, thought Rhett, *all those hours and hours spent in meetings to straighten things out again to undo the damage they caused.*

Deo stopped pacing and got behind the podium, "Men who think they have to know and prove things for themselves are just doing it for their own low self esteem."

Deo puffed out his chest and strutted around on stage, "You have to think for yourself!" He continued imitating a proud person strutting around with his chest out. Several in the audience laughed. "That's pride, that's all it is," Deo added with a sideways glance.

Deo puffed his chest out even more as he strutted back and forth, "This is something **I** have to prove for MYSELF!"

A few tittered.

"WOW, is he REALLY something! 'I study for Myself!' — Those are Satan's fiery darts and they are so effective — it – makes - me - sick!"

Rhett's eyes rested on Deo's ever so prominent large red tie again. *How can Deo have such an uncanny ability to foresee what I would naturally object to when he gets to his main point at the end? I don't think I'll make any comments after this one. I don't want to look like a fool, and, I just don't get most of this. Man alive, Deo sure has put a lot of time and energy into this message! Deo really shows how he believes when he speaks, he doesn't just tell us outright,* thought Rhett, *and he helps lead our thoughts to the right conclusions, even when we don't understand.*

Rhett's mind flickered back to the immediate present as Deo said, "We need to be Separate from the World. No other group I know of has the truth we have and are a functioning, viable representation of the Body of Christ."

This was the anthem song of the Assemblies; they were the pillar of Biblical truth in America, and the world, as far as Rhett knew.

As Deo continued lecturing Rhett reflected back a few months ago, on Deo's speech at his retirement party, "The thrust of my time for the future is currently better spent in the preparation of leadership who can take my place and lead you in the future. I won't be able, as available, for personal counseling with many of you. This is not a thing that is not real. It is a very real need. An appropriate need, a need for you to be led, and it's important for you to understand this very clearly that this is something you need and it is appropriate. It is very, very appropriate."

James Stark had publicly commended Deo as the new main leader in Virginia after the retirement party. James had moved to California after his first wife died.

It was Saturday morning when Deo started his first lecture of the weekend, "My messages given this camp are directed towards a select few Bishops with us this morning, to a handful of leaders. These very capable men have the ability to understand what most of you cannot understand. It is fortuitous we have these men with us in this audience. These few intelligent and gifted men will be able to understand what I give and apply it in the future for your benefit and your children's benefit in the years to come. Most of you won't comprehend what I will be speaking on this morning, or this weekend, but you and your children will benefit as what I give instructs and directs your leaders, as they apply what I say this morning and weekend in the years ahead for you, your children and their children. Is that a good thing? Yes, it is a good thing! It is a very, very good thing."

Rhett had thought, *Ah, so it is starting already, Deos' preparing our leaders for the future and its' challenges. I wonder what Deo will unfold, it will sure be interesting to see what messages Deo gives over the next few years. I just can't predict stuff like Deo can.*

Cary Murdock from Richmond was one of those capable leaders. As Cary's daughters got older he proved himself worthy by speaking publicly for several years, faithfully following Deo's standards for the most part. As a self-proclaimed ruling elder everybody knew Deo had the authority to anoint Cary as a Bishop. Some had opposed Deo in the local Richmond leadership meeting, but Deo's words had weight and the grumblers were now silent; Deo's judgment stood. Rhett hoped they would see it more clearly later on; he had helped Deo cut the resisters off. There were always problem makers who gunned on any authority figure. Rhett hoped to become a Bishop himself one day, or maybe a deacon, but for now he needed to focus on raising his young children.

As Deo's message dropped to a mesmerizing low droning in a rhythmatic six part tempo, Rhett let his thoughts drift off again to the activities of the last week; a fun, busy time.

Last Sunday his family had a full day with their Christian friends. The entire local Christian Assembly in Richmond, Virginia had played Ultimate Frisbee© on a deserted school field in Short Pump. An older couple in the Assembly opened their home up for everybody afterwards. Rhett, his wife Sabrina and their four children ended up visiting with everybody else until 11 pm that Sunday night, as usual.

Monday evening was cut short by everybody being tired and heading off to bed early.

Tuesday was a treasured family time of catching up on chores and playing a few games in the evening.

Wednesday was another Richmond Assembly meeting. Rhett and his family stayed late afterwards, visiting with friends. The forty-five minute drive put them home after 11 pm again. *Wish I had more time to be with my family,* contemplated Rhett.

Thursday was a catch up evening with the family, getting packed up for the weekend Christian retreat and trying to catch up on sleep again for the weekend retreat.

On Friday Rhett got home from work, loaded the van, and they ate fast food on the way to the camp retreat. He looked forward to the uplifting spiritual messages, but the florescent lighting all week at work didn't make sitting indoors for several hours during the weekend that appealing. Actually, it was hard to take mentally.

Rhett glanced from the sunlit windows back towards Deo, who was now standing by the podium. The laptop cast a bluish reflection on his face in the dim light as he showed a slide on the Big Screen up front.

God designed us to have natural sunlight, Rhett thought again for the ninth time that morning, *so we won't get as depressed, and standing some would stop my back from aching so much.*

"Any of you done something wrong? I have! All of us have! Sometimes it makes us feel like running around and telling on each other! Ha Ha! Well, what should you do when you do something wrong? When you hear something that bothers you? It helps to talk to somebody about it. Talk to somebody who can help you. There are leaders here who can help you," said Deo.

Rhett gazed around at his many friends sitting near him, most offering placid expressions as their evidence of zoning out. *Deo is right, this is going over their heads. Most of us just don't get it. He ought to know everybody is tired after staying up until 12:30 am the last two nights. But the sunshine sure will be nice on the eyes, visiting at the play-ground with my friends as we watch our kids play and our brains get a break. Deo sure knows how to push the limits of human endurance!*

Far from being mesmerized himself, Rhett was increasingly aware he should have just let the rest of that pitcher of orange juice go to waste after breakfast. Now he was paying the price. His kids would also enjoy a brief jaunt out of the meeting. As Rhett made trip number three to the bathroom with his son, he caught a few whiffs of the lunch drifting out into the hall, and his stomach growled.

Dawson smelled it too, "Dad, I'm hungry."

"Shshshsh, it'll be over soon," whispered Rhett.

Upon returning, he paused in the back with his eight year old son, glad for the chance to stretch out for a few more seconds. His attention was drawn by the silence to Deo, frozen in the front center of the stage, silently gazing downward towards the front rows of the audience.

As Deo sorrowfully shook his head, Rhett and a few hundred other people craned their necks to see what was catching Deo's attention.

I'll bet a young man sitting in one of the front rows dozed off, Rhett thought.

This didn't happen often, and for good reason.

Hopping off the stage, Deo stood right where the chairs began, cordless mic still on, looking intently at the second row where a young man gently snored in a relaxed slumber. Deo continued gazing at him, breathing heavily into the mic, the silent audience watching with anticipated educational entertainment.

The young man awoke with a start after several seconds of just heavy breathing coming from the speakers. After a little nudging from his buddies, he noticed Deo staring at him from a few feet away.

The audience remained hushed behind him.

The young man sat up with a jerk, flushing red.

Deo softly chuckled as he hopped back up, saying, "Now thaat I have ALL of your attention, I'llll continue!"

That's the young man I saw at 12:30 am last night when we were heading off to our tent. He was counseling with an older man about his failing romance with a young girl. Guess it didn't help staying up late talking; now she thinks he's a fool. Why did Deo do that to 'em? Doesn't seem fair somehow, is his message more important than the counsel he got the night before from the older man? No, he was missing out on Deo's message, shouldn't have stayed up so late! But man! These messages sure are drawn out, but we aren't supposed to be getting much from these messages, it's directed towards our leaders, thought Rhett, stifling a yawn as he sat down again by his wife.

Deo's voice rhythmically went on; gradually fading low, a lulling lullaby-ish breeze of soft words, and Rhett's mind kept drifting, eyes drooping. *How could one word mean so much?* reflected Rhett, as Deo varied the topic but kept coming back to that same word - 'Choice'.

Rhett watched one of Sabrina's best friends in the row ahead yawn as she put her arm around her husband. Mark and Rhoda Shifflet's young children had quietly looked at coloring books for the first few hours, but were now staring off toward the high windows on the right side with glazed eyes, their faces offering no hint of expression or critical thought.

Their lack of expression matches most of this audience, thought Rhett looking around him, *these kids would love to be running around outside. Deo will likely end soon, surely he won't go much longer since there is an afternoon AND evening meeting. This is more like an intense adult Bible study camp, not the family camp it's supposed to be! The fear of ridicule is lengthening the attention span of the young people sitting in the front, but does God motivate people that way? I guess so, it says to fear God and so we ought to fear God's human authority here on earth.*

"YOU ALL LISTENING UP?" shouted Deo.

Rhett and Sabrina sat upright immediately, as did most of the audience, all jolted in unison.

Deo whispered, "You need to listen close - listen carefully, listen very carefully to what I am saying."

A few babies cried out. The parents tried to hush them before hurrying out with embarrassed smiles, clamping a hand in a futile effort to muffle their infant's reckless screams of disapproval.

Deo stopped pacing and faced the audience, "You can be moved, - AND changed, - AND corrected by input from ministry, — — OR — — you can be independent! — The CHOICE is yours! Let ministry be a controlling influence with you! Make the RIGHT choice!"

Rhett's brother-in-law Jarvo thought Deo sounded angry when he yelled liked that, but Rhett knew Deo was just trying to keep up the attention of the audience so they could be helped in their Christian life. The preacher's new surge protector made it a little easier on the eardrums now, and protected the amplifier against Deo's dynamic speaking range.

The meeting finally ended with no comments afterwards.

Sabrina asked Rhett if he had any breath mints left as they woke up their youngest and packed Bibles and kid's books into their large orange bag. While waiting for a chance to merge with the crowd towards the auditorium backdoors, George Taylor, one of the three leaders in the Richmond Assembly, strolled by with his arm around his wife. He caught Rhett's eye and smiled, then with a knowing nod, "Isn't Deo giving some great messages?! That's a lot of meat to digest! I'm getting the recordings to see what I missed the first time!!"

"Uhh, he, uh, certainly had some interesting points there!" But, turning with most of the crowd heading towards the cafeteria, Rhett thought, *It was so drawn out and repetitive, the three hours could have been condensed into about forty-five minutes. Maybe I just missed the point. I must not be smart enough to figure out all the stuff Deo is getting at, just like he said at the beginning.*

A top salesman for a moving company, George Taylor assisted high ranking corporate executives and politicians with their moving needs. Possessing solid genuineness and a winning smile reminiscent of Franklin Roosevelt, he radiated good will and solidity, every bit as good a citizen as an astronaut, as he walked and talked. George's wife was helpful in bringing him back to earth. Like a few months ago when she decided to bake a loaf of bread for the wife of a vice president. After asking George to deliver it on one of his trips, she confided with Sabrina: "I tried a new bread recipe and it got a little overcooked. I hope they like it, I've never tried it before myself!"

On their way out, Sabrina whispered, "I need to talk to her," indicating a friend nearby.

Stopping to wait, Rhett noticed his brother-in-law Jarvo was already deeply in conversation with Cary Murdock, the newly appointed Bishop from the Richmond Assembly. Rhett was glad Jarvo was talking to Cary, a serious man, serious about scripture. Although quite intelligent like his father who was the head of the science department at a local university, Cary chose to be a small construction company owner. He took no pay as their minister in Richmond, spending his personal time in study and counseling. When Cary was a teenager he was teased on the football field because of his seriousness about the Bible. They called him 'Consecrated Cary'. Cary still liked playing football with the young guys in spite of being in his mid forties; he was still in good shape. Rhett liked Cary because he thought for himself, coming at things from a different angle, and was fair with people. *Cary's not a Groupthinker, he might help Jarvo,* thought Rhett.

"Howz your father, — Rhett?" asked Deo, passing along with the cafeteria bound crowd oozing out of the isles, his smile revealing the gap between his front teeth as he added, "Enjoying his retirement??"

Momentarily distracted by Deo's thick eyebrows looming and quivering over his dark rimmed eyeglasses, Rhett wondered if they really were quizzically forming their own opinions about him.

"He's doing fine!!" said Rhett, smiling and nodding.

There was really nothing else to say, since Rhett had answered the question, so Deo, with his arm around his wife, just smiled back and kept walking, moving along with a respectable distance between them and the rest of the hungry multitude. Rhett didn't know why Deo always asked him that. Besides, he rarely talked to his father, so there was not much to tell.

2·

Jarvo

He disarmed people with his casual personality, which was the main ingredient for his own successful plumbing business.

Descending from a long line of Virginia aristocrats, Jarvis Alexander Madison V also laid claim to being a descendent of Pocahontas, the famous Indian girl of early American history. Years ago Jarvo spoke of it when he and Laura were courting, as they approached a museum exhibit featuring Pocahontas. The display read, "Many people erroneously claim to be descended from Pocahontas..." Jarvo took the kidding good-naturedly, but the issue never was entirely cleared up.

While Rhett waited for his wife as she chatted with an old friend about home schooling problems, he stifled the hunger pains, watching from a short distance as Cary Murdock earnestly tried to deter Jarvo from the reckless path he seemed so bent on following.

It was disturbing that Jarvo was not at peace with their Christian Assembly fellowship.

He isn't reading his Bible enough, Rhett thought in self-denial of where Jarvo was heading.

Please, Lord, help Cary to help Jarvo, Rhett silently prayed, *so Jarvo won't leave our fellowship which is honoring to you, where Your truth is spoken, so Jarvo won't need to be marked for avoidance by the leaders for causing division in your Body.*

Rhett thought, *I sure would hate to lose fellowship with Jarvo if he gets marked. I won't be able to talk with him anymore, maybe for my lifetime!*

"Everybody seems so hungry after that long meeting," said Sabrina, as they held hands and worked their way through the packed dining hall, "where do you want to sit?" Sabrina hated to pick which group of people to sit with.

"Let's sit — over there," said Rhett, with a glance towards Michie and Rae Hobkins, then after leaning down and hoisting his daughter up out of the crowd, "Our kids'll enjoy visiting with their kids."

Rhett really enjoyed visiting with Michie. It was on his "list of things to look forward to" when they had moved to Virginia in 2000.

After chatting a few minutes with Rhett, Michie leaned forward, and after a quick glance both ways, said, "I feel like wearing a shirt that says 'HERETIC!' on it!!"

"Why?" asked Rhett, with a now puckered forehead, "I don't think Deo was directly his message towards you!?"

Michie's lip curled into something between a smirk and a sneer, and, still leaning forward, said, "I think Deo's ENTIRE message on heretics was DIRECTED at ME."

Sabrina abruptly left the table, scared and uncomfortable.

Rae stayed, rolling her eyes with a nervous laugh.

"Deo is just trying to keep us ALL on the right path in serving the Lord!" Rhett said, "He is warning us if we do not make the right Choice then we will become Heretics, because we know the truth and are responsible for it. It is black and white; we are on one side or the other. How hard is that to understand?!"

Sabrina came back to the table. Fortunately their conversation was drifting into a debate on acceptable types of facial hair for men.

"We need to have Unity so the World will see our light shining for Christ and then believe," Rhett reasoned with Michie, "God looks in our heart, but the World looks at our outward appearance. It is so important to have our outward appearance be a testimony and not reflecting fashionable beards."

Michie replied, "Come on, Rhett. Beards are against the leader's rules!"

"We don't have rules here," said Rhett, "just the leader's application of Biblical principles."

Michie rubbed his chin, and then with a thoughtful expression, eyes upturned, "Hmmm, I feel like growing a beard."

Rhett looked at him sharply. It was hard to tell when Michie was joking. Michie ignored him and took a bite of his French Dip sandwich. Rhett decided to try his sandwich out too, *Hey, this is good! Mark Shifflett has outdone himself again in the cafeteria.*

Mark planned all their meals for the retreats, glad to do it for free and help out where he could. After spending a day before the retreat scheduling the food deliveries, Mark still strayed into the kitchen several times a day during the retreat to give the volunteer cooks direction when needed.

Driving home that Sunday night from the weekend retreat, Rhett and Sabrina fell into a discussion, so typical of them after leaving a busy weekend retreat. This time it was about their children.

"I felt sorry for Julia. She was sitting up front with some girls her age and couldn't get up much," said Rhett, "that is a loonng time for a ten year old young girl to endure sitting through all those many hours of meetings." He thought back on the weekend, *Too bad those spiritually challenged parents with poorly trained kids have to stand out in the hall during the long meetings. Our bathroom trips give us a little stretch. Maybe we ought to hang out in the hallway more. Nah, our kids can take it. Besides, it shows we have it together more, sitting through the meetings. We aren't fringe people.*

When Rhett or Sabrina took the kids out with them it made it difficult for other people to tell exactly who had to go to the bathroom. Ministers frowned upon excessive bathroom use for adults during the long messages, but it was understandable kids would need to get up once during a meeting, maybe twice. Three times? That was pushing it! Rhett could still sit inside with everybody else, the status quo, but still be able to get outside the meeting hall for a few short stretch breaks.

Sabrina said, "I didn't get anything out of this weekend! It was exhausting, and it was exhausting for all my friends. Everybody complained about it, even the women who rarely complain. We all sat for hours. I felt like it was a waste of time for the women, all the young kids and all those poor teenagers. The only thing I got from it is we need to make the right choice to allow ministers being a controlling influence, and we need to be separate from the World. I already knew that!"

"It had to be pretty bad for you to be complaining about it."

"There were a lot of women complaining that hardly ever complain!"

"Well", said Rhett, hesitantly, "I didn't get much out of it either; there was a lot of repetition about a few thoughts. I think Deo is just trying to cover all the angles for everybody. I hope the next camp retreat is more family oriented. I feel sorry for Hank! He flew all the way from California to hopefully get to know Karla during the camp weekend, instead he spent the weekend sitting through long meetings."

I'll write Deo a letter, thought Rhett, *since Matthew 18 says if you have a problem with somebody you need to go to him first to try and resolve it, then bring one or two others for witnesses, then to the Church. If he doesn't respond after all that, then treat him as a sinner.*

Matthew 18 was preached heavily by Deo.

Rhett contemplated his critical e-mail, wondering what the fall out would be, *Pleasant words promote instruction, but I need to be honest also.*

Rhett wrote to Deo, in part:

Please consider the women and children during the recent weekend retreat, and those who have traveled from other parts of the country to be there and visit. The camp should be more family oriented, but they seem more like an intense adult Bible study course. What do you think about covering less material, or condensing it? I think you could have condensed the first 30 minutes to 5 minutes.

He thought himself a bit bold to be revealing his true thoughts. He got really brave, and in good conscious to Matthew 18, by adding at the end:

Heresies will come. I want to be on guard on this for others, and also for myself. Solomon set an example of being very wise, but failing when he got older. I have known other men like this. I don't want this to happen to myself. I don't want to see you lifted in pride and fall. Older men dedicated to serving the saints are very valuable. My impression is you could be lifted up in pride, and as a consequence putting too much value on your messages and not much value or importance on the time it is taking from other things.

My impression is, things have gone very well in Virginia in the past. There is some division starting but it remains underground due to fear of being hammered by you from up front, and being intimidated by you.

In Christ,
Rhett Stuart

For there must also be factions among you, that those who are approved may be recognized among you.
1 Cor 11:19

He didn't get a response from Deo during that hot humid summer. Rhett and Sabrina kept up a busy pace with raising kids, fixing a broken shaft on the washing machine, and dealing with a weakly running dishwasher.

"There is too much gunk in here that's clogging it all up, the filter must be all jammed up again."

Rhett sat on the kitchen floor while they finished dinner. He had quickly eaten Sabrina's homegrown basil pesto and pasta so he wouldn't have the job hanging over his head that evening.

Ruth sat eating at the table in their breakfast nook extension off the kitchen, and catching his eye, "Maybe just get a new dishwasher Dad."

"Noooo, we don't have the money," said Rhett, "but I'd LIKE to get a new one."

"It's-the-MONey, the MONey-is-the-PRObIem," sang Ruth, eyes twinkling.

"Finish up your dinner, sweetie!" said Sabrina.

"Hey, onebody took the last piece of bread!" said Dawson.

"Onebody?" asked Sabrina.

"Yeah, it wasn't nobody or twobodies, so it had to be onebody," explained Dawson.

Rhett reflected on their summer with his head stuck in the dishwasher. They were having a lot of fun being with so many friends, and so often - usually three or four times a week year round, with Assembly functions and visiting each other. The almost constant routine contact was allowing them to build close, personal, intimate relationships for all of his family in Richmond, something Sabrina really needed.

Maybe we ought to make efforts with other people, thought Rhett, reaching for his cordless quarter-inch impact driver, *No, that wouldn't do, I don't even know anyone else outside of our fellowship, and we are so busy with our Assembly friends. The truth is so hard to explain to other people I meet once in a while. People are just not interested, they reject it. We are in the last days, they just don't want the truth anymore. Most people outside our group are just leaven. And, bad company corrupts good habits. Everybody knows that. Some people inside our Assemblies have some problems too, but those are people who can be helped and worked with.*

"Okay, it's the thread again!" said Rhett, "it came out of the torn filter again. Sabrina, where's the needle and that black polyester thread?"

A few weeks later Rhett drove his car six hundred feet out his gravel driveway, turned left, drove three hundred feet down the gravel road, and then turned left into Mark

Shifflett's driveway. It was very convenient Mark was an excellent mechanic, since their homes on their private dead end road were twenty-five minutes out of town. It saved Rhett and Sabrina some driving back and forth, dropping each other off at the dealership.

As they stood on his newly asphalted driveway, Mark locked his knees and looked soberly at Rhett. "Jarvo just sent me an e-mail harshly criticizing the Leaders. Jarvo feels Deo Trophy and the leaders are just trying to control people and turn us into another denomination. I responded, but I don't think I am getting anywhere with him."

Rhett replied, "It's so sad; I wish Jarvo could see we need to follow the leaders as they follow Christ. We're supposed to go to the Bible for our answers; we're not just another man-made religious organization. We're organized by God."

Outside the wall of their association was the rest of the world, the people with problems who didn't have it together like they did. There were some outside, for sure, with limited success in their families. But the Assemblies had a good track history of low divorce rates, alcoholism (alcohol was forbidden), drug use was almost non-existent, and sexual immorality was rare. The people outside of their Assembly wall were not doing the will of God; some out of ignorance, some willfully.

The Assemblies were the only religious group Rhett knew of who functioned as the Lord wanted Christians to; they had it together and needed to let their light of Unity shine for the World just as the early Christians did. They were separate from the World, and their Unity would help lead others to Christ.

A month later at the regional inter-Assembly Christian retreat over Labor Day, Rhett watched his family suffer through another extraordinarily lengthy and confusing message from Deo. Rhett intercepted Deo in the aisle on his way to the cafeteria while Sabrina was gathering up the blankets and books into their large orange meeting bag.

Catching his eye, Rhett asked, "Did you get my e-mail?"

Deo stopped and gazed earnestly into Rhett's eyes, his eyebrows moving slightly independent of his serious intent expression. It seemed Deo was looking through Rhett's eyes, into his soul, as he said, "I did get your letter, and I am sorry I have not responded to you. My schedule is busy, but my intention is to respond and I will. I thought you made some good points in your e-mail, Rhett."

Deo smiled kindly.

Rhett nodded, "I'll look forward to your response then."

Deo bowed his head slightly, in humility and in consideration of Rhett's e-mail.

"It may take me a little while to respond," Deo said, still looking towards the ground, then back at Rhett.

Well, he heard me out and that is all I can do. I've expressed my burden and done my part, thought Rhett, as he left Deo talking to somebody else who had just walked up, *I'll just let it go. Noth'n else I can do about it.*

After visiting with Mark and Rhoda over lunch, Rhett noticed Jarvo standing off by himself, watching the two volleyball games packed with young people.

"Hey Jaarvo, how's your life going?" said Rhett walking up, anticipating some friendly chatter with his good friend, and brother-in-law.

Jarvo looks so grim, thought Rhett, *but why?*

Jarvo's usual expression reflected a just-under-the-surface humor, as if something funny had just occurred to him and he was thinking of the best way to share it with his friends so they could laugh together, which they often did. His rebellious cow lick on the top back of his head gave his witty jokes credibility, his sturdy figure hinting at his livelihood.

Jarvo once told Rhett and a bunch of other people that while he was doing some personal shopping at a grocery store, bending low to get some cans off the bottom shelf, a woman pushing her shopping cart around behind him commented, "You must be a plumber!"

Jarvo was taught to make his own living in life. He would probably always be a plumber like his father Jar.

"Rhett, I think we are just becoming another religion. I think Deo's Orderly Following is false doctrine."

Rhett thought, *Jarvo's grim expression shows he really does think that.*

"Deo is a liar, he has told a lot of lies, and he is dishonest!" Jarvo added, turning a wary eye towards Rhett, "I watched the video on his message against snow-boarding three times and he told about forty lies in it. I counted 'em!"

"Jarvo, that is divisive! You can't talk about a minister of Jesus Christ that way! He was just trying to make his point so we could understand it! Snow-boarding costs a lot of money and is materialistic! Deo Trophy has helped sooo many people in his twenty-five years of ministry, like Toby Tait, and his Orderly Following ministry has helped reduce a lot of conflict among us, helping us keep our Unity and Light for the World! We aren't becoming some new religion, we go by the Bible. How can you be SO DIVISIVE about a minister?!!" said Rhett.

Jarvo was ready with his response well before Rhett finished, "Deo has redefined 'Separated from the World' to mean we need to just follow him. Did you know the word Pharisee means 'Separated Ones'?! Being Worldly also means being religious and self-righteous!"

Rhett said, "We need to FOLLOW LEADERS as they follow Christ! Deo is JUST drilling into us as Christians we should walk separate from the World, and we SHOULD IMITATE leaders as they follow Christ! Where will you go? There ARE no other Christians who are a viable representation of the Body of Christ, functioning as the Lord wants us to!"

Jarvo glanced around for unwanted eavesdroppers within earshot, and said, "If all the truth in the world was a giant pyramid, then they think they're some elite group who alone live in the tippy top part of that pyramid. Rhett, come on, there are a lot of other Christians in the world trying to do what the Lord wants them to do. YOU are being sooo RI-DIC-UU-LOUS!"

"JARVO," Rhett said, "There are NO Christians that have the truth we have and are functioning as we do, like the early Christians. Do you know of any? I don't!"

Sobbing in grief for his divisive and wayward brother-in-law, Rhett was stricken with the fear of losing fellowship with his brother-in-law for a long, long time. The thought, *If Jarvo should leave our Christian fellowship; I will need to shun him for his divisive behavior!* – struck fear in his heart again.

Rhett valued his brother-in-laws highly. When Rhett was a boy he enjoyed playing, some, with his older sister Lorna. But he always wanted a little brother to play with. When Rhett's younger sister Laura, and then Rosie, were born, he cried both times his mom had called from the hospital with the bad news it was just another girl. Rhett learned to enjoy his relationships with his sisters. However, as the years went by, the realization his sisters would likely provide him with brother-in-laws slowly dawned on him.

Laura's marriage to Jarvo Madison and Rosie's marriage to Randy Greens provided much treasured friendships.

With a sense of urgency engulfing him, Rhett left to find Deo Trophy so they could sit down and talk with Jarvo about his blasphemy towards leaders. Maybe Deo could talk some sense into his brother-in-law. Simon Roland, the leader under Deo from the Fredericksburg Assembly where Deo lived, saw Rhett walking by, obviously shaken.

"What's wrong?" Simon asked Rhett. Simon worked for the Federal Government, approving or disapproving of things that involved millions of dollars and lots of jobs for large corporations.

"Jarvo is being really divisive," said Rhett, stopping and blowing his nose with a fairly fresh handkerchief, as coolly as possible under the circumstances.

"Deo, being from Fredericksburg, isn't aware of all the issues in Charlottesville, even though he frequently speaks at our regional gatherings," Simon said, "What do you think about getting Lyle Cooper involved? I think he would be a better person to talk with Jarvo."

Simon was Deo's right hand man, the only one who was sometimes allowed to speak when Deo wasn't available in the Fredericksburg Assembly. Rhett took Simon's advice.

"Whatz up?" asked Lyle, seeing Rhett walk up.

Rhett said, "Simon says you'd be the best person to talk with Jarvo."

They found Jarvo outside, and the three of them sat across from each other on the wooden picnic benches behind the main auditorium in the shade. It was private there and they could talk freely.

Jarvo again started debating, but more carefully this time, with less intensity: "Deo's youngest son has solicited three women for sex, who knows how many times he's solicited other women? He's been charged with Sexual Assault and Battery, and he says he might solicit sex again. He doesn't really know if he will or not!."

Looking off towards the children swinging in the yellow seats with the chains squeaking for grease, Lyle said, "Jarvo, you are bringing up issues we beat to death recently in our general leadership meeting. The conviction was reduced to simple assault. Archie Stark addressed this last year and carefully looked into it along with Cary Murdock. They concluded Deo's son is mentally handicapped and unable to truly comprehend and understand his sin. Deo needs to move forward with his ministry."

Jarvo said, "So a man in his early twenties who is smart enough to drive a car, get married, have two kids, and is working full time doesn't know when he is being immoral. Surely he knows what he is doing!!"

As Jarvo brought up the old issues, Rhett's heart sunk within him. *Jarvo is not being reached; he's being persistent in casting doubt on Deo Trophy's ministry by attacking one of Deo's grown children. Minister's kids can really have the spotlight on them; it just isn't fair to them.*

Finally Rhett, with tears streaming, interrupted: "Please Please Jarvo. THINK about what you are doing and where you are heading with your family and your daughters! You are speaking harshly against a minister appointed by God, a long respected leader! Jarvo, you really ought to be MARKED for avoidance for being divisive, talking about a LEADER that way!" said Rhett.

It was getting difficult to keep the emotion out of his voice, it felt so strained. This was so stressing, so surreal.

"Well Rhett, I just think Deo and some of these leaders are trying to get between me and my kids. You know, like I want to have my daughters sit by me in our meetings. Deo wants them sitting up front. I just don't feel comfortable with that."

"If you want your daughters sitting with you, you can," said Lyle, "We won't stop you!"

"Uh, that is pretty trivial," said Rhett, "and Deo says young people get distracted easily sitting in the back."

"I don't think it's trivial! I think these leaders are trying to take over as the head of my home and I don't like it!" said Jarvo, "they're splitting up families!"

As Jarvo continued debating, Rhett rose up to his feet, "Lyle, I have nothing more I can think of or say to change Jarvo."

Lyle smiled, "Okay Rhett, thanks for staying here and talking with us! I'll just talk to Jarvo by myself, thanks for your help!"

Rhett left in tears, which was rare for him, his head whirling in a tornado of despair, *This is so helpless, what has gotten into Jarvo?*

As Jarvo and Lyle stayed talking together at the picnic table for over an hour, Rhett went to his car and sobbed for awhile, then blowing his nose yet again, went back to the building to find one of his many other friends to socialize with.

An hour later Jarvo walked up nervously, "Rhett, I really am sorry, I should not have been telling you those things about Deo…."

"Okay, Jarvo. I'll accept your apology," said Rhett, shaking his hand. But he thought, *Something is really wrong with Jarvo, Satan has gotten to him.*

A few weeks later Rhett asked his six year old daughter, "Ruth, where do you want to go for your outing?"

"Bike riding at Deep Run Park, then ice cream at Breuners'!" said Ruth, her eyes dancing with sparkles.

Ruth sure knew how to throw out the smile sparkles.

Since Rhett and his son Dawson went on an annual men-and-boys trip to the mountains each summer with other young fathers and sons from the Assemblies, he promised his daughters to take them on an afternoon outing for some father-daughter time.

The afternoon was hot and humid on the mountain bike trails, so after loading their bikes on the back of the SUV, Rhett and Ruth headed over for a promised ice cream in a giant waffle cone. After finally deciding to split a large cookie dough, Rhett and Ruth finished their treat after exchanging several eye rollings and laughs with, "ahh, this is sooo gooood!"

As they got into their SUV Rhett's cell phone rang. Rhett looked at the screen. It was Jarvo.

"Hell-looo..." said Rhett, after debating answering at all. This was Ruth's special time with him.

"Rhett, I want to talk to you about where I am coming from, please please hear me out!" said Jarvo.

"Okaay..." said Rhett.

"The ministers are trying to control us too much, they are not allowing the Holy Spirit to work in our lives," said Jarvo.

Rhett said, "Jarvo, our Christian fellowship is a fortress for our families. If you leave that, then you're exposing your family to the evils of this world!"

"Our God is a mighty fortress; we need to trust in Him, not a group!" said Jarvo.

"And so God's providing you with this group. Jarvo, listen, okay? We have a disagreement. OKAY? You and I, we have spent a lot of time discussing this. You know what I think and I know what you think. There is nothing more to be said and I am done."

Jarvo said, "Well, I don't think we have talked enough about it Rhett, you see, what you ought to consider -"

"I have nothing more to say to you. So, good-bye Jarvo!" Rhett said, flipping the phone shut with a snap of his wrist.

Ruth looking over with big worried eyes. "Is Uncle Jarvo okay?" Jarvo's youngest daughter was her age and they got along like two peas in a pod.

"No," said Rhett as he put the SUV in gear and backed up, "he is not doing well."

Sabrina was in the mood for company the following week, so they invited Toby Tait and his wife Joy over for dessert with their two young boys on a Thursday evening.

Toby Tait was one person Rhett could think of that had really been helped by Deo Trophy. Toby was raised by his mom and step dad in central Maryland, and never lived near any of the Christians who went to the Assemblies due to his dad's work. His parents didn't want to go to any local churches, believing them to be sectarian, so they drove ninety minutes a few times a month to the Northern Virginia Assembly where Archie Stark is the minister.

Since Toby was home schooled and an only child, he grew up hungry for friends. An extremely gifted musician in his teens, his uncle got him hooked up with contemporary Christian rock music. Toby might have made it big. His large muscular frame, good looks, sincere personality, and piercing grey eyes gave him genetic celebrity appeal, plus he had connections with popular bands in DC and Northern Maryland. But Toby's parents were worried. They didn't want to lose their eighteen year old son to the World, the World outside of the Assemblies. So they called Deo. Deo was glad to talk it over with Toby.

Toby had told Deo, "I am on a spiritual journey, and I am old enough to make my own decisions."

Deo replied, "Yes, you are old enough to make your own decisions and you can leave if you want to, but I don't buy that spiritual journey stuff. Would you be willing to talk about it?" and Deo had talked him out of it by directing Toby's thoughts with carefully worded questions.

A few years later Toby got a job as a graphic artist down in Richmond, thoroughly enjoying his close friendships in the Richmond Assembly, now that he was finally near a Christian Assembly with people he could spend time with. He married Joy four years ago.

Rhett watched Toby chase his young boy around the living room, remembering the time he asked Toby how long it took him to learn to play the guitar. Toby, his fingers running all over the acoustic guitar strings making sounds Rhett never knew acoustical guitars could make, said, "Uuuhh, I never did learn, I just started playing."

Rhett envied that kind of talent; he tried for months to learn several basic cords so he could sing some choruses with his family in the kitchen after dinner during the long winter evenings.

Toby snatched up his son by the back of his overalls, and with a, "Phew, it's a really messy one!" headed into a back bedroom for a change-out.

"Oh sweetie, are you going to change him? That is so sweet of you!" called Joy from the kitchen.

Rhett sipped his late evening decaf coffee and thought of last week's conversation with Sabrina as he watched Toby settle back into the leather recliner. "Toby thought it was just fabulous I ironed his shirt this morning," Joy had said to Sabrina. Rhett didn't really care for this, he tended to not appreciate his wife enough, and Sabrina would sometimes mention how appreciative Toby was over small things Joy did. "Toby is just spoiling her, she needs to grow up," Rhett told Sabrina after hearing the comment, "and I buy shirts that don't need ironing."

"Howz Jarvo doing, you talk to him lately?" asked Toby, interrupting Rhett's thoughts.

"Not good, not good – at-all," said Rhett, "Jarvo called me last week. Has it in for leadership. I wish he would think where he is going and where he will wind up. If you undermine God's authority you undermine your own authority as a father. He has a real problem with Deo Trophy, accusing him of having an agenda. I don't think he's got any of his own personal convictions. I told Jarvo, I reminded him about his three daughters. I asked him – Who're they gonna marry? I warned him he's prob'bly gonna leave our Christian fellowship. I told him there's nothing but heartache and chaos for him out there in the World. His girls won't respect him as the head of his home, since he doesn't respect and obey the leadership of those who rule over him."

Toby said, "What'd he say to that?"

Rhett replied, "Jarvo said, "the Lord will provide spouses for my daughters." The Lord is trying to provide all right, but Jarvo's rejecting the Lord's providing mates for our children within our Assemblies. It won't be long before he leaves. There's no other Christian group I know of who has the truth we do and function as the Lord wants us to in Unity. And if there was another group like us, I'd of heard of them by now, I think. Maybe there is, I just don't know of any."

"Bummer. Kinda sobering, how much we can deteriorate when we get our eyes off the Lord and start allowing Satan to lead us and control'n what we do," said Toby.

Rhett took the opportunity to fork in a bite of cheesecake. *Cherry cheesecake, decaf coffee, and a good friend to talk to. Life doesn't get much better,* thought Rhett, heartily nodding in agreement.

Toby took another bite of cherry cheesecake himself, and they listened to the women chatting in the kitchen. *This is really smooth and creamy, must have some white chocolate in it, and the cherries are just the right tart.*

Toby went on, "Deo helped me at a critical time in my life. Got me thinkin 'bout where I was go'n as a young person. After a few hours on the phone, he really helped change my mind. I was head'n right out of our Christian fellowship into the hands of Satan, disillusioned with being on a 'spiritual voyage' and starting a Christian rock band. If it wasn't for Deo, I would have gone out to the World, to disaster. You know, Deo didn't just tell me what I ought to do, he just kept talk'n and ask'n questions until I could see it for myself."

Toby watched his young son buzzing around the room again in his fresh diaper chasing Rhett's son, and added, "I wouldn't have my great wife Joy and our two boys if I'd left! We owe so much to our great ministers, all those messages on marriage, raising kids, personal relationships and being separated from the World. It's SUCH a safe place to raise our families."

Rhett nodded heartily in agreement with a mouth full of cheesecake, and took another sip of coffee. *Having a friend share in the conversation is always a good thing with cherry cheesecake waiting to be eaten.*

After several seconds of quiet reflection on Jarvo and cheese cake, Rhett said, "Young fathers really do need a safe protected cocoon to raise their family, and the Assemblies provide that. Jarvo's attack on the leaders is totally unacceptable; I just cannot believe what he's doing!"

Abhorrent would really be the right word actually, thought Rhett, *but I might be wrong.* Rhett didn't like making mistakes with words. When he was young he was made fun of for mispronouncing words he had just learned of in books.

Young people frequently traveling and intermarrying in the Assemblies spread across the USA had no other option if they didn't find a spouse in their own Assembly. And parents traveling with their unmarried children to visit their older married children resulted in more interstate romances, more marriages, and more grandkids to visit. After eighty years they were highly interconnected, but not inbred.

Rhett once counted all the people he knew in the countrywide address book for the Assemblies. It amounted to several hundred friends his family could stay with in Texas, Oklahoma, California, Newfoundland. *Why would Jarvo want to leave that?* thought Rhett.

One young man from Atascadero, California had several t-shirts made for him and his buddies called "Forbidden Sequence." On the back of the shirts were four simple graphics of a young man, a girl, an airplane, and then a heart with a couple holding hands. Parents really missed their grown daughters when they moved out of state, but they would rather have a good marriage for their daughter out-of-state then a poor local one.

Unfortunately, Jarvo soon left his lifetime and childhood friends at the Assemblies, with his wife Laura and their three sweet young daughters. Rhett made one last ditch effort to try and help him, going over to their house one evening, but then shunned him. Laura threw out a few innuendos about the leaders over the phone during the next few months, so Rhett asked Sabrina to shun Laura as well.

"Bad communication corrupts good habits, we can't have leaven like that," said Rhett to his next door neighbor Mark Shifflett one cool breezy Saturday afternoon as they strung wire up a hill for Mark's new goat pasture, "it's divisive."

I hope Jarvo's really miserable, thought Rhett from time to time, *I hope he comes to the end of his rope and turns his life back to the Lord. What a tragedy!*

Michie Hobkins quietly faded out also, thinking Deo was a real piece of work. Rhett wasn't sure why Michie left, except Deo bothered him. Rhett tried to call him, but didn't get any returned phone calls, so he wrote a letter:

Dear Michie,

I missed seeing you much the last few years. I remember you coming out to the hospital and hanging around when Jonathan fell. Probably because you wanted to be a support, and because Jonathan spent some time in your home and it impacted you also. Jonathan always spoke highly of your family and enjoyed being with you.

I have always thought of you as one of my best friends, somebody I really enjoy being with, for years. I think it is because our minds work the same way, and we have a similar sense of humor. When we moved back here I remember, especially, the time you had us over and you got some pizza, times sitting around in your living room visiting, playing guitars. Why is it we had so little time to do that? You coming out in your early 20's to California to visit, the time you went to Heart Land Camp, hanging over a rope bridge and laughing together, working on my plumbing, and your garage.

We all need Christian fellowship. Don't forget the assembling of yourself with other Christians. Please don't be fooled by Christians you may meet that you know so very little about. A man who isolates himself seeks his own desire and rages against all wise judgment. I think Satan has successfully gotten you out of a safe place to be, separated you from the flock, and will continue his steal, kill, and destroy tactics on you and your family.

Look how your family has prospered up to a few years ago. You have a beautiful family. It will tear me up to see it devastated, like so many I have known who have left. You need help and counsel. But you are too proud, and I think you gave up a year or two ago. Satan divided you against the very men who could have helped you. I'll miss you! And I do love you! Don't wait until some tragedy happens to help turn you back to the Lord and his ways! Be humble now!

Your brother in Christ,

Rhett Stuart

Michie never responded.

Now Jarvo only had his sister Rae and her husband Michie Hobkins, and his parents to spend time with. Jarvo and Michie would hardly get along now, both of them selfishly serving themselves by going to the World, and leaving their Christian friends and fellowship.

Jarvo's dad, Jar, left also.

Actually, Jar was eventually forced to leave.

> Unthinking respect for authority
> is the greatest enemy of truth
> - Albert Einstein -

3.

Jar

Jar was active in publicly refuting the Orderly Following Doctrine well before Michie Hobkins and Jarvo left the local Assembly in Charlottesville.

Jar considered it to be his place in the church to keep people on track with the truth. He explained himself to Rhett years ago: "Norris Stark asked questions and challenged speakers for years, and now that Norris has passed on from this life, that's my place." Some felt Norris' place of publically challenging speakers wasn't ever needed in the Assemblies, especially Deo.

After last seeing his mother at age five, Norris grew up moving around the country with his father and several different women in succession. They ended up in Southern California in the 1920's. Norris left home and became an alcoholic. He was one of California's first homeless, literally living in the gutter at a young age during the Great Depression. His brother brought him around to Maurice Johnson's local church Assembly, and he hung around in the back, sometimes intoxicated, before becoming saved. Maurice truly welcomed the poor.

Maurice came to believe no church should have a name, membership role, or any written rules, bylaws, or regulations. Simply to meet in the name of Jesus, to have no other name, and going to the Bible for the answers to resolve issues was all the Lord required, no less and no more. So Maurice just shut down his large successful up and coming church in Southern California a few years before Norris came, and lost most of his congregation. He suffered rejection by some friends who were well known religious contemporaries.

Rhett's great grandmother was one of the few who stayed with Maurice's little group. Rhett's grandfather was sixteen years old then and had just been saved.

Assembly meetings were advertised as "meetings in the name of the Lord Jesus Christ." Maurice believed the Bible should resolve all disputes, and he preached it. This attracted people of like mind who also believed the Bible should decide all issues. Rhett's dad, Mycroft Stuart, vividly remembers as a child sitting on narrow wooden benches with no backs during hours-long meetings. Maurice's passion for truth seemed unequal, and his zeal for preaching showed while rapidly making his points.

He made no bones about openly pointing people out who needed it, calling down those who dared to go to a "denominational church" to visit, allowing them to fully present their side in public meetings. In 1959 he dealt with a nineteen year old young man who went to a church with a name on the building, and was contending the important thing was for Christians to rally together when they could and forget doctrinal differences.

Maurice started the discussion in the packed room by stating:

> More likely all of us here are fairly familiar with the arguments, many of them gotten out by far abler men than you, Larry. And some have heard them here, when they use to be in denominationalism, and since then; arguments that have been gotten out by men far more able than you, though you may not recognize it. Men far more able than you, as to why Christians should become identified with some human invention in religion in order to do more good for God.

> This is a meeting where heresies may crop out, and where we will not have police protection to keep them from cropping out. That's one of the surest evidences that we're not a sect. In the Baptist church organization, or the Methodist, Presbyterian, the Roman Catholic, or Lutheran, or any organization by men that own their own property or religious corporation, they have in this country (and I suppose other countries) — police protection, and they'll call on the police to arrest anybody that disturbs public worship. I do not believe that true worship can be disturbed by another human being.

After nineteen year old Larry finished his one hour public presentation on why it was okay to be a member of a Baptist church, Maurice started his rebuttal:

> I heard the pastor of the First Baptist, big fine, I understand, looking fellow, said, "Young man's coming in, brother Larry, a fine young man that's being wonderfully used in the Lord's vineyard." I imagine Larry felt awfully humble. I imagine this Baptist preacher didn't use any of the psychology that he used to get 3500-4000 members by that trick. Larry, I've never given you any of that tactic, boy, I love your soul too much. I haven't kidded you and flattered you, Larry. I've dealt with you as a father in the gospel. And I've plead with you and exhorted you.

Maurice finished his own hour presentation by referring to a prostitute who boasted of her occupation, concluding:

> Larry's guilty now of a far worse prostitution. Far worse. Prostituting the holy things of God, and his membership in the body of Christ, trying to make it <u>appear</u> that there's no rivalry between that membership and another secondary membership in something called a Baptist church. The <u>moment</u> you think there's any value to a secondary membership, you of course are giving the lie to the essential and beautiful value of the original membership. As ye have therefore received Christ Jesus the Lord, so.... - *chorus from the audience* - "walk ye in Him."

Maurice and the Christians like Norris who met with him had meetings in homes or rented buildings.

Norris got married on his thirty-third birthday to a young lady within their fellowship, and after his wife of thirty-one years died, he often mentioned he wished he had treated her better. His son James Stark wished his dad had treated his mother better also.

Time didn't change Norris' crusty, gruff, and abrupt personality. After his wife died, he still sat in the back of their meetings in California, usually dozing off at some point.

Norris would lean his chair against the back wall with the now five hundred plus crowd at the twice-a-year state wide weekend camp retreats in Tulare, California, and interrupt the speaker, calling attention to a doctrinal short coming when he felt it was needed. The truth was really important to Norris. It was also really important not to fall all the way over backwards in his chair.

Norris often leaned back in his chair to the point where he might go either way, and balance there as if he enjoyed that feeling of instability. Then he dozed off. Upon awakening, Norris was usually able to go forwards, rather than backwards. His chair came down with a bang, temporarily interrupting the lecture again. Norris ignored the murmured chuckles and curious glances over shoulders from the adults. The kids just turned, staring until their parents nudged them.

Since Norris had some respect as an older man, and his son James was now a minister, Norris was not stopped from interrupting speakers as he had for years.

"Ministers need to be challenged when there is error; the sooner the better," Norris said and believed to the core of his being.

Sooner usually meant right in the middle of a long message; Norris appeared virtually fearless of any man. But as Rhett got closer to him in his later years he found out Norris actually had a soft heart, concealing it with a tough and gruff exterior.

James Stark shared Norris' love for the truth and God's people in the Assemblies, carefully making his own occasional blunt correcting comments after Deo's long messages. Deo didn't complain when James did it, since James was an older more experienced minister held in high respect for his life of service and personal counseling. James was more gracious with his occasional interruptions or corrections, which were usually done in private.

Norris lived in Fredericksburg during the last twenty years of his life, interrupting and criticizing lectures when he felt the need. Deo grew tired of Norris interrupting his intensely delivered messages, enduring them since he first began to lecture. Deo knew someday he wouldn't have to put up any longer with Norris' loud, blunt, and abrupt interruptions of his train of thought as he spoke.

But Norris had longevity.

At ninety-three the doctor told him, "Norris, you need to start eating healthier!" The doctor thought a little bit more, adding, "Never mind Norris, eat what you want."

Norris was welcome at Jar's house, driving an hour during the winters to give Jar and Jarvo a hand splitting firewood. Arriving at 7 am on a Saturday in his large 1970's high powered sedan, he swaggered up the walkway to the front door.

BLAM BLAM — BLAMITY BLAM BLAM!

"ARE YOU UP YET? WE'VE GOT WOOD THAT NEEDS A SPLIT'N!"

After quickly gaining his entrance, "That coffee I smell brewing — Mamie?"

Taking long breaks in the crisp winter air as they cooled off from splitting wood, Jar and Norris sat on up-ended logs in the snow debating the role of Melchizedek, with Jarvo listening in. Norris died at ninety-five years of age in 2001.

Jar was truly inspired by Norris' burden to keep ministers on track, and he vowed to keep whoever was speaking on the straight and narrow way doctrinally also, since Norris was no longer around to do it. Jar inspired his six children to believe the truth was important, to think critically, and respectfully debate.

James Stark didn't mind Jar's questions and comments when speaking in Jar's Assembly in Charlottesville. James was used to it; after all, his father had done this at times to James during his ministry. Also, James Stark was quite blunt himself, he went directly to the point in his messages, there was no question over what he meant. It was the truth that mattered.

Personal feelings were secondary.

However, Deo Trophy didn't like Jar's interruptions any more then he had Norris', "Jar should not disrupt the meetings, it's distracting from my message."

Jar told Rhett in his crisp Virginian dialect several years prior: "When I go to Deo with personal questions, he hammers me on them latehr, from up front, not mentioning my name, but sort of mocking me. I'm not going to him anymore with questions afterweards; I'll just ask him during the meetings."

Jar's quirky personality and nick name seemed out of place with his strong noble face, stately build, aristocratic Virginian heritage, and full name of Jarvis Alexander Madison IV. After graduating from college, with a brief moment of glory as a pole-vaulter, he taught math for a few years, then opted out of the higher education job and took up plumbing. His wife Mamie didn't mind. Mamie was usually pleased with whatever Jar decided to do. That is one of the reasons Jar married her. Jar decided against another young woman after she accidentally burned a hole in the upholstery of his new car with her cigarette ash, laughing it off. Jar liked to be around people who genuinely cared.

Years ago Jarvo had a renter who was giving him much grief, obnoxiously calling him several times a day, for months, to cuss and complain to Jarvo or his wife Laura about trivial things he claimed didn't work right. One time it was a legitimate problem; the sewer needed to be repaired. The weeds would need to be cleared away so the sewer line could be dug up and repaired.

Jarvo dreaded dealing with the renter and asked his dad, Jar, to help so he wouldn't have to be there as long.

When they arrived the renter declared he was due a twenty-four hour notice. He stood with his shorts on in the middle of the weeds to stop Jar from clearing them with a flexible corded nylon weed trimmer. Jar waded in, weed whacking his way all around the man. Jar got closer and closer, and the renter stubbornly stood his ground in the shrinking patch, unflinchingly guarding the weeds.

So Jar touched the whipping nylon cord to the man's bare shin.

The reaction was satisfying.

Jar was able to finish clearing the weeds, then he and Jarvo dug up the sewer and fixed it.

The renter had his day in court and Jar was sentenced to a hundred hours of community service. Jar didn't mind, he was used to helping out for free at Happy Hill. Happy Hill was where all the Virginia Assemblies gathered once a month for regional state gatherings; it was used for normal Charlottesville Assembly meetings at other times.

Deo wasn't the only one bothered by Jar's disruptive behavior in meetings, it didn't sit too well with some of his friends in the Charlottesville Assembly either.

"We are tired of the turmoil and disorder Jar is causing," Rhett was told by a local Assembly member in Charlottesville, "We like Jar being helpful, like bringing wood mulch for the kid's play ground and fixing the plumbing for the Happy Hill building. But he is getting carried away with all these interruptions, and we just need a break from it!"

Deo kept right on regularly preaching the importance of Orderly Following, despite Jar's objections. Jar couldn't always think of the best question to oppose it, but something about it just bothered him.

Eventually Lyle Cooper, the young local leader in the Charlottesville Assembly, asked Jar not to disrupt the meetings anymore by. But Jar just changed tactics and asked his questions at the end of the message instead of interrupting them. The meetings were almost always open at the end for any comments or questions. Lyle then asked him not to speak up during the meetings at all, not even at the end of the message. Jar still intermittently persisted in asking questions at the end of the meetings.

Lyle finally publicly rebuked Jar for asking a short question at the end of a large regional camp lecture at Happy Hill: "I am very disappointed in Jar, he has been asked to not make comments during our meetings," Lyle Cooper said with an emotionally ridden voice as he held the roving cordless mic.

Deo Trophy nodded in full agreement; his counseling influenced Lyle to stop Jar's disorderly conduct. Deo wasn't speaking that time; he was sitting in his usual spot over in the right rear near his grown sons who sat with their wives and young children. Deo was proud of his grandchildren, frequently displaying their pictures on the Big Screen up front before starting the lecture slides on his computer.

Since Jar continued to speak up and challenge when he thought it was needed, and Deo Trophy and other leaders resented it, Jar created what most people would consider a conflict. It wore on the local people, stressing out the women.

The leaders would not back down, claiming Jar was disobedient, and Jar maintained his right to ask questions. So, eventually, Lyle Cooper and five other young leaders in the Charlottesville Assembly marked Jar to be avoided and shunned for causing a division.

Jar finally stopped interrupting the speaker, or even making any comments after the meetings, after Lyle threatened to call the police on Jar.

Nobody was supposed to even talk to Jar after he was marked, but utterly shun him. Almost all of his old friends from the last twenty-three years wouldn't shake his hand or even look at him, pretending he was invisible, as if he had ceased to be a person. Jar was told to sit in the back and leave right after the meeting.

However, Jar didn't give up easily. "I love those people and I want to help them!" Jar told his wife.

He whispered loudly to Mamie, murmuring some during the messages. Afterwards he leisurely visited several minutes with a few people who dared do it outside the large Happy Hill building. Then Jar and Mamie would drive to their home a few miles away in Albemarle County. Jar had a hard time impersonating invisibleness.

Finally, Lyle got a restraining order on Jar and threatened to have the police called if Jar would not be completely quiet.

If Jar could not whisper loudly, he figured he could occasionally give the thumbs up or down during messages depending on what the speaker said. Lyle didn't know what do to with this. Jar wasn't asking questions, but it might be foolish to call the police on an older man who was putting his thumbs up during a lecture.

Jar took them at their word, believing they wanted to walk in truth and were the only viable representation of the body of Christ, functioning as the Bible instructs Christians, and didn't want to leave. If the truth wasn't being given, then Jar needed to correct it. It didn't matter if the police were going to be called or not. The truth was far more important. Being arrested was a trivial thing. So he hung in there, exercising self-restraint from asking questions during the meetings, sitting in back with his wife Mamie, then drove back to their large comfortable estate on a hill just north of Charlottesville.

Jar finally did have the police called on him. He was determined to have his say during a local Charlottesville meeting to apologize for his excessive disturbances, in spite of his gag order and marking.

With Jar heading up to the front, Lyle Cooper, feeling responsible to stop the disturbance, darted up and stood by Jar, and began leading the congregation in singing to drown him out. Jar put his arm around Lyle and waited for the singing to stop.

While they were singing, another zealous local man, Ernest, jumped up on the stage. Jar jumped off, then on, back and forth, evading Ernest who was apparently trying to physically get him off the stage.

After the uproar tapered off, the entire congregation terminated the meeting and quickly left the Happy Hill building, going to Lyle Cooper's house nearby. Jar came along also, so the police were called. Hobbs, Jar's youngest son, pleaded with his father, but to no avail.

The police officer simply said, "You people need to give this some time, and then work it out among yourselves."

Four of Jar's grown children spent time with their parents, but Jar's other two children 'walked in Jar's marking,' and would not talk or visit with Jar, shunning him entirely. Jarvo didn't like his dad's stage performance, even though Jarvo left the Assembly fellowship along with his dad.

Deo sent a long letter to Jar soon after this in 2006, explaining proper Church Leadership to him:

Perhaps looking at what Christ did as He appeared before Pilate would be instructive in this matter. Christ did not rebel. This would have been ungodly. He knew that Pilate was making a request (to answer Pilate's questions) that He, Christ, was not willing to follow. He knew that he must bear the consequences that Pilate was authorized to mete out thus to fulfill scripture.

And Christ reckoned with Caesar (by submitting to Caesar after acknowledging Caesar's authority was from God and that what was happening was wrong) and Caesar meted out punishment as was his authority to do. So again, we must reckon with Caesar and his authority just as a wife and children must reckon with a husband and father's authority.

The consequences the authority chooses to mete out cannot be avoided. We are not authorized to rebel against Caesar any more than a wife or children are authorized to rebel against a father or husband. But the father, the husband and Caesar will all answer to God for how they handled the authority that God delegated to them. <u>Likewise, I will answer to God for the authority that I have in the Body of Christ.</u> I take this very soberly. It is not a light matter to me. And those over whom I have authority will answer to God for their response to my authority.

Deo ended his twenty-six page response to Jar's with some of the following points:

You are to be pitied Jar. And I do pity you. I hope that you may soon give up the struggle against the Spirit of God and allow the peace of God that can keep your heart and mind in Christ Jesus to be reflected in your behavior toward saints that love you and your family.

The use of the cover of "righteous indignation" for your carnal angry outbursts is shameful and must be called what it is – carnality on your part. Your lobbing of distracting comments into discussions and the confusion it causes keep you off track and unable to focus on something long enough to be helped by those who see what you are doing to yourself and to your family and to others. The legitimacy of asking questions in our times together is necessary and appropriate – but using this cover of questioning as a forum for our own carnal promotion of ourselves or our "cause" is not legitimate and the latter should be stopped according to God's word because of the undermining of listeners whom God protects from those seeking such occasions.

Deo also referred to Jar's questions during public meetings as selfish outbursts, Jar's reasoning as "mental thrashing," and Jar's ego and pride were being inflamed by his rejection of Deo's Orderly Following, causing Jar to have those carnal angry outbursts.

But Rhett thought Jar's questions were polite, sometimes in disagreement or in clarification, but politely stated. He knew Jar said some things too strongly a few times in private disagreement, but what Deo was referring to seemed to be something more. Thinking he might have missed something because he didn't live in the Charlottesville area, Rhett asked some others what they thought, but their recollection matched his.

The surprise rebuking of Jar at a large public Happy Hill regional gathering disturbed Jar, but he controlled himself, obeying his gag order by keeping quiet and talking to a few leaders afterwards. He certainly didn't have any outburst then either.

Obviously Deo knew more than Rhett about the situation.

Alexander never did what he said
Caesar never said what he did
- Italian Proverb -

4.

Sabrina in Richmond

Sabrina was very comfortable living in California for the first ten years of their marriage. After they married in 1990, Sabrina and Rhett lived in Loomis, which is twenty minutes north up interstate 80 from Sacramento.

They traveled to Virginia once a year to visit Jarvo (and Rhett's sister Laura) in Charlottesville, and other Christian friends in the Assemblies throughout Virginia.

The Richmond Assembly was enjoyable to visit because of all the children their own children's ages, and it was a healthy, fun loving, vibrant group of committed Christians. The slower paced activity schedule was more to Rhett's liking in raising his small children: One Sunday a month was an all day activity, meetings every Wednesday evening, one Thursday night local leadership meeting a month, and one Friday night sing practice a month. On the third Sunday of every month the Richmond Assembly would drive an hour to go to Happy Hill for a monthly regional gathering with the other three Virginia Assemblies.

People were getting on each other's nerves after a few generations of living together in their Loomis Assembly in Northern California. Aaron Adams, the local minister there, told Rhett: "The people here don't want to go along with Deo's Orderly Following doctrine. I think it would work if they would just give it a try!"

Rhett replied, "I think they are just too independent. They ought to just follow along with you and do what you say. I think this would bring us Unity and peace, and we could then be a light to the world."

In 1999, during one tumultuous Local Leadership meeting in Loomis, with relationships crumbling, Aaron's son spoke up, "Dad, my best memories were of riding on your shoulders at that amusement park we went to once. I just can't go along with your stand against that! I wish we had gone to amusement parks more! You were so busy in your ministry that you didn't have time for us kids!"

Aaron was wiped out, and Rhett decided to back him up the next day during the Sunday morning meeting. His four year old daughter Julia was prepared to say her verse, "Children obey your parents in the Lord." The children usually shared Bible verses after the singing on Sundays.

During the time allowed for comments before the verses, Rhett announced, "My daughter is going to say a verse this morning, children obey their parents, and they should. My wife needs to obey me, and I in turn need to obey God's authority over the Church, so here is a verse for me - "Obey them that have the rule over you and submit yourselves; for they watch for your souls, as they that must give account"."

The air was heavy in silent disagreement with Rhett, most were for notching down Aaron's authority level and it didn't sit well. Rhett wasn't all that popular after backing

Aaron's attempt at implementing Deo's Orderly Following Doctrine.

Aaron left that very Sunday afternoon in 1999, flying to Virginia for a much needed break from all the adversity. He spent a week visiting Deo Trophy, and came back more persuaded than ever the solution was Orderly Following. He first heard Deo speak on it July 4th, 1990, and had really appreciated it ever since then.

Aaron confided in Rhett after returning, "I agree with you Rhett, the people here just need to practice Orderly Following. That is our main problem here in Loomis. When we get that right, all these other problems will dissolve!"

So Aaron, upon returning from Virginia, amped up the preaching of the Orderly Following Doctrine with renewed zeal and vigor. But he just met tougher resistance, causing more conflict, and more deteriorating relationships. James Stark flew out for several days a month to help, preaching against 'Scuttlebutt', but to no avail: The damaging talk about others behind their backs continued. People just had a hard time working through problems as friends.

The Richmond Assembly in Virginia began in the 1960's with three young families meeting in homes. Their kids grew up and married, and others joined their newly formed group. Visiting other areas and having ministers travel to Richmond had kept them well connected with other Assemblies.

"There's twenty acres for sale next door to the lot I'm gonna build on, and your company has an office in Richmond you could transfer to," Mark Shifflet said, urging Rhett to make the move across the country during his Virginia visit in 1999, "as long as you don't mind dust on your van from the gravel road."

Mark, Jim Alberta, and Manny Floyd are good solid Christian guys, with conservative lifestyles. No TV, no entertainment videos, careful with their money, respectful of ministry, and they don't allow their wives and daughters to dress worldly, Rhett reasoned with himself, *they really have their own convictions on things.*

So Rhett and Sabrina moved to Virginia in 2000 to avoid the constant conflict that played an endless loop of tape in Rhett's head with no ending or solution for the Loomis problems, and to finally raise their children in a peaceful Assembly with hardly any turmoil. They could afford some acreage and raise their kids in the same rural neighborhood as their Christian friends in the countryside outside of Richmond. Finally there were other children their children's age to play with.

Before moving, Rhett heard the young energetic evangelist in Richmond, Julian Petros, had recently said in a local Leadership meeting in Richmond: "Okay, we are arguing about how long a slit can be. To end this dispute, none of the ladies should have any slits at all in the backs of their dresses in Richmond!" The entire Assembly rested in that, bearing the good fruit of Orderly Following.

Rhett thought, *These Christians in Richmond are not too worldly in their attire, and Mark and the other young fathers have strong reputations of walking in established standards, so they are good candidates to raise our families together.*

The Richmond Assembly truly walked in Deo's Orderly Following, with the peaceable fruit of 'Walking in Unity', demonstrating 'How good and pleasant it is when brethren walk together in Unity' in their everyday walk, helping lead others to Christ by being a light to the World.

Their local congregation called themselves The Richmond Assembly since, like the sixteen other

Assemblies (four in Virginia, five in California, and one each in: Texas, Oklahoma, Newfoundland, Arkansas, Missouri, Peru, and Mexico), they all considered it a sin to call themselves any name. They believed by taking a name they would not be under the name of 'the Lord Jesus Christ', and also, they would be separating themselves from all other Christians. Division among Christians is sin, so naming themselves was a sin, the sin of sectarianism.

All the ministers often preached how essential it is to be Separated from the World and false religious doctrine, and not to do anything themselves to divide from other Christians.

Rarely did anyone in the Assemblies actually do anything with any other Christians outside their Assemblies, with the exception of annual outreaches at county fairs, where they explained it was wrong for other Christians to separate themselves by having a name on their building and have rules. Claiming the Bible should be the only written set of rules, just as Maurice Johnson had taught many years ago, their group was the only one they knew of that had the truth. But hardly anybody they met was interested.

So Rhett and Sabrina bought twenty acres of dense woods next door to Mark and Rhoda Shifflet. Right after Rhett's job transfer went through, they built a sturdy home with some help from their Assembly neighbors to last them the rest of their lives. As they settled into the countryside twenty miles outside of Richmond, Virginia, they thoroughly enjoyed raising their children with their Christian Assembly friends, who were also neighbors.

As they got older, Sabrina's children often asked, "Mom, can we meet the Shiffletts and play orphans at the fort?"

The tall hardwood and pine trees formed a high green canopy over Rhett's son Dawson and Mark's son Watson as they walked down the path between their properties to Taylors Creek to maybe catch some crawdads and baby catfish in their minnow traps.

But today they were fording the wetlands to check on the progress of the beaver's dam, and then check on their dads' progress upstream.

"Hold still Dawson, I'll swat that horsefly off you," said Watson.

"Just clap your hands on it, don't hit me like last time," said Dawson.

Stealthily creeping through the tall grass to sneak up on the unsuspecting beavers, their heads popped out right over a perfectly still beaver pond. *No beavers this time*, they thought. Poison ivy and chiggers were not on their minds yet, as the beavers took a break in hiding.

"Watson, let's kneel down here and wait for the beavers to come back. Isn't that awesome how fast they are building that dam?"

"Yeah... I'll cover your back for horse flies," whispered Dawson, and then, "Don't move! A dragonfly landed on you!"

The brilliant green dragonfly on Watson's outstretched arm was on the lookout, quickly rotating its head, then suddenly snatched an annoying deerfly out of mid-air that was buzzing around Watson's hair and landed on a nearby twig with the snack neatly trapped within its six legs.

That is so satisfying when they do that, thought Dawson, and said, "Hey Watson, let's go see how our dads are doing clearing the creek with the mini-excavator."

Meanwhile, back at Rhoda's home, she was letting the girls help make a batch of strawberry freezer jam.

"I'll ask your parents if they want to come over tonight for homemade ice cream, and we can use this leftover syrup as a topping!" Rhoda said.

Ruth's eyes sparkled back her answer, as the rest of the girls said, "Goody! Goody!"

The dense woods between their homes provided forts, shafts of sunlight perforating the forest floor as the Stuart and Shifflett gang raked out rooms for their houses. When Rhett asked his children to pray before a meal, or at night, they prayed, "And Lord, thank you for the trees." Children appreciate things like that.

Dawson even liked the trees in the winter. Rhett always thought Virginia trees were ugly until he watched Dawson carefully draw their tall thin winter shapes during a long message Deo gave. It was then Rhett saw the beauty in their natural winter forms.

Plenty of naturally made toys help eliminate the need for canned Worldly entertainment, thought Rhett that winter, poising with his camera to snap a few shots of the neighborhood kids launching from a jump they made at the end of a sled run below their home. Toby Tait was over with his two boys for the afternoon. Sabrina brought out hot chocolate, but she didn't stay out long in the cold because she didn't want to bother with tights under her dress. Tights made her dress bunch up, making it uncomfortable and awkward.

I'll put the pictures on a CD along with the pictures of the kids jumping in the leaves a few months ago, and give them to Mark, thought Rhett, jumping out of the way from an errant sled with two girls heaving snow balls at innocent bystanders as they zoomed past with uninhibited laughter.

Since they all believed Christians should be perfectly joined together in the same mind and the same judgment, the standard of dress and lifestyle was pretty much the same. The girls just put a hand on their dresses to keep them from blowing up as they slid down the hill. Conforming to the same dress code reduced conflict, but it did get some unwanted stares when several ladies went shopping together with their daughters, all wearing shin length dresses and full blouses. Sabrina worried people might think they were part of a cult.

Cary Murdock, their minister, spoke often about how important it is to be connected, and to attend all the functions so the children will not miss out. "Less chance of losing them to the World," said Cary, "if they are connected to the Assembly."

Visiting after the many Assembly activities, home school outings, and impromptu visits during the week allowed Sabrina to quickly make much valued friends with other ladies in the Richmond Assembly. There were never any problems to speak of when Rhett and Sabrina's children were playing with Mark and Rhoda Shifflett's children. Sabrina and Rhoda sent their kids to borrow sugar and butter from each other; Rhett hardly ever had to bring their vehicles to the dealer: Mark was willing to work on them for a reasonable amount right next door.

When Sabrina was very pregnant with their fourth child, Rhoda offered to plan Rhett's big Four-O surprise birthday party with the whole Richmond Assembly for Sabrina.

Building a house, pasture fence, or a barn were all neighborhood events. The many willing hands made the work light.

After a usual Wednesday night meeting in Richmond, as the people sat or stood around visiting, and munching on surplus vending machine snacks one man thoughtfully brought for free from his job, Rhett scanned the room to check on his kids. *Ah, there is Sabrina, it is so good to see her happy, visiting in that circle with her friends. She always looks so alive and cheerful, and so interesting when she is with her friends. I don't know why she worries so much what the ladies think of her. And it looks like the kids are busy, trading stickers with their friends.*

A few Sundays a month were all day events at locally rented parks where the children enjoyed riding bicycles, playing kickball, and baseball.

During one of these Sunday events Deo Trophy came to speak that morning, as he did a few times a year. Calvin Hobkins was down from Fredericksburg also, sitting in the audience. Deo gave a detailed doctrinal study on something and Rhett's thoughts drifted.

Calvin, following close behind Deo, spoke up a few times during the message; benignly pointing out Deo's misquoting of a verse, or a point that didn't fit like Deo was trying to make it fit. This temporarily sent Deo into a tail spin as he recollected his impetus, but he was forced to oblige, since there was really no other option than to be corrected. Calvin possessed a singular gift of amassing much of the Bible to memory. His excellent recall of it equaled nobody else Rhett knew.

Later that afternoon, Rhett spotted Deo getting out of his brand new economy sedan, and decided to have some amusement at Deo's expense. Deo strove hard to keep an anti-materialistic culture in the Virginia Assemblies.

"Nice car Deo, it really looks nice!" Rhett said.

Deo uncomfortably shrugged his shoulders, not liking the insinuation of having expensive or wanton materialistic inclinations. "Yeah, I bought it after I retired; my old one was all worn out. I got a good deal on it."

Rhett smiled inwardly. "It sure is a sharp looking car."

"I had a lot of mileage on my old car. This new one should last me a long time," Deo said.

"I like the way those newer model cars look," Rhett persisted, with a friendly smile. *Why is it is so hard to criticize flattery, regardless of the motive?* thought Rhett, walking away to check on his kids.

Rhett was still feeling his oats later that day during the hamburger cookout. With Sabrina at his side, Jake and Lacy Beth sat across the wooden picnic table under the pavilion. Rhett watched out of the corner of his eye as Lacy Beth took a large bite of hamburger, and then gleefully asked her a question with a straight face, carefully choosing an open ended one that required much more of an answer than a nod for yes or a shake for no.

Lacy Beth struggled through her large bite as they all awkwardly watched, finally answering the question after she was able to swallow. Rhett waiting until his next bite had been swallowed himself, plotting his next move and watching for Lacy Beth to take another large bite. He didn't have to wait long, she was an easy target. He asked Lacy Beth the next question just as she committed, careful to not ask the question too early so she could simply withdraw the hamburger from her teeth and respond. Rhett's playful grin clued her in, all four of them laughing as she struggled through her large bite. Sabrina was relieved Lacy Beth laughed along with the joke.

For the first several years the activity schedule was very nice in Richmond. The many times together each week were allowing Sabrina and Rhett to cultivate close friendships in their Assembly, and they had enough time with their family.

But the year Jarvo left, Cary Murdock said the Assembly was growing and so were the needs. Over the next several months a few more "Friday night sing practices" were added. Most Sundays evolved into long all day events, and Rhett began to feel his relationships with his kids going downhill. A few older men objected, but Cary went forward with it after waiting a few months. Cary had Deo's full authority behind him.

The Richmond Assembly was evolving into a local church community on steroids.

"We are either getting in late, or I am tired and going to bed early. I need more time with my family," Rhett told Toby Tait.

Toby said, "Well, I'm out of that loop somewhat, due to hav'n young kids that need-a-nap."

Most local middle aged men argued young fathers ought to have the little kids sleep in the car at the park, and scoffed at the few parents giving their kids naps at home on the now-every-Sunday all day events. 'Family Time' was scoffed off as a lame excuse to come late or leave early from a function. The three older couples in the Richmond Assembly thought the old slower pace was better, but they kept quiet about it after speaking their mind when Cary first brought it up at the local leadership meeting.

George Taylor didn't like it either, but he was in leadership and couldn't say much about it as a leader who was suppose to be Orderly Following Cary Murdock, who was Orderly Following Deo Trophy. But George did once say, "I would like just a little more time to read my daughter a few books in the evening while I have the chance."

George loved playing football with all his sons and other Assembly boys Sunday afternoons, along with Cary.

George loved sports, but he wasn't allowed to play them in high school because James Stark had preached against it at the time. "Bad Company corrupts good habits; a little leaven leavens the whole lump," James argued from the pulpit. George never did quite agree with all the reasons. He was way too embarrassed to tell the guys at school why he couldn't play football with them. It just wasn't cool. George's dad forbid him to play, wanting to be in Unity with his brethren. But sports was the only connection George really had with his father.

Sabrina's love of gardening complimented her ability to prepare big dinner parties in her home. Slender, sweet, blonde, beautiful, and a scrumptious cook, she was the perfect wife. She didn't mind too much when visitors asked plant questions and admired her large thriving flower gardens, but she did plead needing to be more organized.

On Sundays, Sabrina liked to go out to eat with her friends, "When we have people over, I spend all the time cooking or cleaning up, but when we go out I can just visit and be with everybody," Sabrina explained to Rhett during one of their evening walks down their gravel road, as she waved to Rhoda out weeding her own flower beds.

Sabrina really looked forward to treasured social times with her friends. Home schooling the kids made it a long tiresome week, and the late Wednesday night meetings added to the burden. Recently the Wednesday night meetings were going until 9:45 pm; Julian Petros was having a hard time starting his actual lecture. Visiting for a few minutes afterwards, the forty minute drive home, then finally getting the kids wound down for bed at 11:15 pm made her dread the added trouble of waking them for home school in the morning.

Deo came to Richmond on another Sunday to give a message, "I'm going to speak this morning on the wiles of the Devil with women this morning. I hope this is educational and instructive. This is going to be very biased against women, I am just giving one side of this."

Deo got some of them laughing with his story of Eve and the Serpent, how it was Eve who was deceived. He spent most of his sixty minutes elaborating on it:

> Every woman has an overwhelming urge and tendency to teach and have authority over a man. Some women control it. But all women have this urge. All problems that go on and on and on and on... trace them back, they always start with a woman who said, 'I have an idea!' Now, maybe there are some problems that weren't caused by a woman. Do you know of any? - I don't know of any.

> Remember, Adam had a great relationship with God, face to face, but he was still deceived by listening to his wife. Men who listen to their wives, what happens? Problems, lots of problems. Then they get bitter! That's why the Bible warns against getting bitter against your wife, because you listened to them! When husbands don't listen to their wives, what do the wives think of them? Ungodly, unspiritual? What? ..... That's right, unspiritual.

> Remember, it was EVE who got deceived. At least she got THAT right when she told God it was the serpent who deceived her! And what do women do when they are questioned? Sarah lied, didn't she? Yes, she lied and told God she didn't laugh. It was because she was afraid. Women get afraid, and then they lie.

> Remember the story of Eve and the Serpent... It is the greatest example in the Bible on good and evil, and it explains the source of sin in the world.

Deo gave a few pretty funny impersonations of a woman sobbing while trying to put pressure on her man when she didn't get her way.

He ended the meeting with a warning:

Now as a warning to you young men. Let me tell you, when you get married the bad times will far outweigh the good! So don't tell me I didn't warn you up front about it!! Don't feel disappointed when, as you get older, you can recall mostly bad times as you reflect back in your marriage.

Rhett and Sabrina went with their friends out to eat on that pleasant sunny spring Sunday. Rhett looked at his burrito lying in a basket in front of him, and observing all his close friends sitting with him, thought, *We are so lucky*.

The fifteen or so children were chatting pleasantly at tables near them. Most of the people had quickly cleared out of the restaurant when they all arrived, but the children *were* well behaved.

"How could things get any better than this?" Rhett said.

"What do you mean?" asked Mark.

Rhett replied, "Our unity and relationships — we have a good thing going here... don't you think?"

"We do, but Satan is on the job and wants to destroy it."

"I know," replied Rhett, "we need to stay on guard against his devices."

Cary Murdock thought so too. He often said: "It is very important to have your children connected; you parents do not want to lose your children to the world. Your children will know they are connected by your commitments, your walk with the Lord. It is very important to make sure you come to all the functions and meetings, and on time. Staying late gives more opportunities for being connected. Those who have had problems with leadership will have their own problems with their children, because they are undermining their own leadership when they undermine leadership in the church."

There were *some* problems in Richmond. Rhett's oldest daughter, Julia, wanted to have friends but a few girls her age were downright malevolent. Julia would get ditched, left out, and suffered rude or catty comments. It ran off Julia like water off a duck's back, and Rhett thought of her as undauntable. But after several years Rhett was concerned, and carefully tried to change the situation. Julia just couldn't seem to win their approval.

"This has to be affecting her in a bad way," Rhett told Sabrina during one of their early morning walks, "but I can't do anymore than try and work it out with the dads, but any changes only last a day or two, then it just defaults back to the way it was."

After seven years of living in Richmond, Rhett concluded the real problem was actually the mothers, and it was just trickling down to their daughters. There wasn't much Rhett could do; they couldn't leave the truth of course, the only viable representation of the Body of Christ. These were the only girls Julia's age in their Assembly. Cary discouraged going to other nearby Assemblies to visit, except for every third Sunday when all the Assemblies met at Happy Hill. But the ditching went on there also.

Cary noticed the problems with some of the women and daughters in the Assembly also, and gave a really good series of messages on it. "Women and Girls want connection and approval more than anything else," Cary preached, "Girl bullies will use this need to manipulate and hurt other girls."

As Rhett tried to work through the problems with the fathers, he realized the girl's behavior would not change.

Some parents did well at following the dress and lifestyle standards, but were lacking in the be-nice-to-others department.

Finally Rhett encouraged Julia to just make friends with other people. "You need to expand your horizon; there are plenty of other girls older and younger in our Assembly for you to be friends with that are nice," Rhett said to Julia on a long drive together for the day. So Julia floated around with other people of all ages with the same cheerful outlook.

Rhett and Sabrina put on a teenagers party for Julia's thirteenth birthday party to help perk her up. Since the main 'girl bully' Arina was under thirteen years old, Rhett was able to have Julia's newly made older friends there, in spite of Julia's protest – she wanted the younger girls at her party regardless of how they treated her.

Rhett conspired with some young men to crash the girls-only party, and they all snuck in the basement, surprising the girls during a balloon stomp game. The party was on full throttle the rest of the evening with games, skits, and visiting.

One of the moms told a teenage young man on his way to Julia's party, "We are taking Arina and my daughter out for ice cream to cheer them up since Julia didn't invite them to her party."

Arina lost no time in blaming Julia for excluding her, turning some girls against Julia behind her back, even though it was actually Rhett who had done this with Cary's advice, to only include those thirteen years old and up.

Julia told her dad a few years afterwards, "I wanted to invite Arina because I was afraid she would talk bad about me to others."

"Well," said Rhett, "I guess we found out you were right! Sorry about that!"

There were some rules Cary Murdock asserted that Rhett thought was a little extreme. Cary would have never agreed they were rules, just 'things encouraged and things discouraged by ministry'. But they were carefully followed rules all the same with consequences for not obeying. The consequences were usually indirect public admonishments with no names mentioned. Cary didn't want anybody getting a drink of water during their sing practices, sometimes the singing went straight for two hours or more. Also, no sandals for men, shirts had to be tucked in, and no Hawaiian shirts, even during social gatherings at homes in the evening. Deo disapproved of Hawaiian shirts and had spoken against them for years. Jonathan Ranger was one of the young people who wore a Hawaiian shirt.

Jonathan was one Sabrina's five younger brothers, and came out from California to Virginia in 2000 to help Rhett and Sabrina build their home. He liked it so much he ended up moving out permanently, much to Sabrina's delight. She was homesick for the blue skies of California, and it was nice to have Jonathan near them. Jonathan was an excellent construction worker, furniture maker, and loved rock climbing. Virginia couldn't match the Sierra Nevada Mountain's rock climbing, but Jonathan did find a few places to climb in Virginia.

> Behold, how good and how pleasant it is
> For brethren to dwell together in unity!
> - King David in Psalms 133 -

5.

Jonathan

Hawaiian Shirt Sundays in the relaxed easy-going Visalia Assembly in Central California during the 1990's made Jonathan have a hard time comprehending why it was wrong to wear Hawaiian shirts in Virginia when he moved there in 2000.

"I think I'll just skip wearing them now, Rhett. These leaders think it's wrong. I don't agree with it, but I am getting tired of them talking about it to me. I guess I'll need to do this Orderly Following thing to avoid a conflict," said Jonathan, after a year of living in Virginia.

"Well Jonathan, I think you're unintentionally sending off the wrong message when you wear them. When in Rome, do as the Romans do. I tuck my shirt in now. You'll just be seen as independent and rebellious if you don't follow the rules. You probably don't realize how bright they are because you're color blind."

Jonathan didn't go much for style. As he would put it, when it came to fashion he was the last hog to the trough. Jonathan's older brother Hank told him years ago he needed to start working out to have bigger muscles. Jonathan's response - "I don't even use all the muscles I have now, so why do I need more?" made them all laugh. Hank loved to work out, and felt he could never have enough muscles.

When Rhett was over visiting Sabrina during their courtship, Jonathan's sudden burst of laughter floating down from his upstairs room through the open foyer over the living room was a vivid reminder of his book reading habits, temporarily pausing all conversations within earshot. Even though it was Jonathan who had the problem, he was the one who put the 'Reading limited to short stories and the Bible' on the family's only bathroom door, in the small home they moved to shortly after Sabrina and Rhett were married.

Jonathan also gave up wearing his dog tag necklace after moving to Virginia, the one proving he could legally carry concealed guns. Jonathan was a late bloomer in California. His move to Virginia when he was twenty gave him a fresh start, and he made many close friendships.

Jonathan quickly gained a reputation with his talented construction skills developed by his father since childhood. Like the time the mini-market at the beginning of Highway 20 in Charlottesville had a car driven through the front of it. Jonathan was called out to do the temporary fix. Jarvo's younger brother, Hobbs, was driving past and reminisced: "I saw this large group of men standing around watching, and in the center of them was this flurry of activity. Plywood flying around as it was being cut and nailed up. It was Jonathan, doing a one man boarding-it-up show. Everybody else just got out of the way and watched!"

Rhett had a special young girl picked out for Jonathan before he moved out. Marilyn was quiet, but not shy, and considerate of others. Not wanting to match-make, Rhett and Sabrina quietly observed Jonathan fitting in with the young people, and were happily surprised when Jonathan fell in love with Marilyn. Early on, Marilyn got Jonathan out during a basketball game of Knock Out, and told Jonathan in her soft but crisp quiet voice, "I don't play favorites." Rhett roared with laughter when Jonathan told him, and Jonathan kept trying to win her affection, fighting back periods of despair.

Marilyn was drawn by Jonathan's unpretentious commitment to serve the Lord. Jonathan regularly read his Bible, applying it with humility in his daily life, and aspired to maybe be a bishop someday, Lord willing.

After several months of courtship, hundreds of wedding guests celebrated the occasion with Jonathan and Marilyn at Happy Hill in 2003. Jonathan was so happy and distracted he almost ran into a tree in their borrowed car as they left.

Jonathan and Marilyn were seen around town over the next month, slowly hugging and kissing in the parking lot, as Jonathan took his time opening the door for Marilyn to get into Jonathan's old beat up blue Toyota pickup he still had from California.

Unfortunately, Jonathan broke his promise of giving up rock climbing after he got married. Liking the extreme California image of using his rock climbing skills while installing windows, Jonathan tied a sturdy rope to a wide piece of nylon webbing, and began installing windows twenty feet up at The Center for the Deaf and Blind in Fishersville.

The knot gave way.

The cloud cover prevented the helicopter from flying. The ambulance took Jonathan to a local hospital, which sent him to the UVA trauma center, but it was too late. Jonathan had a large amount of internal bleeding in his brain, leaving his eighteen year old bride of seven weeks to decide if or when she should take her husband off of life support.

Surely this isn't hopeless. Lord, please help Jonathan! Surely he will pull through this and come out of his coma, prayed Rhett when he got the phone call from Sabrina at work.

Jonathan's four brothers, parents, and other friends flew out from California to give their support, including the minister from Visalia, California: Peter Waters and his wife Joy.

The young neurosurgeon diplomatically explained the reason for the large white bandage over the entire top of Jonathan's head with "No Bone" scrawled across his temple in red marker.

Rhett felt the ground falling away from him. Somehow managing to make it out of the room without fainting, he sat down on the floor outside of Jonathan's intensive care room with his head on his knees, trying to keep from blacking out.

Later that day Rhett left Jonathan's room and exited the double trauma center doors of the Neurological ICU.

Deo Trophy was there waiting for him.

Deo came towards him and said, "Rhett, we are praying for you!" and embraced Rhett with a long, rigid hug.

Rhett felt himself getting off balance in Deo's tight hold, and began leaning onto Deo's lean hard body. Since nobody else was in sight, Rhett bent his knee and stuck his right lower leg partially out behind him to keep balance. Deo hugged him even tighter, and Rhett felt himself getting pulled more off balance, leaning on Deo even more, so Rhett stuck his leg out straight behind him, as high as he could, as he balanced on one foot. But it still wasn't enough to avoid leaning onto Deo's rigid chest.

"We are praying for you," said Deo fervently into Rhett's ear, "for you all. I know this is such a difficult time, but I know God is there for me, and I want to be here for you."

I just hope nobody sees my leg sticking straight out behind me, they'd think I was odd, thought Rhett, waiting for the hug to end.

After his very long, awkward hug, Deo said, "I'd like to get the families together to talk about Jonathan. Could you coordinate that?"

Still feeling embarrassed about sticking his leg out behind him, and hoping Deo hadn't noticed, Rhett heartily agreed. After gathering all the families together, Deo told them, in Marilyn's absence, "This is Marilyn's decision. Let her decide if Jonathan should be taken off of life support."

"That was a really helpful piece of advice Deo gave us," Rhett later commented to Hank, Jonathan's oldest brother. They all knew Jonathan would not want to be a burden to Marilyn, and for her to remarry again someday.

After a few days the doctor assured them again there was very little chance of any recovery. Marilyn said she would let Jonathan be taken off of life support. The entire family on both sides supported her. The doctor said it might take up to several days before Jonathan actually died.

Rhett went to Jonathan's room a few hours later with Julian Petros, and checked Jonathan's eye for himself to see if there was any reaction to light, if there was any glimmer of life except for the labored breathing and beating heart.

Rhett knew mistakes were made at hospitals, and sometimes doctors can be wrong. Nobody else involved had any medical background, and there was nothing to indicate Jonathan would ever recover. They came to take Jonathan for a MRI and as the gurney went over a bump, Rhett saw Jonathan throw his arms out in response as if to balance himself.

After a night of not sleeping, Rhett and Sabrina wearily came down the next day to the hospital cafeteria, finding it packed with about two hundred Christian friends from the Virginia Assemblies, mostly from Charlottesville. Rhett fell asleep sitting upright while his friends talked, and then made his way over to a requested meeting with Deo Trophy and the three leaders from the Richmond Assembly: Cary Murdock, George Taylor, and Julian Petros.

"Rhett," said Deo Trophy, "I understand you pushed for an MRI on Jonathan's brain. I thought we all decided there was no hope. Marilyn made her decision to let Jonathan go."

Rhett felt he might have done something wrong by Deo's tone of voice, and said, "I am concerned with Marilyn feeling she should have let Jonathan live, later on down the road. Trauma centers can make mistakes, and I want some evidence to show Marilyn later if she regrets taking him off life support after this is all over. Marilyn is agreeable to this and so are Jonathan's brothers. We all talked about it."

"Well!" responded Deo, "I guess we need some people going across the current sometimes. But keep in mind this is a really tough thing for Marilyn, and if you push for things giving false hope, it will make it more difficult for Marilyn and not easier. Another concern I have is, I understand you invited Tommy Sooner up to see Jonathan. As you know, Tommy has left our Christian fellowship over a year ago, and he should not be here at all. Tommy is out of the will of the Lord by leaving the Christian fellowship the Lord has provided him and forsaking the leaders the Lord has entrusted to Tommy to help him in his life. His mother Lorna Sooner invited him here to the hospital and she should not have done this. Tommy's parents should not be contacting him. Lorna has created a lot of confusion by doing this."

Hmm, why did I invite Tommy up to Jonathan's room? I thought it might sober Tommy seeing his cousin's husband and former friend on life support. Guess it wasn't a good idea. "Ok, I'll let Tommy know he isn't invited anymore," said Rhett.

Cary Murdock spoke up quickly, "We already let Tommy know he shouldn't be here, and he left."

Something about all this just didn't seem right, but Deo had been a minister for twenty-three years by 2003, and knew more than he did. Rhett was just thirty-eight years old at the time.

Although Tommy had appreciated Deo's counsel regarding his parent's problems in his youth, Tommy hadn't agreed with Orderly Following. Wanting to be able to make his own decisions in life, he unexpectantly moved out of his grandparent's home after being surprised by a public reprimand at Happy Hill for working as a bouncer at a nightclub and getting a concealed tattoo, after he had already given a requested confession at a local Richmond meeting. Tommy quickly cut off all contact, knowing he would be shunned anyways after he left, and wanted to avoid being marked. Not that there was much of a distinction between a shunning and a marking, but he wanted to avoid the latter if possible.

After a few more emotional days at the hospital, while Rhett and Sabrina were sleeping on the floor outside of Jonathan's room, Marilyn came out at 3:12 am and woke Rhett up.

"Jonathan's breathing has slowed!"

Rhett quickly got up and followed Marilyn into Jonathan's room. He put his arm around Marilyn's shoulders by the bedside as Jonathan's breathing grew more and more labored, and then stopped. His face turned grey as his spirit left. Jonathan was gone.

"Blessed in the sight of the Lord is the death of his saints," Rhett told her quietly.

Marilyn asked for some time alone with Jonathan's body, and the families were called from nearby hotels. As they sat in the room with Jonathan, Marilyn played a music CD made by their friends a few years earlier. Even though Rhett knew the CD well, every song seemed so different, and new, with so much more meaning.

Coming home to a lawn freshly mowed by one of their Christian friends, Rhett and Sabrina were ready to get some much needed sleep. As Rhett was writing a detailed e-mail to his mother, Sabrina slowly walked from room to room, looking at all the many pieces of furniture in her home Jonathan had made for her, the paneling, the wood trim throughout their home, and emotionally cried out, "Everywhere I look, there is Jonathan!" After a long hug and more tears, Rhett and Sabrina finally got some sleep.

A few days later Marilyn asked Rhett, "Why did the Lord take Jonathan home? I need him more than God does!"

Rhett said, "We live in a sin cursed earth where there is gravity, chance, and circumstance. I think the Devil had more of a part in his death than the Lord. Satan can hinder us and cause death for Christians, but the Lord is always with us. To be absent from the body is to be present with the Lord. What happened was bad, but the Lord can use it for good later, we just need to trust in Him, and He will take care of Satan in His time."

Jonathan and Marilyn's parents and siblings met at Jar and Mamie's large home in Charlottesville after they graciously offered to have a lunch for them; so typical of their Virginian hospitality (This was in 2003, three years before Jar was marked).

Jonathan and Marilyn's families quickly planned the funeral. Julian Petros, the young minister from Richmond, was the only leader there during the planning lunch. Rhett suggested somebody go over the events of Jonathan's life, and Julian suggested it be Rhett. Marilyn and Rhett agreed.

"If it is okay with you Marilyn, I'll read some interesting incidents of his life, and at certain points I'll introduce you and others who want a chance to say something," Rhett told Marilyn, as Jar and Mamie served up an oriental chicken salad to the twenty or so people sitting around the table on their large deck overlooking the Virginia countryside.

Marilyn said, "That sounds really good!" with a soft firm smile, looking Rhett in the eyes. *"Quiet but not shy" was what I told Jonathan about her*, Rhett thought, smiling back.

The funeral arrangements were settled. Julian would scan some photographs in to project on the Big Screen up front, and start out by trying to reach others for Christ who would be there from Jonathan's work. Rhett would read his narrative of Jonathan's life, with Marilyn, Jonathan's dad, and others interjecting memories and stories about Jonathan.

"I want this to be about celebrating Jonathan's life here on earth," said Marilyn in her calm soft voice.

Over the next few days Rhett heard Deo Trophy and Cary Murdock were going to speak at the funeral. *They are the ministers, they know best*, thought Rhett, *but I hope they don't go long.*

Rhett looked out over the packed room from behind the podium. Julian was sitting on a chair a few feet to Rhett's right side working the computer projecting the pictures of Jonathan's life on the Big Screen. *Must be five hundred people here; they're even standing in the back because we ran out of chairs.*

"Rhett, you're on," Julian whispered.

Clearing his throat, Rhett told them of Jonathan's life, including his magic tricks, which almost always ended in failure.

"His most famous trick was his rope trick. When Jonathan was ten years old, he decided to put on a magic show during a Visalia Assembly talent night. He passed over some kids raising their hands, and asked Rob to come up on the stage during their annual talent night. Nobody knows why Jonathan picked Rob Hemlock, a retired school teacher in Visalia," said Rhett.

"Jonathan began tying the rope around Rob's waist, telling the audience when the rope was pulled tight it would magically come undone. Then Jonathan and his assistant grabbed their ends and yanked hard as the audience watched with baited breath. The rope didn't magically come off; it got tighter, much tighter, dramatically squeezing in Rob's middle as he looked very surprised back at the audience with a suddenly skinny waist. But Jonathan wasn't bothered by the long roar of laughter; he simply re-did the trick again during other talent nights. Jonathan's philosophy was, "If I can't do the trick right, I might as well get a laugh out of it"."

Rhett then introduced one of Jonathan's newly made Virginian friends, Art.

Art got up with the cordless mic, and said, "Shortly after I met Jonathan, I found out he liked guns. I was never around guns much when I was younger, but Jonathan was, and he really liked guns. Really liked guns. One time, soon after we got to know each other, Jonathan and I got lost in a bad part of town near Washington, D.C. It was a really bad area, late at night, and we were in a liquor store parking lot in Jonathan's truck reading a map. There were several dangerous looking people walking by and looking at us. I told Jonathan I sure hoped we weren't going to be robbed. Jonathan just grinned as he reached into the back seat, and whipped out a handgun and cocked it. As I sat there in shock and fear, Jonathan told me, 'Don't worry Art! I've got one for you too!' and reaching back, cocked another handgun and handed it to me!"

After comments from Marilyn and Jonathan's father, Rhett ended his thirty-five minute eulogy with, "I can imagine Jonathan in heaven visiting with Elijah, saying "Oh, my friends on earth? They will be here with me soon." Our lives are so short. Jonathan only had a second to think things over as he fell, but he had already made his choice. I know he is with the Lord."

Rhett glanced over at the back left of the packed room of Happy Hill, where Jonathan's former co-workers sat listening intently. Many of them were unsaved, getting the time off with pay to go to the funeral.

When Deo Trophy got behind the podium, Rhett hoped he wouldn't go long.

Deo spoke for about an hour or so in the packed Happy Hill auditorium on Orderly Following and Hawaiian shirts. How, even though Jonathan never understood the reason why he should not wear them, Jonathan finally did submit to his brethren and leaders and stop wearing Hawaiian shirts. Julian was still running the computer and showed a picture of Jonathan when he had first moved to Virginia, wearing a brightly colored Hawaiian shirt.

Sabrina was really bothered that Deo would speak on Hawaiian shirts at her brother's funeral.

Justin (Jonathan's brother who had also moved to Virginia when Rhett and Sabrina did in 2000) commented, "I had to go out of the funeral service during Deo's speech, and I talked to a man I think might be unsaved while I was in the restroom. He told me he could not believe anybody could possibly be so against Hawaiian shirts to speak about them at a funeral! How is that helping him believe in Christ?"

Cary followed with a forty-five minute speech on 'Accountability', how Christians all need authority in their lives to be accountable to, pointing out Jonathan had submitted, even though he wasn't in agreement with some things.

The service was almost three hours long, with Deo in the lead for airtime.

And you will seek Me and find Me,
when you search for Me with all your heart.
- Jeremiah 29 -

6·

James Stark

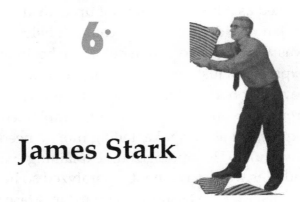

James Stark was fourteen years old when his severely disabled thirteen year old brother died, a tragedy James seldom spoke of.

James was a teenager in Southern California during the 1950's; flat top butch haircuts, white t-shirts, and peg-leg pants. When James wasn't working long hours he liked messing around a little with cars in the desert. Norris' treatment of his mother really bothered him, but there was not much he could do about his father's verbal abuse. Starting to work since the eighth grade, he sometimes had to ditch school for his construction job during high school.

One day a skip-loader bucket knocked him down, and as it came back up it caught his head between the bucket frame and bumper on the tractor. During his lengthy hospital stay he thought more about the brevity of life, how the Lord must have kept him around for a reason, and he committed his life more to the Lord. However, James' muscles near the upper right side of his mouth were permanently damaged, giving him a tough-guy grimace with a hint of disapproval. His face always made the same unintentional expression, regardless of his mood. He looked as if he would not put up with anything.

James didn't like it, but couldn't help people thinking he was coming across harsher than he intended. His facial expression just made it seem that way, along with his cowboy boots and a flat-top hair cut, which was a souvenir from his youth. One woman complained about his grim expression as he spoke, telling him he needed to look more cheerful. He apologized, explaining part of his smile muscles were permanently paralyzed so he couldn't help it.

His brief job as a prison guard in Atascadero, California imprinted an unforgettable perspective of really raw human nature. He moved to Visalia and started his own construction company.

James supervised cooking breakfast meals in the kitchen at the Assemblies' large, twice a year regional camp meetings in California. After several years, he believed God called him into ministry. Over the years it became obvious what James Stark's burden was. James stressed husbands should love their wives, treating them with respect and honor, adore them and nurture them, providing for their personal and emotional needs. Wives needed to respect their husbands, with love and honor, as 'heirs together', and be available for intimacy.

He spoke often about raising children, for parents to have close personal relationships with their kids, loving and disciplining them carefully. And especially how important it was to teach them to love the Lord. He encouraged parents to teach young children work ethics, giving examples of his sons Archie and Byron each holding one end of a single 2x4 stud at very young ages as they carried the board over for their dad - "But the extra time spent when they are young is worth it because they learn good work ethics," he said.

He preached the advantage of children managing money at an early age, and truly set a good example by living what he preached as he toured the country with his wife, even after his own kids grew up and got married. One of the poems he often quoted was:

> I may never be as clever as my neighbor down the
> street, I may never be as wealthy as some other
> men I meet: I may never have the glory that some
> other men have had, But I've got to be successful
> as a little child's dad.

> There are certain dreams I cherish, that I'd like to
> see come true, There are things I would accomplish
> ere my working time is through; But the task my
> heart is set on is to guide a little child, And to make
> myself successful as that little child's dad.

> I may never get earth's glory; I may never gather
> gold; men may count me as a failure when my
> business life is told; But if the one who follows after
> is a Christian, I'll be glad -- For I'll know I've been
> successful as a little child's dad.

> Author unknown

One year he toured the country speaking on 'The Sculpturing of an Adult'.

"I saw a man at the fair in Southern California when we were doing our gospel outreach last year, and he was sculpturing a horse from a three hundred pound block of ice. I'd like to compare that to raising a child during the next few meetings. The ice was slippery and heavy for the man, making it difficult to handle, and also brittle. The ice sometimes melted too fast so a chemical was put on it to slow the melting. Some tools were used to sculpt large pieces quickly, and some were used for fine details at the end," preached James, attempting to get parents to focus on the art of child training.

James stressed the importance of praising young children for their efforts to encourage them, and to avoid being critical. He taught parents to watch out for them during Assembly activities: "There are predators in any group, and the Lord is counting on you to look out for your own children."

One thing James firmly believed and often preached was that lying justified the severest punishment for children: "Children need to know lying is very wrong."

James' own life backed up his words. He had a well earned reputation for being ruggedly honest and investigating situations very carefully. Everything he said publicly had been vigilantly checked out and confirmed with at least two witnesses. He was very careful to allow only verified facts into his brain, having a passion for definite and exact knowledge.

It was as if he owed the sharpness of his mind to truthfulness. James' mind worked more efficiently since he was so honest. His brain didn't get clogged up with remembering which lies he told, or what gossip he heard that was untrue. He just stuck to the truth, his neurons directing him back to the facts.

"I want to let you all know up front I check out any gossip you tell me, so if you tell me something I'm gonna follow up on it," preached James from the pulpit during one of his visits to Loomis, California.

In Rhett's uncomfortable experience it was done within a few seconds as James whipped out his cell phone to get both sides of the matter. Personal reputation and integrity was of the utmost importance, and James' conduct in being careful to fairly and impartially judge complicated situations earned him a good name as his forty years of ministry rolled by. James was virtually unimpeachable due to his extreme carefulness with the truth.

James move to Visalia, California from Atascadero in the 1970's didn't go well. The people in Visalia enjoyed their materialistic lifestyles, and didn't appreciate James Stark's conservative approach to the Christian life. James tried his best to convince people to live more simply but hardly anybody was interested. One Sunday morning James was speaking on a subject he knew was controversial, and looked out into the audience. He couldn't see anybody that would agree with what he said; he suddenly had severe stomach cramps and left the podium. After several minutes he came back and finished his message.

Over the next few years it became obvious James was not going to change the culture in the Visalia Assembly, and James wasn't going to change his beliefs, so he sold his construction company to one of his many Christian brothers he helped get started in home building, and moved to Fredericksburg, Virginia in 1978.

This experience left a permanent impression on his mind, and in his stomach. After leaving Visalia, he always stayed in the back of the room before he spoke. The Visalia experience played lifetime havoc with his stomach each and every time before he spoke for the next thirty years. Traumatic events have long lasting consequences.

Deo Trophy was introduced to the Assembly meetings in Fredericksburg around the time James moved there. Deo supported James Stark and his authoritative ministry. James appreciated his strong support, after all the adversity he had gotten in California.

A big priority for James was to keep the peace in Virginia, and the support he got was a welcome relief. James did not want to get run over again by forceful self-serving men, and what better defense than a good offense.

His truthful and honest public reporting, with witnesses and documentation to back it up if needed, earned him a lot of respect in Virginia. Counsel he took from many other leaders, elders, and deacons helped him keep the peace and make good judgment calls which bore the stamp of his integrity.

James was the king of common sense, having an extremely practical outlook on life. He saw things from both perspectives, and frowned on others taking things out of context, even if it was against somebody who disliked him or had wronged him. He was impartial on a personal level.

The contentious people in Visalia no longer absorbed so much time and energy, and he was able to focus on more positive ministry in Virginia. James really enjoyed speaking on how to have a happy marriage, and raising kids so they were a joy to be with. A lot of families benefited from his ministry in Virginia, as well as in Texas and California, during his frequent interstate travels during the 1980's and 90's.

James also spoke about the terrible effects of child molestation, and angry parents. "The wrath of man does not bring about the righteousness of God," James preached, "and your daughter will have nobody to go to if she is molested."

"A little leaven leavens the whole lump, bad company corrupts good habits. We need to stay away from outside influences that can lead us in the wrong direction, and take up a lot of our time, like television," James often said.

Not all the people appreciated James' leadership methods. In James' zeal to protect the flock he would sometimes resort to what some referred to as strong arm techniques. Like what happened with Albert Murdock, Cary Murdock's father, in the 1980's: Albert liked discussing the Bible openly without consideration of current Assembly doctrinal beliefs. After James moved to Virginia, Albert asked questions in meetings that seemed like they conflicted with current doctrine, so James successfully stopped him. Albert deeply resented this; he wasn't able to talk openly to others about the Bible anymore.

James thought just a few should be in true leadership in each Assembly, and gravitated towards defending them and backing them up as needed to make their authority stronger.

Some accused James of having short man syndrome, blaming this on James' strong handed approach to dealing with people who he thought were causing problems. James himself spoke at times on 'little man syndrome', applying it to himself, and how physical size impacts people.

James gave his opinion from the podium on what clothing and lifestyle standards people should conform to. Individual peer pressure took over from there as people conformed on the group level. He couldn't *make* people do what he asked, but he did use the podium to make it uncomfortable for those who didn't go along with him.

After several years of traveling around the country, James and Glenda's three kids grew up and got married. Glenda then told him, "You just go on ahead James, I'll stay home. My arthritis bothers me more when I travel."

So James began making some short trips on his own. James traveled to Loomis a few weekends a month when Rhett and Sabrina lived there in the 1990's, giving support to the local minister and Bishop, Aaron Adams.

James' place was not to be in charge of the entire country, just to travel and give support as it was needed. James never wanted to undermine any local leaders, just support them, and he was held in high esteem. But some thought he ought to broaden his opinion of who he considered leaders in each area.

Aaron really needed the support. He had bought into Deo's Orderly Following as James Stark had, and was having a hard time implementing it in Loomis.

One time, around 1997, seven men made some accusations against Aaron. James flew out for two weeks, carefully investigated it, talking privately to most of the people in the Assembly. He concluded Aaron was not the problem and wanted to clear him of the accused wrong-doing in a leadership meeting Saturday night. James thought the real problem was 'Scuttlebutt' being on the loose again, the name James came up with for all the gossip going on in Loomis.

James Stark's brother-in-law, Kevin Banks, lived there and he didn't care for Aaron's leadership style.

When Kevin was in his fifties, he made money out of things like using chicken wire in large old sheds to make dividers, renting the space out as mini-storage units. Kevin shrewdly bought some property near a newly announced highway and later sold the gravel in it for the road base. Sharp nosed and intelligent, he was a formidable game player when memorization, strategy, or monopolizing was involved. After being slaughtered by him and his wife one evening in a card game, Rhett and Sabrina never played that game again.

Kevin's kind-hearted wife was easy going, having an authentic love for people. Never complaining during the times Kevin unexpectedly announced he had just invited a few families over for dinner after a Sunday Loomis Assembly meeting, she just quickly produced a large meal.

On one of James' visits to Loomis, Mark London was also out visiting from Arkansas. Mark and his family stayed with Kevin. Kevin had a whole lot to say about Aaron, behind his back, and Mark wrote it all down later in private.

Mark was heading out of town Saturday evening to go back home, and stopped by the local Loomis Leadership meeting.

Rhett was talking to James Stark, Kevin's brother-in-law, before the meeting started as Mark walked into the building. He handed his notes to James Stark, briefly explaining them. Mark was eager to begin his drive home.

Just before the meeting began, Kevin strode up to the front, confident he and several others would topple Aaron in the meeting. Kevin told Aaron who was sitting behind the front table, "You ought to be sitting in the audience with the rest of us, the meeting will not be going well for you tonight!"

But Aaron stayed up front, along with James Stark and Tim Mervin, the minister from the Southern California Assembly. James thought poorly of what his brother-in-law was attempting, especially about the underhanded gossip to Mark London he had just learned of.

James began the meeting, facing the audience from behind the table, along with Tim Mervin and Aaron Adams.

Kevin sat on the front row of metal folding chairs, leaning forward in his seat. Kevin was ready to pounce, and James was poised to respond.

During the first half hour, Kevin started in with his accusations against Aaron. Knowing he was backed by several people sitting behind him instilled self-confidence.

James said, "Kevin, I'd like you to answer a question: Did you make these comments?" Slowly, with deliberation, he read Mark London's notes: "Aaron will squash you like a bug. You cross Aaron, and look out, he will crush you. Aaron is in charge here and he doesn't let anybody forget it, Aaron thinks he is the king here," and so forth, about twelve comments in all. All of the comments were quite opinioned and negative.

Kevin leaned weakly back in his chair, asking, "Where did you get those?"

"From Mark London"

"I don't remember Mark writing anything down when we were talking."

"Did you say these things, or something similar?"

The packed room was now very quiet, all were intently listening for Kevin's response. The water cooler noisily blew out some moist air in the back of the warm poorly ventilated rental building.

The several people sharing Kevin's complaints against Aaron decided it was prudent to keep quiet for now. It was better to wait and see what happened to Kevin. Now it was happening, and they were content to watch and listen.

"Well, I'm not sure I said ALL that," Kevin said, casting a quick glance over his shoulder.

James Stark leaned back, tilting his chair almost to the point of toppling over backwards, and propped his iconic cowboy boots up on the table. He looked over the paper at

Kevin with his unintentional characteristic grimace, "Well, let me read them one by one, and you tell me which ones you said and which ones you didn't say."

And James read them, all twelve, one by one, asking for Kevin's response after each and every one.

Kevin leaned back in his chair. He didn't say much for about three weeks.

James told Rhett the next morning, on Sunday, "I can't believe Kevin did that," with a sorrowful frown and shake of his head.

Several months later, Rhett spoke at a Wednesday night meeting about treating people with respect and dignity. The following Sunday James was in town. Several men surrounded Aaron and accused him of treating them poorly and mishandling the Assembly. James sent Aaron out of town, to Texas, and James responded the next Wednesday night meeting. The men who had challenged Aaron left their wives at home that evening.

Facing the small audience from behind the podium, face flushing red all the way up to his flat-top haircut, James pointed out at the audience so far his shoulders were turned sideways. "You men will PAY for how you treated Aaron someday!!" And James rebuked them during that forty-five minute speech. It worked, the accusers backed off.

James heavily preached in Loomis to just call people up and work it out, not gossip or run people down behind their backs, and set the example by whipping out his cell phone to clear it up right then. James didn't like problems stacking up on him. His mind rested easier that way. His memory matched the truth.

James and Glenda's three children all loved him very much, esteeming him highly. His two sons followed him into ministry around 1990; Archie Stark moved to the small Northern Virginia Assembly, Byron Stark to the large Texas Assembly, and his daughter stayed in Fredericksburg.

Around 2002, shortly after Rhett and Sabrina moved to Virginia, Glenda died after battling cancer for several months at their home in Fredericksburg.

Deo Trophy spoke at her funeral. There were about five hundred people in attendance.

Towards the end of the service, after striding up to the front, James told them, "My wife was molested when she was a young girl. Glenda suffered her whole life from this terrible ordeal. I tried to help her many times, and as I tried, I realized others suffered from this also. That is the reason I spoke so often on this. I wanted to help her and I wanted to help many of you. But, my messages didn't help her. Shortly before Glenda died, she wrote me a note..."

James cried. After a moment of struggling, he regained his composure, and finished —"Her note said "Thanks for your efforts, but I am still struggling." Glenda looked forward to her death, to be released from the battles within her mind, and now she finally is. She is with the Lord. Maybe I've said too much, but I wanted you all to know."

James remarried a year or so afterwards to Marie in California, who had also recently lost her husband to cancer. Marie was a spirited Peruvian, full of zest for life. She didn't have Glenda's personal hang-ups.

Unlike Glenda's ultra-conservative viewpoints, Marie thought it was fun to get her toenails done. The polish was clear, because red might cause too many problems with some older men and women who were used to things ultra-conservative. Pink wouldn't have gone over that well either, and besides, she didn't like pink. Red was her style.

So James moved from Fredericksburg, Virginia to Loomis, California to live with his new wife, leaving Deo Trophy in charge of the Assemblies in Virginia. James still spent most of his time traveling to the Assemblies, as he had his whole life, to Peru, Newfoundland, Texas, Oklahoma, and Virginia.

Marie really liked the excitement of traveling, compared to Glenda who had usually stayed home. Marie loved and appreciated her new husband, and they quickly bonded with a new, close, loving relationship.

His father's new wife bothered Byron. He had always thought ultra-conservative was the Lord's way. He kept his reservations mostly to himself.

Archie's own wife died of cancer about the same time as his mother, but Archie moved much faster than his father, choosing his new fiancée two weeks after the death of his wife, much to the consternation of many women. Archie's own three children kept quiet about the rapid family change.

Being away from his grown children wasn't concerning to James. Deo Trophy would likely outlive him and would be there for his kids to counsel with. After they moved away, James' sons still stayed in close contact with Deo Trophy of Fredericksburg.

Unknown to most people, James figured he didn't want his kids to be dependent on him throughout his life, that would be unhealthy. Although his personality didn't blend well with Deo's, he certainly didn't mind his kids getting regular counsel from James' staunch supporter, Deo Trophy.

When it became known Deo's son was sexually immoral in 2005, James became concerned about Deo's judgment, and registered it to him.

He began to think Deo was not the best person for his children and grandchildren to rely on.

God is our refuge and strength
A very present help in trouble
Therefore we will not fear
Even though the earth be removed
And though the mountains be carried
into the midst of the sea

Psalms 46 - the sons of Korah –

7.

Groupthink

The most important thing for Christians on this earth is to be a light to the unsaved. Rhett and his friends were taught their light would shine by the unity resulting from endeavoring to be perfectly joined together in the same mind and the same judgment.

The Virginia and Texas ministers made the judgment calls for standards of dress and lifestyle. When everybody else followed the minister's judgment calls, it demonstrated unity to the world. The world would observe their unity and testimony, and then hopefully turn to the Lord. In California the ministers voiced the judgment calls, but with input from the older respected people.

This worked well in establishing unity for the Assemblies since the 1950's. One problem was the standards, such as dresses or skirts for women, stayed in the 1950's. There were always some on the fringes who were Worldly, and allowed immodesty such as skirts above the knees, skirts with slits, or a little makeup. Pants for women were most definitely taboo. Earrings in

Virginia were discouraged, that would be considered "Worldly." There was no rule against them per se, but everybody knew women should not wear them, and hardly anybody did.

Leroy Luther, the minister in Oklahoma, came out in 2007 to speak in Fredericksburg, Virginia. His message that Wednesday evening was on women's need for modesty.

He preached, "Sandals expose women's feet, which is provocative. Bright colored clothes also attract ungodly attention to a women's sexuality."

"These thoughts just suddenly came to me," Leroy excitedly shared afterwards.

Leroy Luther had left the Loomis Assembly in California to be a minister in the small Oklahoma Assembly. He had been too rough with his movements and words on the basketball court with the young men in Loomis, like saying, "THROW IT TO ME! I GOT A SHORT ONE, GOT A SHORT ONE!" when one insecure short young man was covering him during a basketball game.

Preaching to the young men the next Sunday backfired. Other events continued piling up, and people didn't let Leroy forget his habitual misconduct and arguing during basketball games, even though Leroy gave up playing. So he moved to the small unorganized Oklahoma Assembly to implement Deo's Orderly Following there.

Cary was implementing Deo's Orderly Following in Richmond also.

"Why don't you just untuck your shirt?" Sabrina said every few months on Sunday mornings before Richmond Assembly meetings, "I really think it looks nicer to have you and Dawson have your shirts untucked."

"We aren't in California anymore, and if I do it here then I'll look independent and rebellious. I think it'd be okay for Dawson to have his shirt untucked this morning though, he's only six."

But when they were on vacation Rhett untucked his shirt and wore his sandals, feeling a little bit of a rebel.

Ministry encouraged everybody to just listen to music produced by their group. Especially Archie Stark, he thought the Assemblies needed to be self sufficient. The regional camp retreats provided an opportunity for people to sing, and these 'special numbers' were recorded. Copyright permissions were obtained, and the CD's, like the one Marilyn played right after Jonathan died, were distributed several months later. Sometimes it was several years later, because nobody got around to getting the copyrights for awhile. Some listened to music produced by others outside of the Assemblies, but it was generally frowned on.

Not everybody believed in this unity created by the leaders, which created turmoil at times. Like the split in 1986 in California. A Texas minister's involvement resulted in a mass marking of two thirds of the Visalia Assembly several years after James Stark had left California. Dudley Franklin had some issues within his own family a few years prior, but the Texas Assembly assured people out of state that it had all been cleared up.

Dudley's preaching greatly expanded the reasons for marking others with his no-nonsense I'm-right-whoever-disagrees-is-ignorant style of speaking, hand picking stories out of the Old Testament to support his doctrinal theories. He became the driving force behind the California mass markings after coming out to help 'deal' with the problems. James lived in Virginia when this happened, and solidly backed Dudley.

Peter Waters ended up in charge as a young minister in the greatly reduced Visalia Assembly, after Dudley Franklin went back to Texas to recuperate from the mass markings of about two hundred people he instigated.

Peter was one of the California ministers who were more lax with their rules than the Virginia and Texas Assemblies. "People need to have their own convictions on things," Peter Waters believed, "I shouldn't be forcing them on people."

Peter's reputation suffered for allowing less modest apparel. Peter even allowed shorts for men for a few years until he succumbed to pressure from ministers out of state.

"Faults? Is somebody claiming I have faults?" Peter questioned with a warm, hearty laugh, "Well, they won't have to look too far!"

Peter Waters was still in his early twenties when he moved up from Southern California to Visalia. His seriousness about Christ helped him pick up an unwanted dent in his door; somebody kicked it one dark evening at an Assembly meeting because they just didn't like his genuineness.

Randy Greens, Rhett's brother-in-law in California, lived in Visalia, and looked to Peter as a father figure. He complained to Peter about the shortcomings of his own father. Peter simply replied, "I wish I had a father," while tilting his tousled blonde head down, blue eyes towards the ground with a somber expression of undeserved regret. Although they were very close, the Orderly Following doctrine was subtly driving a wedge into a small weak crevice, eroding their relationship as it slowly impacted the entire Visalia Assembly. Randy was becoming convinced by ministry outside their Assembly that Peter was a 'weak minister'.

Peter's large frame got him through framing homes for twenty years before deciding to go into ministry. He drove an American made pickup that was usually about six years old, with a faded Bible on the dash he reached for at lunchtime. As far as Rhett knew, Peter and his wife Joy never got in any arguments the thirty-four years they were married so far; they just got along.

"Ah just let Peter recuperate for 'bout foorty minutes before talk'n to him when he gets home, he perks up after a litt'l bit," Joy said to Sabrina during one of their visits to Visalia. Coming from a large family with brothers in Texas may have helped Joy remember stuff like that.

Peter and Joy's marriage success was part Joy too, her cheerful outlook, cherubic countenance, and easy going personality helped avoid conflicts. Maybe it was part of Peter's easy going personality, or lack of a father, that made him not want to control adults in the Visalia Assembly.

Peter figured since he was self motivated to serve the Lord, others ought to be also. "Christianity shouldn't be legislated on adult Christians," Peter reasoned.

But Rhett was really impressed by the harmony in Virginia, with the unity in dress and lifestyle. There were no trouble makers getting out of pattern with the rest of the group, like in California. The few young women who wore too tight of a sweater, and young men who played too much volleyball or took up snowboarding were dealt with publicly in Virginia. They were not pointed out by name, but most people knew who they were when Deo Trophy gave his analogies, innuendos, and the scriptures to back up his reasoning on why they should conform to Orderly Following.

Sometimes everybody knew exactly who they were, like the time a few young men were criticized about their excessive volleyball playing to discourage them from playing so much. Afterwards, they didn't play so much.

Nobody was immune to or could escape from Deo's faithfulness in public ministry. It was a no-brainer to conform. Conforming to the group is much more pleasant than the alternative. Nobody wants public ridicule.

However, after living in Virginia for several years, it occurred to Rhett in 2006, shortly after Jarvo left, that the lack of controversy may not be all of a good thing. At first it was impressive to have a public message delivered by Deo Trophy with hardly any comments or questions afterwards. It seemed to Rhett, what was said by Deo was enough to think about without others throwing in their two cents at the end. Rhett hoped nobody would make any comments after sitting there with his family for four hours, even if it was important. Anybody who didn't clue in and made comments afterwards in Virginia were regarded as 'not tuned in much' by many. In California, several people usually made comments after the message, sometimes they would insert one during the message, and it was socially acceptable.

The monthly Thursday night local Richmond Assembly Leadership meetings were also a very refreshing change from all the controversy in the Loomis California Assembly Leadership meetings. Cary spoke for sixty minutes, Julian for another sixty, then there was a few minutes for comments from just anyone, and that was it.

In Loomis, Aaron would talk for twenty minutes or so, and then it was open for anybody to talk or make comments. When James was out visiting in Loomis he spoke for thirty minutes, and then opened it up for anybody to express their concerns. The comments James and Aaron made were to temper the emotions during the meeting. But Cary and Julian usually dominated almost the entire time in their leadership meetings, just as Deo normally did.

However, as time passed, there was a low grade of disturbance in Rhett's mind. Most things just went smoothly and unchallenged in Virginia. Men and women were taught, under Deo's Orderly Following doctrine, to just do precisely what they were told by those who controlled the podium. This brought unity and peace, and consequently they would be a light to the world. Then, as others looked on and saw their togetherness it would help lead the unsaved to accept Christ. The result was little controversy, which was peaceful, but seemed, somehow, unnatural.

After converting Cary Murdock to his doctrine, Deo put together a study, and after having it tempered by other leaders around the country in 1997, had it printed and distributed. One year later, in 1998, he traveled around in one of his rare trips around the USA to preach it many hours in each Assembly. Rhett and Sabrina still lived in Loomis, California. Rhett didn't appreciate the private criticism of some claiming it was too controlling. He had thought, *They are just revealing their weak spiritual condition in wanting to be independent and rejecting authority.*

One older man in California with some health problems had a heart seizure while reading Deo's Orderly Following study in 1997. When he died seven months later of cancer, he warned his grown children on his deathbed of Deo's Orderly Following, telling them, "We are not Robots."

The key points in Deo's Orderly Following doctrine:

1) In the Church, leadership is to be obeyed and followed (Eph 4:11-16, 1Th 5:12-13, Heb 13:7, 17, 1Ti 3:4-5). Our duty is to obey those that God has placed in positions of authority. They are to be obeyed because that is pleasing to Him, not because the individual merits it. This is very important to understand and truly believe.

2) <u>God</u> puts leaders in <u>and takes</u> them out. Those under authority <u>do not</u> have the privilege <u>to install or remove</u>. They only have the <u>privilege to recognize</u> either what God has done and is doing or that an individual has misunderstood what God wishes to do with them. <u>This is an essential difference between man-made "hire and fire" mechanisms of sectarianism and the divinely ordered Body of Christ.</u>

3) It is undeniably clear in the scriptures that God chooses to direct the lives of those that are His through the agency of leaders in positions of authority.

4) If we can obediently do what one in authority directs us to do, then the one in authority is responsible before God for what was done. (Consider the accounts of Sarah misleading for Abram's sake and Joab seeing to the murder of Uriah for David's sake.)

Deo underlined some words for emphasis.

With the exception of Jar's comments, when he was able to speak up, not much was controversial in Virginia. Deo came down hard on some fathers for allowing snowboarding, and using religious curriculums for home school, but the few conflicts soon settled down and fizzled out. Some things bothered Rhett, and he wanted to say something, but it was definitely not the norm to stir things up with counterpoints or criticism. The few occasions people did ask disputing type questions, like Jar, the others looked on with shock and disappointment.

Since there was very limited interaction with any from outside their group, and not much challenging within, it was easy to just go along with Deo. It was usually okay to ask questions for clarification. It was not okay to challenge publically, or privately afterwards.

Most teaching, books written, and messages given by anybody outside of their Assemblies was discouraged by the leaders, since the preachers were sectarian. Deo preached the only book the Assemblies needed was the Bible, and emphasized the doctrine of not getting involved with politics, or even voting. Sometimes he would go over a book he had read, but he certainly didn't recommend that for others. Deo certainly recommended Bible study based on his own messages.

They had separated themselves from the rest of the Christians in the world who were denominating and having a name on their buildings. Any Christian who was met was quickly assessed to see if they wanted to 'be a part' of the Assemblies. If there was no interest in coming to Assembly meetings, then most Assembly people had no interest in spending any more time with them. Most people of the Assemblies would even object to having the word "Assembly" capitalized.

Cary Murdock certainly didn't challenge Deo Trophy. Cary was one of Deo's strongest supporters. Cary had almost left the Assemblies when he was in his late twenties, but Deo had talked him out of it.

When Cary's teenage daughters started wearing their sweaters too tight, it was predictable Deo would soon do a message on modesty and put a stop to it.

"Toby, you ought to have your wife wear looser sweaters," Rhett told his friend Toby Tait confidently one evening over another fabulous creation by Sabrina; pecan pie with vanilla ice cream. "Deo will probably speak on modesty at our regional gathering, and if it was me, I wouldn't want to have the spotlight turned on me when I am sitting there with my wife."

Sure enough, Deo let them all have it at Happy Hill a month later in intense modulated points.

Deo said, "I was sitting in my car with my son, and I saw this young women walking in front of us in the cross walk with a large split up her skirt. My eyes were — RIVETED! I lost track of who I was or where I was!" A man quietly pointed out to Deo after the meeting that Deo's own wife had a small slit in her skirt.

Although a bit upset, Cary put up with Deo's admonishment and conformed.

Cary Murdock's father, Albert, was drawn to the Assemblies because of their willingness to go to the Bible for answers, lacking a set of undisputed doctrine. Albert and his wife stayed and raised their children in the Assemblies. Albert Murdock's intellectual outlook on life was influenced by his job as the head of a local universities science department. Unfortunately, it didn't blend well with James Stark's construction boss leadership style.

James Stark's authoritive We-have-got to-have-unity-in-our-beliefs personality clashed with Albert Murdock's quiet intellectual small group discussion approach of reasoning-through-scriptures,-we-need-to-walk-in-our-own-convictions.

James thought Albert was trying to mold people's minds with leading questions, and put a stop to it. James knew Albert did this as a university professor with his work and didn't want him to change the Assemblies doctrines. Dudley Franklin, the minister from Texas who came to Virginia to deal with people before James, had already tried to shut Albert down. The second encounter with James left Albert sitting in the back of the meetings, rarely speaking up for years.

Unlike his son Cary, Albert quietly thought the Dudley Franklin instigated 1976 wholesale markings in Virginia, and the 1986 mass domino markings in California, were unbiblical, and his continued quiet lack of support made James Stark and Deo Trophy uneasy. Albert's four grown children gave him some influence. Albert Murdock's son being Cary Murdock, the minister in Richmond, Virginia, and his daughter was the wife of Joshua Jude, the minister in Atascadero, California.

Cary Murdock resented James Stark's strong arming of his father, privately saying around 1999: "My dad is the rightful minister in Richmond. If it hadn't been for James Stark, he'd be the leader here."

Deo Trophy didn't care for Albert Murdock's self professed quest for truth either, but he befriended Albert's son Cary. Deo saw the value in Cary's intelligent mind and simple but dynamically poised speaking style. So he took Cary Murdock under his wing to teach him the value of Orderly Following in the mid 1990's. Deo claimed it was this effort with Cary that lead him to his extensive Orderly Following study and lectures, although he had been vehemently promoting it since at least 1985 at regional Virginia camp retreats.

After James left Virginia, Deo assumed the position as the main leader. James had balanced Deo out when he was around, but Deo was now having trouble finding his own equilibrium without the senior minister around to whack him back in line with common sense when he needed it.

Major differences in standards and doctrinal beliefs were addressed in country wide leaders of the leaders weekend meetings in Texas, about twice a year, to make sure the whole country was in unity and on the same page with doctrines and standards.

In 2007 Rhett's dad called and told him about the leadership meeting in Texas. James Stark had led out, and asked the leaders to consider if four time honored traditions were based on the Bible, or just traditions. Two of the standards James brought up were if it was okay for women to wear pants, and if drinking wine was okay. Mycroft thought the meeting was good; it was a brain storming session with no conclusions, which confused a few leaders who weren't used to that format, but most liked it. Julian Petros spoke of it when he got back to Richmond; he was excited to be able to talk openly about their beliefs. The other two standards discussed were if it was okay to vote, and if it was okay to join a union in employment. Voting, unions, pants for women, and drinking wine were considered taboo by most, due to the public ministry on the subjects.

In Virginia, Deo explained what was wrong or right by giving one of his confusing long winded and strongly worded messages. His intensity and emotion at times gave no doubt to what he wanted to have happen.

Many of the people in Virginia were born and raised in the Assemblies, and it seemed a normal way of life to them. The few people who drifted in from the outside world quickly conformed to what everybody else was doing, or left. Most left.

The Orderly Following doctrine created a very loyal-to-Deo-Trophy environment. It was almost like Deo felt he had illusions of invulnerability, all he did should not be questioned, except to clarify what they thought Deo wanted them to do.

Deo claimed he knew the will of the Holy Spirit with who should be involved in situations, and could read the hearts of others. He said "You can read my heart, and I can read all of your hearts," in a message he gave, calling it "Accountability for Speech."

As time went on, it got worse. James Stark had always traveled a lot but now only came out a few times a year to visit since he was focused on getting to know his new wife, Marie, in California since 2002, and wasn't much of an influence anymore in Virginia.

"I think we are falling into a Groupthink pattern here," Rhett said during one of his few chats with Deo, "The Nixon administration just all agreed with each other and it was disastrous. We need leaders who can think critically and are not afraid of challenging what we believe. The important thing is going back to the Bible for the answers, and the truth."

Deo looked thoughtful, as if he was trying to hide his annoyance with a less alert intelligence, looked down at the ground briefly as his brow cleared, and then, after a brief pause with his head still tilted downward, humbly said, "We certainly need to carefully consider what we believe."

Rhett thought, *I expressed my concerns and that is all I can do. Like Deo preaches, I talked to him about it like Matthew 18 says to do.*

Deo changed the subject and asked Rhett, as he frequently did, "Howz your dad doing out in California?"

"I think he's doing fine, but I haven't talked to him for awhile," Rhett said, as he usually did.

"Deo always looks like he wants to talk more about my dad," Rhett told Sabrina while driving home on a windy rural road after the weekend camp retreat, "but I don't leave him any opening and he can't say anymore without it being awkward."

"He always asks about my dad too," said Sabrina, "I don't really want to talk to Deo about my dad either, it's personal. Why do you suppose he does that?"

"I dunno," said Rhett, already preoccupied with a new thought that just hit his mind.

Deo Trophy's ridicule of imaginary people who opposed his views in his messages was very effective in helping people see his point. Sometimes his public ridicule would be against somebody he did not name "but everybody knows who it is."

Sometimes Deo named or even showed the person, like the time photos of Sammy Shifflett were was put up on the Big Screen at a regional camp weekend retreat. Sammy was Mark Shifflett's younger brother, a sixteen year old from Richmond who liked to joke around a lot, probably to hide insecurities caused by his parent's marital problems over the years.

His mother's adultery almost caused Sammy's father to leave her for good, but James Stark talked Sammy's father out of it, and the marriage in time was a strong one. "Your marriage can be stronger and better than it has ever been," James confidently told Sammy's father. This comment became a guiding light to Sammy's father in his marital recovery. James was a builder of relationships, mending bridges and bringing people together in mutual friend-ships, if possible.

As Deo was walking by earlier that year, he saw Sammy getting his picture taken. Not one to stand on the sidelines, Deo jumped in and goofed off in the picture with Sammy. They had a good laugh along with others standing around watching and laughing with them.

Deo unexpectedly showed these pictures on the Big Screen in front of a four hundred person audience months later. The ridicule was obvious and direct. Rhett wasn't there but heard of it. Out of pity and compassion, Rhett invited Sammy over for lunch the week afterwards.

"I felt a rage against Deo I don't think I've ever felt against anyone. I listened to Rap music regularly a few years ago," Sammy said, "And all that anger and hatred I had heard just came up in my mind against Deo, so I just got up and left."

Rhett certainly didn't want to be divisive, but he didn't think what Deo had done was right, so he told Sammy as they sat at the breakfast nook table, "There are some things you can't do anything about; the Lord has to deal with it in his time. For now, just worry about the things within your control."

The incident with Deo helped Sammy, the trial sobered him, and he went on to be happily married a few years later to a nice girl from the Atascadero Assembly in California. But Sammy's humor about evaporated.

Well, when the President does it
that means that it is not illegal
- Richard Nixon -

White Collar Crime
Investigator

Rhett focused on his main priorities in his life after losing Jonathan to death in 2003, and Jarvo to a marking in 2006: Marriage, raising children, and his job as a white collar crime investigator. He worked for a Fortune 500 company, arguing with attorneys and doctors for twenty years from his fluorescent lit cubical.

The natural daylight had a strong pull for him, and taking a new outside field position was a welcome relief in 2008. He received more training on systematic investigation techniques to help determine when people are deceptive.

He still looked forward to his vacations though, and Sabrina agreed to go on a family vacation to visit Christian Assembly friends in Newfoundland, Canada.

"Let's drive there with our camping equipment, take the ferry and go with the Newfoundlanders on their annual August camping trip," Rhett told Sabrina.

So on August 1st, 2008, in a fully loaded van with camping gear packed on top from a friend's borrowed roof rack, and three mountain bikes hanging off the back, they headed north "like a pack of dirty turtles," Rhett joked with his kids. *Funny how I say the same jokes my dad did when I was young,* thought Rhett as they pulled out of their driveway, waving to Mark and Rhonda's family out in their yard yelling well wishes for a good trip. Watson would feed the dog for them while they were gone.

"Ok kids, that's enough!" said Rhett, after several seconds of hearing his kids yelling their goodbyes. All the hard rock music from his struggles as a youth had sensitized his ears.

The thirty hour drive gave Rhett plenty of time to think. During the last several months in 2008 some puzzling things happened. Usually there was full disclosure on Assembly matters, but secrecy shrouded recent events. Cary Murdock and Julian Petros were involved in a secret meeting in Virginia with a visit from Temple Austin in February.

Temple, a large and hearty Texan with a ready warm smile and a booming voice with a drawl, had ministered in the Texas Assembly for twenty-two years. Byron Stark's move to Texas from Virginia sixteen years ago was a welcome relief for Temple. It was hard to work full time as a sales manager and be the only minister for three hundred people. Texas was the largest Assembly.

Byron, being James Stark's son, grew up traveling around the country with his father's speaking engagements and ministry, and found it natural to be a minister in Texas. Texas had a reputation for disorderly following for years. Deo regularly complimented Byron with his ability to discern problems since Byron was in his twenties.

Byron told Rhett a few years after he moved to Texas, "Daddy told me the Texas Assembly is a large ship, and it will need to be turned slowly."

Byron had slowly turned the ship, so now they were quite orderly in their following in 2008. Many disorderly young men in their late teens and early twenties had been marked by Byron, providing welcome relief for young families, and those who thought it important to keep the standards of dress and,lifestyle.

Rhett called one troubled young man in Texas shortly before he got marked. Rhett asked, "I just want to see how you are doing, your dad is worried about you. What is the main thing that bothers you?"

The young man told Rhett, "I simply want to enjoy my life and go snow skiing and stuff like that. Bryon preaches against recreational sports like water and snow skiing, and those are things I'd like to do."

Cary Murdock mentioned a secret meeting with Temple and Julian briefly in February during a Wednesday night meeting, just saying, "Something has come up, and we are trying to work things out."

Then in March of 2008, Cary and Julian left for a secret meeting in Texas. In April they left for yet another secret meeting.

"Please pray for us, we are trying to work through some difficult problems with our brother James Stark," Cary said upon his return in April. Cary spoke on Fear that Sunday, how, "Fear can be your belly, and fear can be your god."

That is a surprise, James has always had an impeccable reputation, thought Rhett, sitting in the rented hall with the rest of the one hundred and twenty or so person audience in the Richmond Assembly, *That's really too bad, James has had a lot of integrity, and he has been ministering on raising*

children, marriage, anger, and child molestation for the last forty
years and has helped so many, including myself... Maybe James
is right and all these other leaders are wrong... No, that could
not possibly be so!

Rhett asked George Taylor and Cary Murdock after the
meeting, "What's wrong with James?"

"James attitude is quite poor, he is very contentious. We
all saw it with our own eyes," Cary said confidentially,
"Trust us on this one."

Julian walked up, and said, "Cary is right. James is very
defensive about our concerns for him."

Then in July, Julian and Cary went out for a leadership
meeting in California.

Rhett sometimes helped out with the public speaking
when the three local Richmond leaders were out of town.
The year before he spoke on "Approval" when the Virginia
ministers had all gone to their important annual countrywide leadership "leaders of the local Assemblies" meeting
in Texas.

"We all need approval desperately, but we need to get it
from God," Rhett said to encourage his many friends,
"When we fear people we try to get approval from people,
but when we fear God we want approval from God. God
wants to be our father. When we were young, we wanted
our father's approval. As we became young adults; we
need to transition from wanting our physical father's
approval to wanting God's approval. We should be able to
cry out "Abba, Father," which means "Daddy, Father," and
have an open and honest relationship with God through
Jesus Christ."

When Cary and Julian were away in March, Rhett filled
in again, and spoke on avoiding extremes: "We can be
worldly by being influenced by the leaven of Herod which

is the lusts of the flesh, or become worldly by being influenced by the leaven of the Pharisee's which is hypocrisy, and the lusts of the spirit."

"Solomon said he's seen a wicked man perishing in his wickedness, and a righteous man perishing in his righteousness. Hold on to the one, keep doing what is right, but don't let go of the other, and remember we can all be wicked. Micah told us the Lord requires for us to do what is just, to love mercy, and walk humbly with our God. We all have an old sinful nature and we need to have mercy on others. But, we need to keep doing what is right, and not become proud and condescending like the Pharisees."

Rhett suspected he got a lot more out of his own messages than anyone in the audience. James Stark had told him studying and giving things publicly did that.

What could possibly be the problem with James Stark? Rhett pondered when his cell phone rang in their van, while heading north on Route 1 in Maine.

"How is your trip going?" asked Mycroft Stuart, Rhett's father.

"Our trip has been uneventful, which is good! We are having a great time in Maine. We went through New York City at 2 am Saturday morning when everybody was leaving the bars, that was very educational for our kids," Rhett replied, "We got a lot of curious stares as I tried to maneuver around all the taxis with the top of our van loaded with camping gear and three bikes hanging off the back."

Mycroft laughed at this mental picture, and said, "Hey, I need to fill you in with some things that are going on, if you have a few minutes. Have you heard much about the James Stark situation?"

Rhett replied, "I've heard a little. Cary and Julian asked me a few times "How is your dad doing with the James Stark thing?" Why, what's going on?"

Rhett hadn't known much, because usually his dad didn't talk to him much about leadership issues. His dad was an older retired man who helped people in personal situations when he could in Visalia, California. Mycroft wasn't given to divulge personal information to people like Rhett who were not directly involved. Mycroft also went to the country wide leadership conferences the bishops, elders, deacons, and local leaders from each area went to, and Rhett assumed Mycroft was probably involved in the James Stark situation. Mycroft had known James since they were teenagers.

Mycroft asked, "Did you hear of Deo Trophy's public report of it a few days ago on August 3rd at Happy Hill?"

"No, we had already left for our trip to Newfoundland."

"Well," Mycroft said, "We were all at a leadership meeting in California last month, in July, with about thirty-five of us working through the issues with James Stark. Temple Austin told us Deo Trophy exaggerates, but not about important stuff. Then later in the meeting Deo told us how James Stark was acting in a February meeting earlier this year. Deo said James was really rude and interruptive the entire time during their three day February meeting earlier this year."

"Did James really do that?"

"There's a dispute over it," said Mycroft, "one of the witnesses is Carson Frund from Newfoundland, along with Temple Austin, Deo Trophy, and Byron Stark. Carson disagreed with Deo's version, and said, "Deo, that's not true! James just interrupted a few times during those two days," and Deo responded, "Yeah, you're right." Then

Matt Warren, an older brother from San Diego California, asked, "Deo, wouldn't that be a lie?""

Rhett thought this was quite interesting. He had a lot of respect for Matt with his integrity and perception.

"What about Deo's August 3rd message?" asked Rhett.

"Well, Deo exaggerated even more about James being rude and interruptive."

"After Matt rebuked him two weeks earlier?" asked Rhett.

"Yep!"

"What about Byron Stark? How does Byron view his dad's behavior in the February meeting?"

Mycroft paused for a moment, then said, "Well, Bryon backed up Deo on his August 3rd message in Virginia. You see, Byron spoke for five hours at this California leadership meeting last month about how Byron thinks his dad has changed a lot since James was remarried to Marie several years ago. Remember me telling you about James speaking last year at our 2007 regional country wide leadership meetings, about our standard of having women wear dresses being biblically based, and how the Bible doesn't actually forbid alcohol?"

"Yeah, Julian Petros thought it was a great meeting," said Rhett.

"Well, Byron and Deo didn't like it. They think James is advocating women wearing pants at times, and drinking wine in moderation. James has been encouraging the leaders from each area to justify what our standards have become with what the Bible actually says. Byron Stark and Deo Trophy are still bothered by James' challenge to old standards."

Rhett thought, *Even Byron thinks his dad has problems.*

"What about Temple?" asked Rhett.

"Temple thinks James came on strong, but he's keeping quiet about Deo's exaggerated account of the February meeting of this year."

Rhett usually talked to his dad every couple of months. Being a busy father of four and holding down a full time job didn't allow much time for evening phone calls to his parents with their busy Assembly schedule.

It rained most of the time Rhett and Sabrina were in Newfoundland, which is unusual for August, normally a sunny, pleasant time of year. The Newfoundland Assembly held meetings in a building James Stark had purchased years ago with his personal funds for them to use, renting it to Al for one dollar a year.

Al Taylor, the minister there, related to Rhett things were now strained in Newfoundland.

"I read a letter this last Wednesday night, that James was asked to take a break from ministry for awhile, and Carson Frund left right after the meeting," Al said, "I am wondering how this camping trip will be since we haven't seen each other since then."

But Carson Frund had to work, and the camping trip went well. It was a pleasant time of hiking, bicycling, and especially visiting and getting to know the Newfound-landers. Rhett and Sabrina's kids had a blast playing games and mountain biking near a coastal campground with the Newfoundland children.

Al Taylor, coming back from town one afternoon, excitedly explained, "I heard of a really good fishing pond from a local man at the store. The man told me there are two and three pounder trout in there," said Al, with a wild gleam in his eyes. "I'm gonna go with my wife to find it this afternoon, and tomorrow morning we can catch us some trout. I think I'll bring my pole this afternoon."

Al's wife said, "Al, a man told you about a good fishing spot last year and you didn't catch anything."

Al graciously smiled. He left with his wife after a nice lunch, but upon returning late that evening, Al mentioned in passing the disappointing news they had not found the pond.

"I have a better idea where it is now," said Al, "whoever wants to catch some trout can go with me early tomorrow morning."

Al's wife didn't say much about her afternoon of hiking through brush in a skirt and swatting mosquitoes.

Something told Rhett to opt out, and he slept in. After Rhett had a leisurely morning of hiking around the lake with the kids, Al and several men came back from the fishing expedition. Mosquito bitten and tired, they fought through the brush and swamps all morning, but only found a shallow pond with no trout.

"Maybe we will have better luck next year," said Al. His wife was busy cooking up a late lunch.

Rhett and Sabrina were hospitably put up in Al Taylor's home the following week. Al's son slept in the living room, and his daughter provided tour guide assistance. Al's other sons were happily married and living nearby.

Rhett was intrigued by the James Stark conflict, and wanted to confirm what his dad had said of Deo Trophy's exaggeration with Carson Frund. Carson was one of the four people at the February meeting earlier that year in which Deo was accusing James of having such poor conduct.

Carson was still very busy running his successful restaurant and hotel business, but did make time to go the following Wednesday night meeting after the camping trip.

Visiting privately after the meeting, Rhett said, "I heard your restaurant is so successful it rated number one for a large portion of Canada."

Carson said, "Well, my son runs it with me, and we have a great chef and wine specialist."

Serving wine at Carson's restaurant created some controversy with Al Taylor. Al believed recreational wine drinking was wrong.

Carson asked, "How is Jarvo doing? What caused him to get marked anyhow?"

Rhett said, "I didn't know anything was wrong with Jarvo until I approached him at a regional camp. I thought everything was fine until he started telling me Deo was a liar, and exaggerated."

Carson looked thoughtfully at Rhett, then repeated the same story Rhett's dad had told him on the way up, how Deo had not told the truth. As Rhett listened, his brain suddenly connected what Jarvo had told him a few years ago, with what his dad had told him on the way up through Maine on Route 1.

I welcome this kind of examination because
people have got to know
whether or not their President is a crook

Well, I'm not a crook

I've earned everything I've got

- Richard Nixon -

Mycroft Stuart - Just the Facts

Mycroft was cut out of a completely different mold than his own father. Taking after his mother's sharp wit, he was hard to manage as a young child, mainly due to a lack of training.

When Mycroft was six years old, he rode his bicycle up to his grandfather who was sitting on the front porch of his craftsman style home in Glendale, California.

Mycroft stuck out his tongue, "Pfffft! Pffffffttt!", — and then saucily —"NAH nah, nah nah, NAH NAAAH!"

This unglued grandfather from his rocking chair and he bounded after Mycroft.

Mycroft stood on the pedals, pumping hard, smugly thinking he could easily pedal faster than his old grandfather could run, until he felt a huge whack on his bottom.

Mycroft grew up in Glendale, in Southern California, during the 1940's and 50's before surfing became popular. His father Gilbert never learned to drive, always taking the bus to work. When Gilbert lost his construction job he couldn't find work because he couldn't drive, so he became a janitor at Walt Disney's studio, when Walt Disney was known as a man rather than a giant playground. Gilbert's natural tenderness towards people made him especially vulnerable due to the mental trauma of seeing a nephew drown in a Central California irrigation canal near Fresno in his twenties, making him cautious towards everything in life. Also, Gilbert's father had a temper, and as the oldest, Gilbert had gotten the brunt of it, adding to his quiet, repressed nature.

When Gilbert was sixteen years old he was saved after going to Maurice Johnson's Maranatha Tabernacle. Soon afterwards Nels Thompson came from the East in the 1920's, convincing Maurice that no churches should have names, denominating and separating Christians. Maurice let him speak several times on the one true church.

After Nels Thompson finished his public series of lectures, Maurice shut his successful church down. He lost a lot of his income, having only a small group of committed Christians remaining of his large congregation. The ones left shared some of his zeal for doing the Lord's will, standing in the truth. Bill Baker's father much needed financial support kept Maurice going through some rough times. Mable Stuart and her three sons, one of them being Mycroft's father Gilbert, were some of the few who ended up with Maurice.

After a seven year courtship, Gilbert got married to a girl in the Southern California Assembly. Their only child was Mycroft.

When he was fourteen, Mycroft took pity on a new-born blue jay that fell from its' nest, naming it "Scuttlebutt." After nursing it to an adult with an eye-dropper, Mycroft let it go. Mycroft got into body building, winding up with a physique resembling an uncartoonized version of Joe Atlas. He got a job guarding the gate of his high school during his physical transition, but quit after being roughed up by some kids who were ditching class. It bothered him the teacher who saw what happened didn't try to stop it.

His tall muscular physique got him another job at a local gym for a week. He quit the gym in disgust after observing some narcissistic muscular men flexing in front of the mirrors.

Still going to Maurice Johnson's little group, he and his parents took the bus, making several transfers to get to the small Southern California Assembly meetings, sometimes held in homes.

Mycroft found a book on management at his uncle's home during a summer vacation in Eureka, and the theories behind what makes people tick intrigued him. The two of them came back home from an errand one afternoon. His uncle pulled up as close as he could to the vehicle ahead, within about one inch, as it was his uncle's custom, then stopped and sat there for a few minutes. Mycroft sat also, wondering what his uncle was thinking. His uncle looked over at him for a few seconds, then said, "Mikey, whatever you do, remember this — marry a woman who is a Christian and you will be a lot happier in this life."

Mikey fell in love, courted, and married a Christian girl from the Riverside Assembly, where Kit Jude was the minister, and where James Stark lived.

Still devoted to natural physical health like his mother, he went to chiropractic school, but changed his career after he took some required classes on financial incentives for treating people. He was more interested in adjusting people, not taking their money.

His college degree and experience selling magazines door to door with crews of high school kids helped land a job as a sales manager for a large insurance company after a brief stint as an investigator. Moving to Visalia, California propelled his success as he built up a large network of loyal insurance agents. His wife June set an excellent example of hospitality locally, as well as putting up Assembly guests traveling through the area, both in state and out of state, with her large multi-course meals and chatty personable friendliness. In time Mycroft reaped the benefits of her efforts, gaining close friendships around the country.

Quiet and non-confrontational, Mycroft bore no resemblance to the naughty little child he once was, except sometimes his serious grey eyes would twinkle while telling one of his dry jokes.

"Ask me where muscle beach is," Mycroft urged his young daughters.

They would ask, and Mycroft, poising in classic muscle man form, puffing out his large chest and flexing one of his large biceps, slowly turned his fist outward and pointing off to his right side, said in a deep voice, "Thaat Waaay".

Mycroft would sometimes incrementally set his glass of milk down closer and closer to Rhett during dinnertime, until it ended up totally infringing into Rhett's personal space right next to Rhett's plate of food. It would subconsciously bother Rhett, but he would ignore it, intent on eating another delicious dinner his mom had made. Rhett would finally catch on consciously, and they would both have a laugh over it.

Unfortunately, the large corporation consumed a lot of his time when Rhett was young, and Mycroft's family suffered some as a result, but Mycroft tried to set an example balancing family and work.

One of his favorite poems he memorized and quoted with dramatic emphasis to teach Rhett, and remind himself of, was -

> WHENEVER Richard Cory went down town,
> We people on the pavement looked at him:
> He was a gentleman from sole to crown,
> Clean favored, and imperially slim.
>
> And he was always quietly arrayed,
> And he was always human when he talked;
> But still he fluttered pulses when he said,
> "Good-morning," and he glittered when he walked.
>
> And he was rich - yes, richer than a king,
> And admirably schooled in every grace:
> In fine, we thought that he was everything
> To make us wish that we were in his place.
>
> So on we worked, and waited for the light,
> And went without the meat, and cursed the bread;
> And Richard Cory, one calm summer night,
> Went home and put a bullet through his head.
>
> Edwin Arlington Robinson - 1908

Mycroft's quiet polite nature was a product of his deep seated belief that everybody has a God given worth, and needs to be treated that way; this belief permeated his very being, affecting all of his interactions with others. To avoid defensiveness, he would usually compliment others before doing any occasional, casual criticizing. A few men accused Mycroft of manipulation, due to his virtual abhorrence of bluntly telling people what he thought of them. But Mycroft's quiet and genuinely friendly person-ality gained many friends locally, and across the country.

Mycroft's perceptive intelligence was tapped by James Stark, who had no problem being blunt. They had spent time in their late teens while Mycroft was courting his wife in Riverside where James then lived, and maintained a close relationship over the years.

Rhett was quietly mulling over his father and the James Stark situation while coming home from Newfoundland, now southbound on Route 1 in Maine, when Ruth interrupted his thoughts.

"Dad, where did the Indians go?"

"Oh, some of them became truck drivers, some of them doctors or attorneys," said Rhett.

"Dad, was that an Indian driving that truck that caught fire on our way up?"

"I don't know. Seems to me it might have been a cowboy."

"Why Dad?"

"Well, as I remember it, the cowboys were the ones with things catching on fire."

"Daaady, come on, tell me if you think it was an Indian!'

Babomp Babomp — Babomp boop-boop!

Rhett snatched his cell phone off the consol of their minivan - "Hello?"

"Hi, how ya guys doing?" asked Mycroft.

"Uh, good! How you do'in?"

Rhett's mind picked up. He was really curious and wanted more details. The thirty hours drive back home was giving him plenty of time to think.

"I'm doing fine! How was Newfoundland?" asked Mycroft, who preferred hearing how other people were doing rather than talking about himself. Interesting people are interested, that is what Rhett had learned from his dad.

"Pretty good! We had a great time," said Rhett, telling a short summary of their trip, then asked about the leadership problem. The more particulars Mycroft told his son the stranger the James Stark situation became:

"I thought it was a good idea when James Stark spoke during the country wide leadership meeting last year in March of 2007. James had all the leaders engage in a brain storming session discussing if women should wear pants, and if drinking alcohol was really forbidden by scripture. I was comfortable with the brainstorming format James chose for the meeting. I've done it myself with my agents. It takes getting used to, and some up front explaining. I think James should have explained the format better beforehand. Anyway, I liked being able to honestly discuss if our beliefs matched up to the Bible," said Mycroft.

"I can imagine some of those people not even knowing about brain storming sessions, but I remember Julian Petros was excited about the meeting and being able to discuss things openly."

"Well, I think most of us really liked James Stark's open format discussion in discussing landmark standards we've had for fifty years. Deo Trophy, Byron Stark, and a few others didn't seem to like it. I don't know why Byron did it, but he came in with his hat on backwards one of the mornings. I think he was making fun of something his dad had said. I don't really know what to make of it," said Mycroft.

"What happened after the March 2007 meeting?"asked Rhett.

"Well, in September of 2007, at another countrywide follow up leadership meeting in Texas, James started out speaking, and Byron stood up, interrupting and accusing his father," said Mycroft.

"What did he accuse him of?" asked Rhett.

"He said "You have an agenda", "You can pull rank when you want to," and "You're not listening to your brethren, Daddy". He was pretty strong about how he said them too."

"What did James do?" asked Rhett.

"James just sat down and was quiet the rest of the weekend. James told me afterwards he figured he would try and work things out later. James considered taking Byron out right then, but didn't think it was appropriate. I think James was really sad about what his son was doing."

"So James just took a back seat the rest of the weekend?!"

"Yes he did. Then Deo Trophy spoke on "The Mind of Humility" for about ten hours, the second day at our country wide leadership meeting. It was obvious to me Deo was directing his message at James Stark. When Deo was done, there was no time for questions since it was late at night, so we resumed our discussions the third and last day."

"Did James get it resolved with his son later on?" said Rhett.

"James tried to. They talked and e-mailed. Byron accused his dad again in an e-mail, "You can pull rank whenever you want," which really saddened James. The conflict really bothers him because they're both ministers. James figures if they can't work out a conflict between them, how can they help others? So Byron and James got Carson Frund from Newfoundland involved, since they both have great mutual respect for Carson," said Mycroft.

"I'll bet that really bothers James and Byron. I can't imagine them having a difference they can't resolve between the two of them. That is really odd," said Rhett.

"Yeah, James still doesn't know what the problem is. James told me that whenever his mind hasn't been occupied with an immediate task, or counseling, or in ministry over the last year, his thoughts have always returned back to Byron, and what could possibly be wrong," said Mycroft.

"Did they ever get it worked out?" asked Rhett.

"Sort of. Carson helped them both understand each other better. Byron finally explained that what he actually meant by his father having an "agenda" was that his father "had a plan", "not hearing his brethren" meant "he needs to listen more", and when Byron accused his father of "pulling rank" he actually meant "not being effective"," said Mycroft.

"That's a real definition change!" said Rhett.

"Wellll, James agrees with you on that. James said as he commonly understands it - "not hearing his brethren", "having an agenda", and "pulling rank" would all be disqualifications from ministry. Recently Byron claimed he just wanted to help his father "be more effective." Anyway, when James thought their dispute was finally resolved, he called for a meeting in February of 2008 in Texas with a few other leaders to make sure everything was worked out between him and his son Byron," said Mycroft.

"So they got it worked out between them then, that's good," said Rhett, flipping on his turn signal to pull off the road. *Wild blueberries on the side of the road! Only in Maine!*

"Hey, can I call you back in a little while? The kids have been clamoring to pick some wild blueberries."

"Sure, give me a call when you're done."

Rhett called back an hour later, and Mycroft continued, "So, in the February meeting this year, James Stark goes in with his son Byron, Temple Austin, Deo Trophy, and Carson Frund, thinking the meeting he had requested was to wrap up any remaining disagreements between him and Byron. But when the meeting started James found out the meeting agenda had changed, and they all thought James Stark had some real problems and were there to help him. James strongly disagreed. They debated how authority ought to work in the Assemblies. Deo just kept quiet, and took notes."

"So they changed the meeting agenda on him, the one James had called for himself?" asked Rhett.

"Right, James had asked for the meeting, and they changed the agenda. He found that out when the meeting started. At the end of the meeting James agreed to submit for the sake of unity, but he didn't agree with them."

"Seems to me if he was willing to go along with them, then that would have settled it," said Rhett.

"James told me he thought the meeting ended peaceably. But then James got this long letter dated March 12th from Deo, accusing him of being proud, and that James thought himself to be a "superior intellect". Deo asked Carson Frund, Byron Stark, and Temple Austin to sign it, which they did. James began to suspect something was very, very, ominously wrong when he got the letter."

"Keep going," said Rhett, "but I'll need time to absorb this, I might need to call you back to repeat some of it."

Mycroft said, "Well, we found out recently Deo Trophy had a secret meeting in March of 2008. Deo picked fifteen select leaders from the Assemblies all over the country, including Al Taylor from Newfoundland. The meeting was in Texas to express their grievances about James Stark, without James' knowledge. Deo told the fifteen leaders to keep the meeting a secret. At least one man wouldn't even tell his wife what it was about."

"What was it about?" asked Rhett, "Did you ever find out what they talked about in the March meeting?"

"Carson Frund is one of the few who will tell us what was said during the secret March meeting. The meeting was strictly to talk about James' problems. Al Taylor talked with his overhead presentation explaining a long history of problems with James in Newfoundland, since James has gone up there to minister for over twenty-five years. Carson didn't agree with some of what Al was saying, so he interrupted the presentation, and said "Al, there is another side to this!" Deo stopped Carson and said "We can talk about that later Carson, now is not the time." Then Deo told the rest of the leaders, "Carson is referring to some things with no witnesses to verify it." But Carson, as a witness on his own behalf, never got a chance to give the other side of Al's accusations," explained Mycroft.

"Did Carson say if anybody besides Al Taylor presented anything?"

"A few others did. Sean Lane was upset because his son was out visiting in California, and was wondering if he should go snow skiing with the young people of the Loomis Assembly. So he asked his grandpa what he should do."

"What did James tell him?"

"James told his grandson he was twenty-one years old, and to make his own decision about that. So he called Deo to get his advice."

"Deo gave a really strong message back here against snowboarding, that it is a frivolous waste of money. But why would Deo put on a meeting without James there? That's weird, Deo has preached a lot about the Matthew 18 process," said Rhett, "has Deo had a problem with James in the past?"

"I think so"

"Has he ever talked to James about his concerns?"

"No. James didn't even know about the secret March meeting with the sixteen leaders."

"I mean, you know, if Deo has a problem with James, and so Deo goes to this meeting in February and just keeps quiet and takes notes, what's that all about?" asked Rhett.

"I'm still sorting this out myself. We haven't done things like this in the past, having meetings behind other people's backs. I agree with you, I think Deo should have tried to work this out with James first, and James should have been at the March meeting to answer for himself, you know?" said Mycroft.

"Yeah, James has preached that for years, don't gossip with each other without the accused person there! Has Deo been gossiping to Byron about James?" asked Rhett.

"We don't know. There are some e-mails between Deo and Byron that have little cutting comments about James that were inserted by Deo, but other than that, I don't know," said Mycroft.

"So Deo goes to this February meeting and says hardly anything, then handpicks these fifteen people and has a secret meeting all about James in March without him knowing anything about it, and then finally has the April meeting with James in it. That doesn't sound like Deo tried to work this out with James at all!"

"I'm forced to agree with you," said Mycroft, "Deo also sent some e-mails on March 27 to Byron, Aaron, Temple, and Carson about some of his ideas, calling them 'The Dilemma,' about what could possibly be the problem with James Stark."

"What did Deo say?" asked Rhett.

"Deo speculated on his opinions about James' problems. He said "I have put these slides together in an effort to say what I see as succinctly as I can." He says they were just a guess and he was just trying to make sense out of what he knew."

"Did James know about the Dilemma Slides?"

"No"

"Sounds like Deo's following a Political rather than a Biblical process. How long has Deo had a problem with James?"

"Bach Jude got this e-mail from Deo that shows Deo had a problem with James for about five years. One of the problems is everybody is using Deo's notes to find out what was discussed in detail in the February meeting. Deo thinks he has enough on James to bury him with his past," said Mycroft.

"And he never talked to James about his concerns?"

"Uh, no, I don't think so," said Mycroft.

"Did they agree on what James' problem was in the March 2008 meeting?" asked Rhett.

"They agreed James was not hearing his brethren, thought himself to be a "dominant man", and had a problem comprehending. James found out about the March 2008 meeting later from Carson. Al won't give James a copy of his presentation," said Mycroft.

Rhett mulled this over in his mind, *As a retired Royal Mounted Policeman, I'm sure Carson is familiar with procedures of justice in Canada, and this doesn't seem to even be following basic standards of fairness for our judicial systems in the USA, let alone for a "viable representation of the Body of Christ."*

Mycroft continued, "After this March meeting, Deo called for an April meeting with forty-four of us. I was invited to this one, as well as James and all the other leaders."

"Hey, could I call you later when we get back home? We're going to make another stop soon, and I need some time to think about what you've told me," asked Rhett, "do you have any significant e-mails you could forward over to me?"

"I'll send you a bunch of e-mails I've got. This is a lot to take in at one time," said Mycroft.

"Sabrina, something is *really* wrong here," said Rhett after he hung up, "and I don't know what it is."

Sabrina said, "I sure hope not!"

As Rhett reflected on what his dad told him while now driving south on Route 1 in Maine, he heard a voice deep within him say, *"Rhett, get involved."*

Rhett returned home, deep in thought, and over many conversations and copies of e-mails from his father pieced more of the puzzle together.

Carson had returned to Newfoundland from the March meeting with increasing concerns, but at the same time thought everybody else was in agreement with Deo. Carson had a few reservations deep down, but there were leaders at the meeting who saw the issue clearly with James. Carson felt it was likely legitimate, and hoping to see it clearer later on, he just kept quiet about his reservations. Deo had asked them to keep the March meeting a secret. Deo assured all of them there that they would really be able to see the problem clearly with James in the upcoming April meeting.

Tim Mervin and Peter Waters, both ministers from California, were not invited by Deo to the March, 2008 meeting. Tim was the oldest of the leaders and had the best personal example with his family by far than any of them. Tim from Southern California, and Peter from Visalia, were unaware there had been a secret meeting in March.

Carson decided to go along with things after the March, 2008 meeting, since all the other leaders seemed in agreement with Deo and Byron. Deo started giving Carson more adverse opinions about James, sending Carson an e-mail after the meeting, stating:

> If James were to have his past thrown on the table (which he knows that I could do and his family could do but none of us do) he would be likewise blown away.

Deo also commented in the e-mail to Carson, referring to their dispute over how authority should work in the February 2008 meeting:

> So if this concept does not carry the field then James is left to attacking the messenger or submitting to a new order. I think he has registered quite emphatically that he will not submit to a new order as long as he is mentally competent and not disqualified. So we shall see what James is able to bear in April.

Carson requested proof of James' past family problems, but Deo wasn't able to provide anything to support his claim about blowing James away. Deo just claimed he lived two blocks away from James for years and knew a lot about problems with James' family. Carson inquired of this, and found Deo lived a few miles away and rarely had been in James' home over the years, their families rarely socialized. Carson began to wonder about Deo's honesty.

In April of 2008, Mycroft Stuart was invited to the large Leaders of the Assemblies meeting in Texas, along with James Stark, Tim Mervin, and Peter Waters. Forty-four people in all were at the meeting.

Byron Stark started the meeting by saying, "I am asking you leaders to judge a dispute between me and my father!"

Deo quickly added, "We are here to help James be more effective in his ministry!"

Some leaders from the March meeting expressed their concerns for James. He had problems comprehending and not hearing his brethren. It was mentioned briefly that James claimed to be the "dominant man."

Deo announced, "There are volumes of information regarding James that are pouring in!"

Matt Warren's son Blair, from San Diego like his father, asked, "How many reports, Deo?"

"Many" said Deo.

"Less than a hundred?"

"Well, yes, less than that"

"Less than twenty?"

"Not that many"

"Less than ten?"

Everybody could hear Blair clearly due to his excellent voice projection. He was sometimes asked to make announcements in large crowds in lieu of a bull horn.

"I don't think it was that many," said Deo.

"Less than five?" Blair persisted.

"Well, three or four," said Deo.

Blair got it narrowed down to the three reports they already knew of, plus one more.

Blair was quick to smell a rat; he worked as a supervisor on the docks of the San Diego Harbor, dealing with difficult personnel issues within the unions.

James calmly said in the April meeting he did not think Temple Austin should be involved in this. Immediately after saying this James apologized for it, saying it was the wrong time to talk about Temple. James also apologized for it later in writing (Temple's children had left their Christian Assemblies, and Temple had given poor counsel to a couple who ended up in divorce).

James wanted to point out Deo's twisting of the facts in the April meeting, but most of the audience had already been turned against him, so two men, Blair Warren and Luke Alastair from Southern California, cautioned him to wait; he likely wouldn't be heard impartially, and it would just look like he was getting more defensive, which he was already being accused of. Most of the leaders already thought him to be guilty. The more he said of Deo's dishonesty, the more it looked like he was getting defensive and attacking others. Deo had already accused James of attacking the credibility of the witnesses, and had warned, "Don't let him get away with it!"

Deo said during the April meeting: "Everybody that was at the March meeting are all of one mind, to a man, on this issue with our dear brother James. There is a lot of evidence and information against James that was covered in our March meeting with fifteen others, besides myself. I don't want to go over it now and unnecessarily expose James, but trust us, we have information that is collapsing in from all over the country, serious problems with James, and I am just asking you bear with us and support us in this difficult and delicate problem. If you are thinking this is just a Byron and James conflict, well, it's much bigger than that!"

Deo refrained from mentioning who all the fifteen attendees actually were.

Later on, during and also after the April meeting, a few decided to check up on Deo, asking around to find out who of the fifteen people were in the secret March meeting, and which of them were actually with Deo on this. It was discovered that they were NOT of "one mind, to a man." In fact, the opposite was true. Many of the fifteen March meeting attendees had questions and concerns, but had been told by Deo in the March meeting to be patient, and wait until the April meeting when more evidence would be presented, and they would then be able to clearly see the problem with James.

However, the people in the April meeting were lead to believe that all sixteen in the March meeting were together, and had secret knowledge condemning James. The perception that the sixteen men were together played a big role in influencing these additional leaders in this April meeting, giving credibility to the vague accusations against James. This inaccurate perception was an extremely misleading illusion.

One person asked, "How were the fifteen people chosen for your March meeting?"

Deo answered, "I picked them myself!" pointing to his own chest.

Deo asked James to leave the room. The question was then asked, "I think we have a consensus here, pride is part of the problem with James." Four people objected, three of them being Mycroft Stuart, Matt Warren, and Peter Waters.

Then, at the end of the meeting, Deo and Byron asked, for the sake of unity and for the safety of the flock, to just have everybody agree to ask James to take a break from ministry for awhile, and it was better for the leaders to keep quiet about the details for now, and also better for Deo and the other fifteen in the March meeting to not release the evidence condemning James, for now.

"I am asking that only leaders talk to James about this situation," Deo told the leaders from California, which they agreed to. Deo assured them a few leaders would be working directly with James.

This was a change from what James Stark and other leaders had done in the past, in which a full disclosure was quickly and truthfully made public in all the Assemblies to everybody in a matter like this. James didn't like it, but he was shut down for now, and couldn't dispute it. This was totally different than how he handled things, but he wasn't handling things now.

Since three people had signed on with Deo after the February meeting, and fifteen in the secret March meeting, the forty-four in the expanded April meeting all agreed with Deo and a few others like Byron. There seemed to be a lot of unity in everybody else seeing the problem with James, especially the sixteen in the March meeting.

Most of them just believed Deo, a minister of many years, and agreed with Deo to have James take a "much needed break" from ministry for awhile. A lot of them were not quite sure themselves what the problem was with James, but they expected to see the problem more over time, since they didn't have all the understanding and information Deo and Byron had.

Deo, Byron, Temple, and a few others who "saw" the problem with James, said they weren't sure what the problem was exactly, they didn't know what was wrong with James, but there was something wrong, that was for sure.

The whole meeting perplexed Mycroft, but he couldn't put his finger on it. Not quick to form conclusions, he was puzzled, but didn't know why. There were a lot of men who could "see" James had some problems, but Mycroft couldn't formulate the problem himself in his own mind, and Deo didn't want to talk about the critical information from the March meeting.

Mycroft's wife had always distrusted Deo, but Mycroft chalked that up to a woman's attempt of laying claim to her own intuition, which could very well be flawed.

Mycroft and a few others, like Matt Warren from San Diego, had misgivings about James being presumed guilty, in effect, without hearing his side of it. Most people who sinned in the Bible could have their sin summed up in one verse. But after many hours and days of explaining, the problem with James still wasn't clear.

Lyle Cooper, the young minister from Charlottesville, told Deo after the April meeting, "It bothers me that you said there were volumes of reports coming in about James but there wasn't, just the three or four we already knew about!"

Deo said, "I said VOLUMES of INFOMATION are coming in. I meant there was a lot more information coming in about the three or four reports we already knew of. I wasn't trying to say there were a lot of additional reports coming in."

The California ministers and elders agreed to not give out reports in their own areas, but were still unsure exactly what the problem was themselves. Mycroft Stuart and Peter Waters, who worked together on problems in the Visalia Assembly, also agreed to do what Deo asked, and not disclose what was going on to anybody else in their own Assembly for now.

The California ministers began looking into the matter, asking more questions of Deo, Byron, Temple, and Carson. The leaders in Texas and Virginia were surprisingly agreeable with Deo's assessment.

Their first accusations against James was: "James has a lack of comprehending what is said to him, and James' harmful conduct."

James' response was: "That's right, I'm listening for the meta-message, I always do this."

The California elders and ministers including Mycroft, after spending time with James, were quickly coming to the conclusion James was listening just fine, his mind continued to be as sharp as it always was, and he could comprehend very well, probably better than they could. James was sixty-nine years old and was still as sharp as a new utility knife blade. His conduct did not seem harmful. So the leaders from California requested a meeting as soon as possible to hear James side of this, and allow James to respond to the accusations.

Deo Trophy, Byron Stark, Temple Austin, Cary Murdock, Aaron Adams, and Joshua Jude responded to their request for another meeting in a letter dated April 25th, 2008, concluding:

> There is no need for another meeting in the near term (next few months) to hear "James' side" since no case is existing against James. There is a need for continued looking into the concern of *the cause of James' lack of comprehending* clear dialogue from brethren.

> But if we disclose that something has or is changing with James then we are opening ourselves up to be "viewed" by those who have not had these same experiences that we have had as attacking James or undermining confidence in James without sufficient cause.

> We did not present a case against James at Temple's (February 08 meeting) or at the April 08 Burleson meeting. No case has been put together. **Therefore, there is no case that needs to be answered by James having his day in court so to speak at this time.**

Mycroft thought he better move fast and get James Stark's side of it while he could, and drove four hours the same day from Visalia to Loomis to talk to James. Carson had flown out from Newfoundland to see James also.

Deo, hearing Mycroft was already driving up to visit with James, and hoping Mycroft would come to the same conclusion, commented to Carson in a text message: "Mycroft Stuart is a quality brother, and a very stable, very well grounded thinker. He is not a politician but a straight shooter. He is extremely quiet but his mind is very sharp, and very active. He does not miss much in interchanges, and is a real quick study."

Things just didn't add up for Mycroft, creating a new problem and challenge for Deo. Deo was perceptive and intelligent himself, but that of itself doesn't make a man morally right or wrong. Gifts and knowledge of the truth can be used for good or for evil, depending on one's motivations.

Two days later, Deo put out a request that no one talk to James at all, not even anybody considered to be in leadership.

Tim Mervin, the minister in Riverside, California, was one who thought James was sharper than he was. Tim complained of needing a larger brain at times. He finally learned to read and write by the time he was six foot tall. His lack of ability with reading and writing didn't stop him from loving the Lord, and genuinely ministering to others.

His seven children all grew up to love the Lord, and married spouses who did. And now some of his grandchildren are in their teens and early twenties, and following the same example their grandfather set by committing their life to the Lord. It didn't matter if Tim got distracted during a message and changed the subject, or forgot what he was speaking about; he could always get back to the subject later, or maybe the next Sunday.

Tim was an Anti-Deo, the opposite of Deo Trophy in so many ways, loved and respected by many. Deo very seldom had any guests over except to lecture and counsel, talking to them for hours about their personal problems. Tim opened his home almost every Sunday for whoever wanted to come over and just visit, and many did, often it was eighty or a hundred people at a time.

Deo was a controller. Tim was an enabler.

After the accusations were cleared up, Deo Trophy and the Bishops sharing his concern then accused James of wanting to be a 'Dominant Man'. James said if he said it in the February 2008 meeting as they claimed; he apologized and certainly did not believe it. After a lot of debate the accusation was refuted.

Once the California leaders, including Mycroft, had refuted the 'comprehension', 'not hearing his brethren', and then the 'dominant man' accusations against James, then Deo, Cary Murdock, Byron Stark, and a few other Bishops focused on accusing James of combative and defensive behavior in the April meeting. That accusation was also refuted by the California leaders, especially after James apologized for the comment he made about Temple Austin during the April meeting, this time in writing.

The last and final accusation a few months later was focused on James' rude and interruptive conduct during the two day February 2008 meeting, supported by Deo's exaggerated account. Byron Stark backed Deo on this.

Mycroft and the California leaders were concerned about restricting the information from everybody else in the Assemblies, and the exact reasons why Deo Trophy, Byron Stark, Cary Murdock, and some others were so content on just letting James take an indefinite break from ministry. Deo had said a few leaders would be working with James, but nothing had happened for months.

The California leaders were able to have a few meetings with Deo during the summer. During one of them Carson unwittingly spoke of Deo's 'The Dilemma' slides from the March 27th, 2008 e-mail; the California leaders hadn't heard of it until then. At first Deo gave an unintentional impersonation of a deer in the headlights, then quickly explained himself away, knowing he couldn't back up his many suggestions that bore a strong resemblance to slanderous accusations against James behind his back by saying: "I put the slides together in an effort to say what I see as succinctly as I can," and also, "I am only trying to make sense out of what I know."

The people in Northern California, in Loomis, were in limbo. What exactly was wrong with their minister? Ward Morgan had recently become a Bishop in Loomis, with James' help, and wondered what it was all about.

The leaders set up a country wide regional meeting for the entire weekend upstairs at Bach Jude's home in Long Beach, California in mid July, 2008, starting Friday.

James' problems were well presented by Deo and Co.

During the meeting, a few interchanges caught Mycroft's attention.

Temple Austin, from Texas, said, "Deo does exaggerate, but not about important things."

Deo said, "I do exaggerate at times, but there are those here in this room who are riding shotgun so I don't hurt myself," and Deo pointed to himself as he said "I."

The question was then asked, "How will we know when Deo exaggerates?"

Cary Murdock from Richmond said, "Just ask him!"

Mycroft followed that chain of reasoning and speculated to himself how it might work to interrupt Deo during his long messages with questions like that. He concluded there must be a missing link.

A few hours later, Deo grossly exaggerated regarding James' conduct in the February 2008 meeting, and was admonished for lying by Matt Warren, the older man from San Diego.

James Stark was asked to leave halfway through Saturday's meeting by Bach Jude and Ward Morgan, who were becoming sold on the idea James was the problem, and having a hard time seeing that Deo was dishonest.

Shortly after James left, Byron Stark asked to present some thoughts he had, and then spoke for five heavy emotionally laden hours in the small, nearly windowless upstairs meeting room at Bach Jude's home in Long Beach, California.

Byron was so overcome with emotion that Ward, the minister from Northern California, went up to help comfort Byron and support him. Byron spoke of the years of agony in dealing with his father, how his father's new wife had made him more liberal, and how he knew his father so well, because he, Byron, was so like him. "I resent the problems I have had that my father still shares."

Byron swayed almost all the leaders, except Mycroft Stuart. Mycroft was used to long sales presentations, and had learned to reserve forming his opinions until well after meetings like that.

Deo Trophy asked for a document to be signed at the end of that July meeting, and it was quickly drafted by Joshua Jude, the Bishop in Atascadero, California. Joshua was Cary's brother-in-law and, like Cary, had extensive contact with Deo over the last several years, with many e-mails.

Deo urged that only the leaders who were named Bishops should sign it. The elders, like Mycroft Stuart and Matt Warren, weren't included in being asked to sign, just the Bishops who controlled the podiums. This was a change from how things had been done in the past, when men considered deacons and elders would have been part of the decision and signed their names.

Tim Mervin and Peter Waters signed it only after Deo assured them they would soon hear James' side of it (but Deo never followed through on this). Then almost all of them, except Mycroft, went to James' hotel room and asked James to confess his sinful resistance to men who were trying to help him with his problems. Mycroft was waiting for the ether to wear off after the long emotional presentation.

When everybody got back home, some of them, like Carson Frund, wondered over the next few weeks what had come over him, and why they had bought into Byron's five hour sales pitch. There was no facts given that should have swayed them.

Mycroft reflected back on how Byron had once urged an attorney, "You have got to make that emotional connection with the jury," Byron had encouraged, "in order to convince them."

James was still very concerned about Deo's exaggeration and misleading problem, and certainly would not agree or apologize for any false accusations. On the other hand, many leaders thought James had probably overreacted in the February meeting. The whole issue was becoming who was a witness, was the witness credible, and whose story agreed with whose. Carson Frund was a witness, but he was quickly becoming discredited due to 'flip flopping'.

James felt he should apologize, in spite of his concern about Deo's dishonesty, and sent this e-mail to Ward Morgan, the Bishop from Loomis, California, who forwarded it to the other leaders, including Byron and Deo.

From: James Stark Sent: Saturday, July 26, 2008 2:56 PM
To: Ward Morgan

Dear Ward,

First I want to thank you and The Lord for all the efforts you and others have put in to sorting out this situation for the benefit of our small representation of the church which is His body. As you requested yesterday, I want to put in writing what I have expressed several times in your presence, and I believe toward the end of the last meeting I was allowed to attend in Texas this past April. You felt that many, possibly most had not picked up on what I said, or I hadn't said it there even though it has been expressed in conversations where you were present since.

I believe that for me to challenge Temple Austin and Deo Trophy relevant to their decision and their testimony regarding the February meeting at Byron's home when Byron turned the April meeting over to me was wrong. I believe that was not the time to do that and it contributed to the difficulty brethren had in moving on to the facts relevant to the situation. I believe in what I did at that time I was not guided by the Holy Spirit. I have asked the Lord to forgive me and I believe he has. I ask all of my brethren to forgive me.

As to the February, 2008 meeting at Byron's home. I want to say that I wish Deo's letter had only addressed the question of whether in my efforts to defend what I believe is truth I had come on too strong at times, and not gotten into areas where the letter is inaccurate or where only God can successfully go.

There is no doubt that there was disagreement, there is no doubt that at times I was intense and passionate in what I said. If there were times when I went beyond the bounds of what I believe is acceptable in such a situation, I am not aware of it. There is no doubt that Temple, Byron, and Deo feel that I went beyond what they believe is acceptable. I am sorry they feel that way, and wherever I did in fact go beyond what is acceptable in God's sight I am sorry. Many times since I received Deo's letter of March 12th, 2008, I have asked the Lord to help me see or remember such times and to forgive me even though I don't remember such. I would ask the same forgiveness of my brethren.

I am grateful for and I rest in the truth of the following scriptures:

He who covers his sins will not prosper, But whoever confesses and forsakes them will have mercy. Happy is the man who is always reverent, But he who hardens his heart will fall into calamity. Pr 28:13-14

Search me, O God, and know my heart; Try me, and know my anxieties; And see if there is any wicked way in me, And lead me in the way everlasting. Ps 139:23-24

You know my sitting down and my rising up; You understand my thought afar off. You comprehend my path and my lying down, And are acquainted with all my ways. For there is not a word on my tongue, But behold, O LORD, You know it altogether. Ps 139:2-4

With Christian love and sorrow of heart,

James Stark

One week after James' apology letter went out, in Virginia on August 3rd, 2008, Deo Trophy gave his public report to a large audience the day after Lyle Cooper's son's marriage at Happy Hill in Virginia, and went even further in his exaggerations of James' conduct than he had two weeks before, when he was admonished by Matt for lying.

Deo made no mention of James' written apology the week before.

Matt Warren was out visiting for the wedding, and called Mycroft - "Deo just exaggerated worse in Virginia than he did to us in California two weeks ago! And this time it was publicly in front of a large group of people! And Deo is telling us in California not to even talk about it or say anything publicly!"

Mycroft got a copy of Deo's two and one half hour 'reporting out', and had it transcribed. Deo offered no apology for talking publically about James in detail after he asked the California ministers not to.

Rhett got the entire transcript, and noticed near the end Deo made a persuasive emotionally charged pivotal point:

> What I saw in that meeting, I have never seen before. What I saw in that meeting, I would eventually say none of you except for Byron have ever seen before. I won't expect you to believe what I saw if I try to describe it. But I saw was, James Stark, who resisted everything that was said, resistance, resistance, resistance.....You couldn't communicate. I saw rudeness that I have never seen before. When you are trying to talk to him, he would top you and talk over you and I am telling by just interrupt you once or twice or three times, continuously and this went on for two and half days. We are not talking about a few interruptions. You know, when you have a dialogue, may be intense dialogue with some body, people cut people off. I am not talking about that. Heat may get elevated for a moment and then calm down. I am not talking about that. I am talking about resistance, intense resistance, unrelenting, rude for two and a half days! Now, if you would say, that is not the James I know, than I would say, me too, that is not the James I know. But that is what we saw for two and a half days, and at the

end of two and a half days we just said, stop, stop. He was exhausted, James was exhausted, we were exhausted and just said, let us stop. Then we stopped.

Deo also said during his presentation:

James was having trouble comprehending him from his ministry and brethren in some situations. That is a hugely mild statement for what had been observed. James is going to spend some time in rest and recuperation that was needed.

Deo said nothing about any of James' apologies, or that James had agreed to submit to them at the end of the February meeting, even though he didn't agree. It was a very one-sided against James account, and anything that reflected well on James was never mentioned. Deo instructed the audience to not look into anything for themselves, the leaders were handling it for them.

Luke Alastair from Southern California later put it this way in a letter to Deo Trophy:

I believe James has proved himself over many years of being an honest, forthright, and a non-politically motivated minister among us. So when James Stark expresses the following about your March 12th letter it gives me pause:

"In approximately 40 years of service to the saints known to us I am sure at times I have been misunderstood, misquoted, quoted out of context, and my words repeated with a "spin". I feel some or all of this takes place in your letter. Your response does not reflect either my attitude toward you, my feelings toward you, nor where I am in my understanding of the situation that brought us together in February.... There is not even the appearance of impartiality in the way you have handled this request for help with my son Byron... My prayer is that the Holy

Spirit be allowed to help us find the basis for peace, take advantage of it, and move on in a Godly way."

Matt Warren, tall and lanky, thought Deo had problems. Matt never learned to read or write that well due to a learning disability. His quiet beautiful wife who had married him when she was sixteen years old sweetly helped him do the paperwork over the years as they sold their motorcycle shop and invested in real estate. Retiring to a hillside home overlooking the San Diego Harbor where their son Blair worked, Matt got a job working the huge crane that unloaded the overseas cargo carrier ships. Like a little boy playing with his favorite toy, Matt could see the boats entering the harbor from his window at home, and then drove down to unload them.

Like his son Blair, Matt's sharp and discerning mind helped with Union disputes over dock workers where he was valued for his honesty. His lack of ability in reading forced him to focus much more on verbal communication, enabling him to pick up on things many others didn't. Matt was also a confidant of James Stark, being an invaluable resource with his perceptive insights of human nature.

Matt's wife sweetly told him at times, "Matt, you are just a little fish; they don't care what you think!" Matt just chuckled; he knew there was truth to it.

He disliked any comments about his investments: "My true wealth is Jesus Christ, and anything of value I have is from the Lord: my wife, family, friends, and possessions. It doesn't take a genius to buy real estate and have it go up in value! Really, it's pretty simple. — The Lord gets all the honor of any good in my life, and we all need to all lift him up with our lives."

Contrary to what was falsely said of him privately and publicly in Virginia, Carson Frund from Newfoundland had never changed his version that James came on strong and interrupted a few times, as others also did during the meeting. Carson had just changed his opinion about James Stark having some of the problems Deo attributed to him.

Almost everybody who had a background in investigating criminals or dealing with dishonesty was becoming highly suspicious of Deo Trophy.

Failure to see conspicuous flaws in a strong supporter was the chink in James' armor of discernment.

Everyone praises a prince who keeps faith, lives with integrity, and not with craft. But, our experience has been that princes who have done great things have held little faith in integrity, and know how to overcome intelligent men by craftiness, and in the end have overcome those who have relied on their word. But it is necessary to know how to disguise this characteristic well, and to be a great pretender and deceiver. Men are so simple, and so subject to their daily necessities, that he who seeks to deceive will always find people who will allow themselves to be deceived. Alexander the Sixth did nothing else but deceive men, and always found victims; he had great power in making oaths and affirming what he would do, but would never do it; his deceits always succeeded according to his wishes because he understood so well this side of humankind.

– Niccolo Machiavelli from The Prince, 1513 -
(paraphrased)

10·

The Investigation

Showing complete disregard for the pubic request from Deo, and the local Richmond leaders Cary Murdock and Julian Petros, to ask general questions of just them, Rhett asked his dad for copies of all the correspondence so far, and to send him more as the situation developed.

The e-mails and letters ended up being nearly a thousand, including reports from many meetings local California leaders had as they worked through this very difficult problem. Rhett had investigated countless incidences in his work over the years, going through volumes of information, and this helped him wade through it. Rhett thought it was worth the effort, because if something major was happening, he needed to look out after his family.

Rhett also got the actual recording of Deo Trophy's two and one half hours August 3rd, 2008 public meeting, listening to it three times while traveling in his car. Being familiar with the situation now, he counted many exaggerations, misrepresentations, and partial truths from

Deo Trophy. Deo kept repeating the phrase, "Byron was just trying to help his father become more effective." He kept reiterating and coming back to that point, as if he really wanted it to stick in the minds of his audience. Byron had started the April meeting saying, "I am asking you men to judge a problem between me and my father!" which conflicted with what Deo was trying to accomplish.

Deeply concerned, Rhett gave copies to Cary, Julian, and George, the three leaders in Richmond, along with verses on falsehood and bearing false witness.

After hearing no response for several weeks, Rhett asked Cary and George Taylor about it. Their response — "We are working with Deo to be more effective," made him uneasy – *Why are they so biased? Deo should have been quickly disqualified, and asked not to speak up in meetings, instead he's the main communication link with the California leaders!*

Rhett contacted the California ministers involved in October, 2008, and they answered his questions with facts and evidence. Cary only gave short general statements, no written information, just broad sweeping opinions and accusations. Julian was more willing to talk, and told Rhett of many accusations against James.

Most of the California Assemblies were in turmoil; hardly anybody not in leadership understood what was happening, and the California leaders had agreed to not talk about it, adding to the huge dispute.

Rhett thought Cary, George, and Julian needed to deal with Deo as a hypocrite according to Galatians 2. He needed to be rebuked publicly for his dishonesty. Julian Petros responded to Rhett over a lunch: "Deo was just speaking during his report of August 3rd, in the context of the amount of resistance James gave during part of the meeting and not characteristic of the whole meeting."

Rhett replied, "The three hundred or so people in the audience didn't understand it in that context! Is Deo going to correct his false statement to the same group of people?"

Julian changed the subject.

Later, Rhett asked Cary about the status of his concerns with Deo.

Cary said, "Deo Trophy's exaggerations are similar to what Jesus said "If your eye offends you, pluck it out, if your hand offends you, cut it off." The Bible does use some exaggerations to make a point at times."

Rhett looked it up later. What Jesus meant was it's better to lose an eye or a hand than to be cast in Hell. Jesus wasn't making an exaggeration, but an understatement. All of Cary's public comments about James Stark were limited, opinionated, and negative.

Rhett talked to all the leaders in Virginia about Deo's exaggeration problem, including George Taylor, telling him, "We might be able to avoid a split if you guys would only deal with Deo's problem. He shouldn't be speaking up in a meeting, let alone leading out and dealing with the leaders in California. Can't you just sit him down from ministry for awhile?"

"No... No, we can't do that, Rhett," said George.

Rhett called Temple Austin from Texas. Rhett had known Temple for twenty-five years. Like a huge friendly teddy bear, Temple gave everybody hugs and big smiles, acting delighted to be meeting all his many friends again when he was visiting in Virginia.

Rhett had called him a few years ago about a young girl who Cary Murdock counseled. Cary had a conflict with the young girl's parents. Cary offered to help her through her courtship by offering his home for them to visit in, and she ended up happily married. At least everybody thought she was happily married. She found out her husband had a totally different side to him, coming home drunk soon after they were married. Things worked out for them later, but it was a rough ride for a short time.

Temple was glad to talk to Rhett about that, and other things over the years, so Rhett figured Temple would be glad to talk to him.

Rhett said, "Temple, I'd like to ask you a few questions about what Deo Trophy said of James."

Temple's voice sharpened, "Y'all need to talk to your locull leeders, to Cary and Juulian, ah-bout the James Stark pra-blim."

"Well, I did do that, but I'd like to confirm Deo's August 3rd, 2008 comments with you. You were at the February 2008 meeting also, so I wanted to know what you thought about Deo's assessment."

Temple said, "Rhett, ahr you shore you didn't taalk to Julian or Cary a-bout thaat?"

"I already did. Temple, I'd just like to ask you a few questions and get your side of it."

"Weellll, you ought tah be talk'n tu yur local lead'rs bout thaat!"

"Look, I'd just like to ask you about a few comments Deo made. Would you agree with Deo's statements about the February 2008 meeting you were in, that James continuously interrupted for the entire two and half days, and gave intense resistance which was unrelenting and rude for the entire two and half days?"

"Rheett, we muust have a baad phone cunection, cud youu ree-peet thaat again?"

Rhett asked him again, and Temple claimed he had a bad connection again, so Rhett repeated the comments for a third time.

Temple responded, "Waalll, all I can say is Jaames nev'r treated us lahke thaat beefoor!"

Rhett called James, who explained, "I treated those men in the February 2008 meeting like I have treated other men in the past, only this time, for the first time in their lives, and it was Deo, Byron, and Temple who were across the table from me. If they had a problem with me treating other people that way in the past, why should they object when it's directed at them? It wasn't a bunch of young people I was talking to!"

Rhett was relieved Temple was being honest, but disappointed he was willing to put up with Deo Trophy's misleading exaggerations.

"Dad, who all sees the problem with Deo?" asked Rhett on his way home from work in late August, "I don't think James is the real problem here."

"Well, there is me, don't forget that, and then there is James of course. Tim Mervin has some concerns, and I think he will be fine, and Matt Warren from San Diego. I think Randy Greens is there but he's only gotten my side of it."

"Witnesses don't render judgments, they just give testimony to the evidence. Don't you think the witnesses are being the jury and judge also?" asked Rhett.

"You know, Randy Greens said the same thing," said Mycroft, "I think that's really a key element to this." (Randy is Rhett's brother-in-law from Visalia, California)

A week later Mycroft called, and told Rhett, "James did a study on witnesses. We sat down with Peter Waters here in Visalia and went over it. Peter just can't get around the scriptures; I think he's coming around more on this."

Rhett was checking things out in Richmond, spending several hours over two or three occasions talking with

Julian Petros, the youngest leader of the three in Richmond. Julian answered Rhett's questions, contending James really had problems, and why he should not be ministering.

Among other things Julian told Rhett was James' first wife, Glenda, was ultra-conservative probably due to her being molested when she was young. Julian said Glenda heavily influenced her husband to be ultra-conservative. Then when Glenda died of cancer in 2002, James remarried Marie who had also lost her husband to cancer. Marie was a spirited Peruvian, and she liked getting her nails done by a pedicurist. Julian told Rhett that Marie had come to Virginia with pink toenail polish, which was frowned upon by the conservative ministers in Virginia, and she was cutting her hair short also, which was also frowned on.

Rhett broke Cary and Julian's rule yet again, and called James Stark to ask about some of Julian's accusations. James answered, "Marie had silverish toenail polish put on just prior to our trip to Virginia, and when we went to Newfoundland right afterwards, I took it off with carburetor cleaner. Marie cut her hair once after we got married, because part of it got burnt off on one side from contact with our stove." James voice had an "I can't believe we are talking about trivial things like this" tone to it.

At the Labor Day regional camp at Happy Hill in September, 2008, Deo Trophy announced he and Cary Murdock would have a question and answer session outdoors that afternoon. Rhett thought that was odd because Deo had asked the California ministers to not discuss the issue openly with anybody in depth, so why was Deo doing another one?

I wonder why the meeting is outdoors. Maybe Deo doesn't want it recorded, thought Rhett.

Heading over to the meeting with Julian, Rhett decided to test his honesty, "Julian, did James ever say he would submit to those men in the February 2008 meeting, even though he didn't agree with them?"

Julian said, "NO!"

Rhett was stunned, surely Julian knew this key element. Deo had never made any mention of it, but all the California ministers were well aware James had said he would submit, even though he did not agree, at the end of the February 2008 meeting.

After re-phrasing and asking the question three or four more different ways whether James had agreed to submit, Julian finally answered "Yes", and flushed red, putting his head down.

Rhett was embarrassed for Julian, and said, "That works for me."

Julian added, "But we don't think he was sincere."

Rhett said, "We're just fruit inspectors, we can't read his heart. We need to accept what he said and let time prove things out."

"Well," said Julian, "let's go over to the meeting and see what truth we can find out about this."

"I don't think I'm going to hear much truth!" Rhett responded.

That is so unlike Julian, Rhett thought as they walked over to where Cary was talking to the crowd of a few hundred people, *to conceal the truth like that. I think he just has a lot of fear, maybe that's why he accuses James of being fearful, because Julian is. King David lied to Ahimelech out of fear, and feigned madness in front of Achish. That's why kids usually lie, out of fear to protect themselves. Maybe Julian is fearful of having the same dilemma happen to him that happened*

*to James. I feel sorry for him, he's just trying to make it work,
and cover for Deo.*

Rhett was close to Julian, and spent many lunches with
him over the last several years talking about personal
issues, or young people who were struggling in the
Richmond Assembly. Julian was known for his ability to
engage people in conversation about their need for the
Lord where ever he went. Rhett once went with him to a
large hardware store, and Julian testified to three people,
including the lady at the cash register while the line backed
up. They all took it well, reflecting on their need for Christ
as Rhett and Julian walked out to work on Julian's large
bus he used in his evangelistic travels around the country.
Julian just had a special talent for that, and had a lot of
stories to tell of his opportunities to talk to others about
Christ. "There are so many opportunities out there Rhett,"
Julian had said with his thick Virginian accent, "but the
laborers are few." Rhett had thought, *I couldn't pull it off;
people would think I was part of some weird cult if I talked to
strangers like that.* But Julian's enthusiasm had waned in
recent years.

Rhett stood on the left side of the hundred plus adults
listening to Cary Murdock standing and asking questions.
Some sat on the picnic tables, the same one Rhett and Jarvo
had debated over with Lyle a few years back.

Deo sat behind Cary, and mentioned a few things
during the communication meeting, but that was it.

At the end, Deo said, "James told us something about a
Dominant Man Theory he has, that one man should be in
charge of everyone." Deo made a casual uplifted and
outward motion of his hands, then casually turned away
from the riveted eyes of the audience.

Deo didn't say any more about it. Rhett stared in disbelief. *This reeks of dishonesty! Deo knows this is misleading! The 'Dominant Man' accusation has been debated with all the people in leadership, denied and disclaimed by James, and thrown out months before this. Deo is getting away with this because he has kept everybody in Virginia so under informed,* thought Rhett.

Rhett looked around at the naively uninformed Virginian men and women leaning forward with slightly gapping mouths, as if thinking "Has James gone mad?" James had been their minister for thirty-two years, and helped many of them in their marriages and child-raising.

Rhett felt moved to speak. Starting out by saying he could rest in the judgment of the California men, he then finished, "We need to stand in truth, for righteousness, and the Lord's will."

As Rhett spoke, the audience all turned and looked towards Rhett. As Rhett looked back at them all, his eyes went over to Deo. Deo stood, staring at Rhett, with a leering expression, holding his hands pointing toward the ground, wiggling and twisting one hand in a back and forth like a wiggling fish, his sardonic expression emphasizing the pure menace in his eyes.

That, thought Rhett, *is really weird. Something is very, very wrong here.*

As Cary started talking on another subject, Rhett looked back at Deo again, their eyes locked and Deo would not look away. Rhett did not want to avert his eyes, he could not believe Deo's obvious misleading with partial truths, and stared back.

Rhett won the staring contest after a long minute or two; he had learned this with his dogs. It is important to establish some pack rules, because that is how dogs relate to each other, so sometimes the game has to be played by their rules. Rhett rarely stared others down, he once read that executives discreetly avoid it, and he usually emulated this, but this was an exception.

When men cave into their old natures and pervert the truth to gain a following, they become like brute beasts, and later perish in their own corruption, reflected Rhett later.

Rhett talked to George Taylor the following week, explaining his concerns for Deo's misleading statements, and Julian's running down of James Stark for several hours. Rhett got mixed up and told George that James had taken off Marie's colored toe nail polish with WD-40, not carburetor cleaner as James had explained to Rhett.

A few weeks later, Rhett called James Stark again to ask more questions. James asked Rhett, "Did Julian ever talk to you again about what he told you about me, about the pink toenail polish?"

Rhett answered, "No, why do you ask?"

James responded, "I sent Julian an e-mail asking him about the pink toenail polish, and the other things you said he told you. Julian responded he has never told anybody things like that, but is continuing to defend me to everybody, even though it is difficult when he keeps hearing so many negative comments about me."

Rhett said, "Could you send me a copy of that e-mail?! He ran you down for several hours with me!"

Rhett got the e-mail later that day. James asked Julian:

Julian, you are quoted as having said something to the effect that "James was married to Glenda, who was very conservative and he didn't control her, and now he is married to Marie who is very liberal and he is not controlling her. Since they have been married Marie has cut her hair and worn pink toe nail polish." Julian, did you say something like this, do you believe this is true?

Julian responded back to James:

No! I haven't said these things and No, I don't believe they are true. Let me share with you a little bit of what has been going on so you will have an understanding of what I have said and what I believe. Since you have been married to Marie, I have had to field questions from different ones who see a <u>perceived</u> change in what you believe and what you would encourage us to participate in as a Christian. The fact of the matter is, is that we cannot control our wives. They are who they are and each one has their own personality, their own faith, and their own set of convictions. Each wife has their own set of fears and insecurities that are going to manifest themselves in how they respond to their environment. While we cannot control our wives, all we can do is establish our own convictions before them and encourage them to follow. **As I have fielded different questions, I have endeavored to defend you and what I understand you to believe and do.** When questions have been asked to me about whether or not Marie cuts her hair and wears pink toe polish, I have responded with what you have told me. You have told me that Marie does not cut her hair and one time she had toe polish on and you removed it with WD40. (or something like that)

Julian had asked everybody in the Richmond Assembly, including Rhett, not to talk to James about the accusations they heard regarding him.

I can't believe Julian is doing this! Treating James this way, after all those years of helping Julian when he was younger! James helped him get started in ministry! thought Rhett.

Over the next month, as Rhett continued to receive e-mails forwarded from his dad in California, he noticed some from Carson Frund in Newfoundland.

Carson sent a list of concerns to Deo Trophy, itemizing occasions when Deo had not told the truth, but Deo did not respond. Then Carson sent another considerably longer list of facts to Deo that could not be reconciled with the truth, and copied Cary Murdock.

Cary responded:

On Mon, Sep 29, 2008 at 2:35 AM, Cary Murdock wrote:

Carson,

I am fielding what concerns there are. I make mention of them to whomever needs to consider such items. I definitely am encouraging each one to go ask the other involved to get a fuller understanding. I would encourage you to do the very same thing. Would you reconsider your "correction" of Deo's statement that he lived "2 blocks" from the Stark family? I believe that is simply a phrase as in "just around the corner?" If you want to have credibility in an effort to help Deo in this issue, wrangling about something like that hurts you. I think that detracts from the legitimate concerns. Help me know what you were intending to do by making a point of it.

I am well engaged in the issue at hand with Deo about Deo. He has been inquiring and very receptive, even inviting, to input from me and others regarding the subject of exaggeration. I have spoken to him about what I have seen and what others are bringing to me. I am not finished. I have registered with Deo in the presence of others that it is a serious matter. Others agreed.

Deo is an honest man with much integrity, but in all his skill he has hurt himself with poor language usage and technique. Don't hesitate to ask him what you don't understand! I think it is important to follow up on things we don't understand, especially if we are inclined to act on it or share it with others.

Cary

Cary chose to dispute the weakest item of Carson's concerns and virtually ignore the rest. Cary later decided that Deo just needed to be more careful with what he said. It was a weakness, but certainly not disqualifying.

Mark Shifflett, Rhett's good friend and neighbor, asked Cary about Carson Frund, and Cary gave the "two blocks" example to Mark, characterizing Carson with the broad brush of being technical to the point of ridiculousness.

Taking the weakest point out of many strong ones, and then blowing it out of proportion and characterizing the person with it behind his back became a common standard of behavior for Deo and his supporters, including Cary.

Carson regretted including that one point about Deo claiming he lived just around the corner, it distracted from all his other many good points. The truth was, Deo rarely interacted with James Stark socially at his home; it didn't matter if he lived fifty miles or around the corner. Carson was just trying to show Deo was misleading to justify himself when he had sent Carson his e-mail earlier in the year:

> If James were to have his past thrown on the table (which he knows that I could do and his family could do but none of us do) he would be likewise blown away.

This would lead the average listener to think there was a lot of social interaction in the homes, since they lived right around the corner from each other. But it wasn't true, they rarely interacted socially in their homes, and Deo could not "blow away" James with his past.

The problem for Deo was that Carson, as a retired Royal Mounted Policeman, checked up on things Deo told him. When he discovered Deo had mislead or lied to him, Carson changed his mind, of course. Carson's reward for following up with his diligent inquire was being marginalized publicly in Virginia for it, behind his back, for "flip flopping" after he found out the truth later. Carson's other evidence pointing towards Deo's dishonesty was ignored, with no response to his well documented concerns about Deo's dishonesty from Cary or Deo.

Meanwhile, a retired police officer and his wife from Maryland sent Cary a letter expressing their concern for Deo's dishonesty, with a lot of evidence. Cary completely and repeatedly ignored their e-mails and letters. He just told many others, "James sent an e-mail to a married woman," as if it proved James had problems. Cary later put a few sentences of this e-mail on the Big Screen in his attempts at discrediting James. Cary refused to show the entire e-mail he quoted from when asked.

Finally, after a few months of Cary telling him to talk to Deo about it, and Deo not responding, Carson Frund sent the letter detailing Deo's exaggerations out to all the people in leadership who were going to a November 2008 meeting in Texas to try and resolve the raging dispute over James Stark, and if there was anything that should prevent him from being a minister.

The summer of 2008 was thick with confusion, indecision, e-mails, and phone calls as the California leaders sorted through this unexpected situation. Most of the people in the California Assemblies were thrown into confusion; why was all this information so secret in California, yet Deo was going over it in Virginia?

After hearing the August 3rd, 2008 recording when Deo had exaggerated and twisted the truth, some California ministers and elders became convinced Deo was actually the problem.

Deo Trophy authoritatively told the leaders what to do, and the California leaders were submitting because they had agreed to it, but with growing suspicion. It was hard for them to realize there was a genuine and horrible dishonesty with a leader in Virginia, who other leaders were strongly supporting. It was disbelief.

The California leaders began to release some information. As time went on, the manipulation became more obvious, and Deo's flattery, "I am counting on you. You are the salvation of Southern California's Assemblies," with Jon Beamer, a young minister in Southern California, failed to work.

In Virginia, the California leaders and Carson Frund from Newfoundland were ridiculed as 'flip flopping' in private conversations with the Virginia leaders, except Lyle Cooper in Charlottesville. Lyle wasn't sure what to do or think about it, so he decided to be neutral to keep the peace.

"It's sort of like a lynch mob mentality," said Mycroft to Rhett one evening as Rhett commuted home from work, "assessing judgment on somebody without a fair trial, or letting them speak for themselves."

"The Bible says not to follow a crowd to do evil," said Rhett, "like perverting justice by testifying in a dispute under peer pressure, and circulating false reports."

"If these leaders aren't verifying the facts themselves then they are circulating false reports when they tell others of it," said Mycroft, "they have never heard James' side."

"I think the damage was already done before that April meeting," said Rhett, "James doesn't have a chance."

The leaders in California insisted on a meeting in Texas at the beginning of November, 2008: "Everybody will be expected to be there and cooperate," commanded Bach

Jude, the minister from Long Beach. Bach helped plan the meeting to be as impartial as possible, and prevent Deo Trophy or Byron Stark from taking over again.

Bach encouraged Rhett to go to it, "It is open to whoever wants to be there." Usually only leaders of each local Assembly would go to these meetings. Rhett didn't speak enough publicly to be regarded as a leader.

During the next Richmond Assembly meeting, Rhett approached Cary Murdock, and said, "I'd like to go to this November Texas meeting."

"The three of us from our area is already enough," Cary responded, "You need to trust us. We've got it covered."

Rhett thought, *Who should I trust: 1) People who will give me information, facts, and want me to go to the meeting, or 2) People who conceal information, giving sweeping opinions, and say "Trust us"?*

While the controversy raged with the California Assemblies, it was quiet and peaceful in Virginia. Except in Rhett's mind, which was in a big swirl of preoccupied deeply disturbing turmoil. None of Rhett's friends in Virginia knew much about it. Rhett knew, but he wasn't talking. He didn't want to be accused of 'causing a division' by releasing information and 'spreading discord.' Also, it was a choice people needed to make if they wanted to be complacent and just go along with what they were told, or look into things for themselves.

So far, Deo's Orderly Following was holding up like a well built and heavily armed Naval destroyer in Virginia and Texas. Everybody was submitting to him, whether they thought it was right or not. The Orderly Following Doctrine was infallible to his followers.

As the leaders in California sorted through their confusion, disbelief, and growing suspicions, they continued to be ridiculed and marginalized in Virginia.

"These leaders are flip flopping back and forth all over the place," Julian Petros snorkeled, "they are so weak and indecisive, they don't know what to do."

These men were some of Julian's good friends in the past! Julian is evidently devoted to fearing Deo Trophy, with his heart and soul, taking the Orderly Following a lot further then I ever thought it would go, thought Rhett.

Deo Trophy had given some good messages over the years, with the MP3 recordings being passed out in California. Many people had held him in high regard. Luke Alastair from Long Beach wrote to Deo, "The way you present and speak on subjects "clicks" with me. I know my safety is to put personalities aside and focus on the facts of the situation."

The time came for the November meeting in 2008, and after some debate Rhett opted out.

"I will find out what happened from others," Rhett told his dad, "Cary Murdock does not want me to go, and I don't want to create more controversy by going than there already is." *And it will be nice spending time with my family instead of burning the weekend at a meeting in Texas,* he thought.

After an enjoyable weekend with his family, Rhett got a phone call from his dad Sunday night.

Mycroft said, "The meeting ended well! On Saturday James Stark was finally able to tell his side of it, but Deo Trophy didn't respond to any of James Stark's comments, he just ignored James, and took up Carson Frund's letter with his concerns about Deo's exaggerations and tried to

problem addressed in Virginia. Ward Morgan is excited about finally getting James back in ministry in Loomis and helping him out there!"

The next evening Rhett went to pick his parents up at the Richmond airport from their flight from Texas.

George Taylor was on the same plane and walked by, intently reading an e-mail on his cell phone. He never saw Rhett or heard him calling to him. Walking over to his cousin, Al Taylor from Newfoundland, George showed Al the e-mail. Rhett wondered what it said.

The version Rhett got from Cary Murdock the following Wednesday night was much different.

"I don't want to report out on the meeting last weekend in Texas in much detail," Cary said on the following Wednesday night, "I am trying to sort through it."

Rhett was puzzled that nothing more was said in Virginia about Deo's dishonesty. Cary commented months later after finally reading the written report from the November Texas leadership meeting: "I don't see how Deo's exaggeration issue has anything to do with this."

Rhett thought, *Why is Cary having such a hard time seeing Deo had a problem? Cary in his own words said "he has hurt himself with poor language usage and technique." If a minister's words can't be relied on, then he shouldn't be speaking at all in my book.*

Rhett called Tim Mervin's son later that week, who said he had called his dad to get updated during the Texas meeting on Saturday night. After hearing a status update, he said, "Dad, you have got to do something! You are the senior minister! You need to make it happen and get this turned back around!"

Rhett also talked to Matt Warren. Matt said that James and him went for dinner that evening with their wives after the Texas leadership meeting ended on Sunday. Matt asked James if he would pray for the meal, and James prayed, "Lord, please help Deo, that he will be okay after this weekend."

Things went pretty much back to normal in Richmond that winter. The messages were neutral, people visited for an hour or so after meetings, and the teenagers, young married men, and middle aged men who thought they were still teenagers played football at the park. Cary encouraged them, "The football is an Assembly event, if you can't play you need to go and watch to be a support." Rhett decided to not do this, his kids usually got sick in the cold eastern winter winds.

There were some comments from Deo, "We have to stick together, we can't break rank," but otherwise, it was fairly quiet.

In Loomis California, where James Stark lived, it was far from quiet that winter. Ward Morgan, the local Bishop in Loomis, had moved there three years before from Southern California. He was soon involved in helping others with personal counseling and public speaking. It was greatly appreciated. He was consequently named as a Bishop by James Stark with the support of local people.

His large build, dark evening shadowed whiskers, and booming voice was in contrast to his humility, kindness, and genuine heartfelt care for others. He could have gotten a football scholarship, which was believable, looking at him. Rhett had once seen him and another very large man casually lift a grand piano from its side onto the pedestal when they were setting up for a regional retreat camp.

But after the November 2008 Texas meeting, Ward started to change. It all began during the summer of 2008. Ward was the one who supported Byron Stark at the July

Southern California leadership meeting at Bach Jude's home when Byron was emotionally distressed, talking about his father for five hours.

Ward had been supportive of James, but after that July meeting, he viewed James Stark with some suspicion.

It was Ward who told James he shouldn't go alone to a meeting with just the Virginia leaders in September, 2008 when James was out in Virginia visiting.

Right after the November 2008 meeting, Ward was excited about getting James Stark back in ministry. So was the rest of the Loomis Assembly. They hadn't taken kindly to Grandpa (as some referred to James) being taken out of personal counseling there by strangers in the East. A few had just bailed out, leaving the Assembly over all the confusion.

Deo Trophy didn't even know them, he had only visited Loomis a few times. Once to preach against the young men having sports cars, and then to preach on his Orderly Following nine years before, in 1999. One there had the impudence to say publicly, after he finished, that Deo's Orderly Following could be the start of a new cult.

Most people didn't have a problem with James in his own area. So when it finally got resolved, they were excited their local minister, Ward, was going to facilitate James getting back behind the podium again in Loomis and help with much needed personal counsel, finally putting an end to the situation.

But Ward didn't have any meetings with James or the local men in Loomis. Some of the local leaders set up a meeting, but it just dragged on without anything being accomplished. Ward just asked a few questions and the meeting ended. Ward started to change; he was a much different Ward than the Ward of the last several years. Even his old friends in Southern California were puzzled.

The people got frustrated in Loomis. The concerns about what exactly was going on created a tremendous turmoil not only in Loomis, but throughout California.

Lyle Cooper, the young minister from Charlottesville, was concerned, and called Ward, asking, "Ward, have you been in contact with Deo Trophy?"

Ward replied, "Yes."

Lyle asked, "How much have you been in contact with Deo?"

Ward answered, "A lot."

One man in his twenties, who also lived in Northern California near Loomis, had been greatly helped by Ward's personal counsel, looking to Ward as a father. He was surprised and bewildered by Ward's sudden personality change and demeanor, and said, "Ward changed a lot in the last few weeks, I don't know what happened, but he changed!"

Ward's married daughters lived in Texas and Virginia, under the sway of leaders who were in turn under the sway of Deo.

Ward unexpectedly stepped down as a Bishop and minister in Loomis, then reinstated himself a week later to stop Tim Mervin from speaking. Tim had driven nine hours from Southern California to speak there since Ward had stepped down, but just sat in the audience as the newly self-reinstated Bishop Ward spoke.

This was the most disturbing time of Rhett's life, far more disturbing than anything else; more than Jonathan's death. As the facts came forward, revealing the truth, Rhett became more and more disturbed until it consumed his mind. How could he have been so sucked in by Deo?

And why were men like Julian and Cary, men Rhett knew well for years, suddenly supporting Deo against obviously damning evidence?

Rhett became so absorbed and preoccupied in his thoughts, his children learned not to ask him questions. They just started patting him until he roused from his intense, engrossed concentration, and, staring blankly at them, tried to understand what they were telling him.

It lasted for months, and Sabrina was worried: "Rhett, you are really missing a lot of cute things the kids are saying, they are growing up so fast!"

Rhett stopped by on his way home from work to talk to Julian at his home in December, 2008. Rhett wanted to talk about their conversation during Labor Day weekend, and Julian's letter to James, saying he was defending James when he was actually arguing hard behind his back that James had problems.

Rhett read the transcript excerpt of Deo Trophy's August 3rd, 2008 public reporting out. Julian defended Deo, explaining again, "Deo was just talking in the context regarding just a portion of the February 2008 meeting."

Rhett read the excerpt transcript two more times, then said, "Deo is not saying that Julian! People are being led to a totally different conclusion. Why hasn't Deo corrected these public comments?"

Julian was silent.

Rhett said, "Julian, I asked you three or four times, every way I could think of, if James had submitted to those men at the end of the February 2008 meeting and said he would go along with them, even though he didn't agree. You finally answered "Yes" when I asked you the fourth or fifth time. Deo and you leaders haven't mentioned that at all, but painted him very poorly."

Julian said, "I thought you were asking me in the context of James' conduct, and not about what they were discussing during the meeting."

"Julian, I am not buying that."

Rhett showed Julian the e-mail to James Stark, denying he had said anything negative, but was defending James.

"Julian, you ran down James for hours with me, you certainly were not defending him!"

Julian explained, "I was just telling you what other people were telling me!"

"Julian, I'm not buying that either!"

Rhett left Julian's home office, greatly disappointed and puzzled over what was happening. It was so disappointing, and so, so surreal. He couldn't get the other leaders involved in addressing Julian's problem because they were going along with Deo's dishonesty.

Art, the young man who had spoken at Jonathan's funeral, had gotten married to a California girl. He heard that Deo had a problem exaggerating from his concerned father-in-law, who was referring to the November leadership report that George Taylor typed up, that the Virginia leaders were suppose to be working with Deo on it. Cary had never read it in Richmond.

Deeply concerned, Art asked Julian Petros to confirm this. Julian denied any problem with Deo exaggerating. When Art's father-in-law heard of this, he got Matt Warren on the phone, and they conference-called Julian in December, around the time Rhett had met with Julian. Matt reminded Julian of the meeting when Deo announced he had a problem exaggerating, that Julian and Cary were riding shotgun to protect himself from doing that. Matt asked Julian to get back with Art and tell him the truth. But instead Julian advised Art to not talk to his father-in-law anymore about it. Art was counseled to start cutting off relationships with his father-in-law, who had problems with leadership. Art and his wife had one child with another on the way.

Deo continued to give long messages at the regional meetings in Virginia at Happy Hill, and at their December 2008 retreat in the mountains of Virginia, near Lexington. At the regional camp in December, Deo told the audience - "Your faith is going to be challenged in 2009 like no other year in your life!"

Cary Murdock spoke on trust, the Assemblies needed to trust the Bishops, including himself, and not check into things for themselves. "The Lord has entrusted those to you to do this for you, and look out for you and protect you," Cary gently and authoritively instructed the audience from the podium. George Taylor got out of his seat, asking for a mic, and heartily agreed.

The New Year's party was at their rented hall in Richmond, near the Short Pump area. The theme was "Find Waldo©." Some young married men unwittingly picked Rhett as the main character for the night, not knowing much about the conflict. Rhett decided to go all the way, finding a costume that would equal the occasion, but with the sinking feeling his family may not be with them much longer.

This is so ironic, Rhett thought to himself, *I'm Waldo© and likely within a few months they won't be able to find me, I'll be gone.*

Byron Stark heard that the California men were going to follow through on the November agreement to reinstate his father James back into ministry, and sent out an e-mail to the California leaders on December 30th, 2008, concluding:

It is simple to see that my father is not willing to resolve issues with those who see issues. He only wants his ministry back. Of course with ministry comes power and influence and the opportunity to persuade with smooth words. This would be utter chaos and departure from truth. The word of God clearly describes a minister that deals with himself first and always. *1Co 9:27 But I discipline my body and bring it into subjection, lest, when I have preached to others, I myself should become disqualified.*

Those of us who see that my father has a problem have been very patient with you brethren that do not. Now, for you brethren to push for restoring my father to ministry is a recipe for chaos among the saints we know.

My father is strong and persuasive. He is desperate. The only way he can get back to ministering is resolve the issues, or work through leaders who do not see them. Which way would honor Christ? Humble himself and work through the issues, or use leaders who have never really seen the problem. Christ instructs us to resolve issues and come to peace, then we can proceed in helping others. <u>Working around the leaders who are being faithful to what God has revealed is Satanic.</u>

Please do not think there will be peace if my father is restored to ministry by a group of leaders in California. I believe if you do this independent of ministering brethren across the states, you will be responsible for creating confusion beyond anything we have experienced in my lifetime.

The issues were not revealed to you, but you have heard testimony to them. Those of us that bear this burden are comfortable with it. We have also endured the burden of criticism and accusations, suspicions, slander and distrust. We can bear this also, for the testimony of Christ. For Christ this is a small thing. But for Christ we must come together and work together.

Your Fellow Soldier in the Good Fight of Faith,
With Love and Respect,
Byron Stark

The California ministers were shocked by these opinionated and slanderous accusations. Rhett was shocked too when he got the e-mail from his dad.

Byron was a childhood friend of his, and had loved and respected his dad as a boy and young adult. Rhett and Byron had gone on backpack trips with their dads, playing together, standing on each other's shoulders. Since Byron was shorter, he was usually the one who stood on Rhett's shoulders as Rhett staggered around Byron's front yard. They wore old blue jeans with holes in them, way before their time. The derby hats Byron and Rhett wore were way behind their times.

It was sad how things were turning out now. Over the last few years Byron had seemed tense. The tenseness now clearly showed up in his face, his lower cheek area, the part of the face that sometimes has dimples. Byron didn't have any dimples, but he did have some tight muscles there which never seemed to relax. The muscles pulled his face into a peculiar and unnatural permanent smile.

Now, perhaps my relation to Nixon isn't of the most tender manner. I've read a lot about him.

He has a technique that I am disconcerted with, because he appeals so forthright, all the time, **as soon as he gets entangled, he tries to get sentimental.**

He tries to distance himself from a response by turning sentimental, and that I find very difficult.

- Former Swedish Prime Minister Olof Palme -

11 ·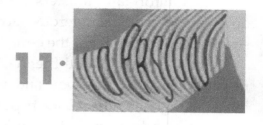

Letter of First Admonishment

T his is like a giant chess game Deo is playing, Rhett mulled over in his mind, *with 1,500 people as the pieces.*

In January of 2009, the California leaders were at a disadvantage strategically. They had not dared at first to think even to themselves that Deo was anything less than sincere, and went willingly along with Deo. After all, Deo had been in ministry for almost thirty years, being endorsed by James Stark himself.

The California ministers and elders had been careful to adhere to their agreement to not talk about the situation or their growing personal suspicions, or say anything publicly, or have communication meetings in their own Assemblies. Most of the people in their own congregations in California knew little about it, although some had heard Deo's one sided reporting out in Virginia, and Byron's in Texas.

On the other hand, Deo had talked extensively about it in Virginia, and his public communication meetings with contrived congeniality in August and September of 2008 helped sway people to his viewpoint. The Virginia Bishops were also making contact with some of the people in the California Assemblies in an attempt to sway them.

The information was restricted, and many people wondered what the problem was with the California leaders.

The California leaders wanted to reinstate James Stark to ministry, and also have a communication meeting to let their friends in their own areas know what was going on before Deo and his Bishops tried to take control of their own Assemblies in California.

They decided to send out a letter reinstating James to the Virginia leaders, include a letter addressing Byron's slanderous accusations against his father, then have a communication meeting open to anybody in the California Assemblies right afterwards.

Rhett knew their plan and waited to see the reaction back in Virginia. The letter went out late Saturday night, or early Sunday morning depending on the time zone, and by Sunday morning Cary Murdock and Julian Petros in Richmond were well prepared to vent on the California leaders from behind the podium for daring to defy Deo Trophy and his league of Bishops and leaders.

The Reinstatement Letter, in full, stated:

Jan 4, 2009 05:38:20 AM, Peter Waters wrote:
To our dear Brethren gathered at Burleson, Texas:

The controversy surrounding James' ministry has been a very heavy, difficult, and challenging situation for all of us. Our desire is to bring peace and resolution in a way that we can all live with and with what we believe will bring honor to Christ. We are asking from all our brethren patience and cooperation in this decision. We believe we made significant headway and resolve in Burleson, Texas, and because of that headway and resolve we have asked James to resume his ministry among us.

We did not believe that there would be a meeting with all the principles or a re-assessment of James prior to James resuming his ministry among us. Our understanding was that Ward, together with the Loomis brethren, would work from the basis of our conclusion at Burleson, Texas and report by Nov 30 that James would be back in ministry, unless they found some significant new problems. In our evaluation, the things we have become aware of since Burleson are not reasons for changing what we understand the direction and conclusion to be.

Brethren, we believe that by having James resume his ministry to the saints we know, we will help bring peace to this situation in a Christ honoring way. Our heart is to continue working with our brethren on any open issues until we can be together. We are committed to working together for as long as it takes. We plead for you to support this for unity sake. We understand that some still have concerns for James at this time.

Taking some thoughts from a recent e-mail to a number of us; "We have complete faith that when a man covers his sin he does not prosper! We have complete confidence that if a man is consumed by pride and lack of humility he cannot hide it! We have complete confidence that the Holy Spirit will make that known to us, and that it is Christ's church! We have complete confidence that if evidence emerges, that godly leaders will be together in judgment!" We believe we can move on with complete confidence in our Lord and His Word.

We also want to register a concern in what seems to be emerging from this situation; a doctrinal difference among us regarding the function of leadership in the Church. We look forward to the opportunity to study together on this very important issue.

As ministers to the Church at large, along with overseers and faithful brethren we are appealing to our fellow ministers, overseers, and faithful brethren for your support in this decision.

Tim Mervin, Peter Waters, Bach Jude, Emery Jacobs, Jon Beamer along with many brethren from California that were at Burleson, Texas

On Sunday, January 4th, 2009, Rhett went on with two of their children, leaving Sabrina at home with two sick kids. Cary encouraged the young families to do this when part of the family was sick and others could go. "Just have whoever is not sick come to the meeting," Cary said from time to time.

Cary spoke that morning, and for forty-five minutes his voice reverberated thick with condemnation, accusing the Californian ministers by name of being: "a tiny subset", "not of a sound mind", "they can't reason", and "they are weak". Most of the verses given were on those who cause divisions and how it is wicked, warped, and sinful people who cause divisions.

"The problem," Cary preached from the pulpit, broad shoulders back with his usual good posture as he solemnly gazed back at the audience, "is the California ministers have independently decided James Stark should go back into ministry again!"

At the end Julian Petros stood up and decisively agreed with Cary. Rhett was really disappointed to hear several ignorant amen's from people in the audience, they hadn't even looked into it for themselves and they were so willing to agree to a one-sided account against long standing ministers.

It was the strongest message Rhett ever heard against anyone, and it was against very credible ministers.

Railing, that's what this is. Cary is bluntly and authoritively discrediting and defaming the California ministers with his opinionated accusations. But the Bible instructs Christians to not keep company with any man who is a "railer", or a "reviler". It's trashing people, to harshly criticize and condemn people's character and commitments. It will take years for the Assemblies to recover from the wounds of being subjected to such scathing public criticism and abuse, thought Rhett.

As Rhett walked out after the meeting ended he saw Julian's mother sobbing. *She is a really sharp lady, she knows something is amiss, I'll bet.*

In anticipated shock, Rhett drove home and related to his wife Sabrina what happened. Rhett knew the California ministers had made all efforts to resolve this. There had been an agreement made in the Texas leadership meeting in November of 2008 to put James back in ministry, yet Cary Murdock had never said anything about this to anybody in the Richmond Assembly. The information was being restricted; hardly anybody else knew what was really happening. The California ministers were simply following through with the agreement from November of 2008 to put James back in ministry since there was nothing left to Biblically disqualify him.

Peter Waters and the California ministers were scrambling, being caught off guard, and trying to figure out how to counter Deo's instantaneous military like precision and strategy, as they learned over the following week of the public discrediting behind their backs on Sunday within hours of sending out their letter.

Peter had evidence corruption was infiltrating the leaders he had known for so many years. He really just wanted to be released from it.

Peter Waters sent the following e-mail to Deo Trophy:

From: Peter Waters
To: Deo Trophy
Sent: Monday, January 05, 2009 10:37 AM

Dear Deo:

Sorry I didn't answer your e-mail the other day. At first I wasn't sure how, and then I let it slip my mind.
I am anticipating some strong reaction to our letters, but the appeal to continue to work on this in our letter is genuine. Byron's statements have clarified where this situation is. We seem to be at an impasse. I'm speaking for myself here, though I believe many will agree with my thinking. I'm sure we are open to another meeting with you all. It would be helpful to know where you all are in light of Byron's statements. Maybe you are preparing a response that will answer this.

Feel free to call or write.

There is conference calling that can be set up, this may be useful at this time.

Feel free to share this with others, my expression here would be similar to all. I will probably share this note with a few on my end.

In Christ, Peter Waters

From: Deo Trophy
To: Peter Waters
Sent: Monday, January 05, 2009 12:17 PM

Dear Peter,

Thanks for getting back to me on this. I can understand letting things slip while a lot is happening. Just remembering it slipped was a gracious thing for you to do. I appreciate this. This is typical for you in my mind to be gracious about things such as this.

You are right to anticipate a strong reaction. What you have done is simply wrong. It is ungodly. It cannot be justified on scriptural grounds. Yes, we will be responding soon.

My heart aches for what you have set in motion. You will be held accountable by God and must be held accountable by your ministering brethren.

Your focus on the guilt you feel toward what has been done to James has been to the detriment of the best interests of the flock. I know you do not see it this way. You want to be with your brethren. I truly believe this. But this guilt that you feel is the fiery dart that Satan has used to ensnare you in this situation since April.

What you have done in your recent letter is addressed the guilt point that you feel. But Peter, it is false guilt. It did not need to be addressed but understood as being false. You now have acted independently. This is not a false thing or just my perception but a real thing. This is wrong. This impacts all the assemblies we know across the US, Canada and elsewhere.

I fear for us all in what you have set in motion. The unraveling has already begin in earnest in California as calls are coming to us for help.

My prayer is that you will quickly recover yourself and come to your senses. It is not too late, Peter. It is never too late with Christ.

To be honoring to the Lord we must be together. May the Lord give all of us the humility to mend the breech quickly for His body sake.

In sadness of heart at the moment but with the hope of Christ's unfailing love and mercy and graciousness for the future,

Deo

From: Peter Waters
To: Deo Trophy
Sent: Tuesday, January 06, 2009 7:37 AM

Deo:

I would simply put the statements back to you

What you have done, starting at least in April has been ungodly and wrong. You, Deo, and Byron, set this thing in motion, not us. We will all be held accountable to God for our part in this. Guilt is good when it motivates us to re-group and do the right thing. It is used by God and the Holy Spirit to help us not violate our consciences.

You are missing another opportunity for peace. You missed it in April when James offered to submit, you missed it when the unraveling begun right after April, where several that were uncomfortable were asking to re-visit it, You missed it right after this last Texas meeting last November when we could have moved forward with peace and a good plan to go back and work the issues as time allowed. If you will accept our letter, accept that If James is carnal God will clearly show it to us, we can still have peace and go on.

I'm not independent, many are supporting this.

With sadness of heart,

Peter Waters

Sent out about sixteen hours after Deo promised, "Yes, we will be responding soon," the Letter of First Admonishment was sent out on January 6, 2008 at 8:20pm. It was disingenuous reparation for the California Minister's defiance of Deo's authority, of daring to allow James to minister and trying to have a communication meeting in their own Assemblies.

Authored mainly by Deo, Ward Morgan sent it out from his computer in Loomis, California, and it cast the

California ministers in a terrible light, coming on the heels of their public defamation. This letter was secretly sent just to the California ministers, authoritatively forbidding the California ministers and elders to have their own communication meeting with the people who went to their own California Assemblies, and ordered them to not put James Stark in ministry.

The First Admonishment Letter from Ward Morgan, like the public defaming meetings a few days prior, also had the diabolically damaging effect of casting another ominous shadow over the reputations of the California leaders.

From: Ward Morgan
To: Tim Mervin; Peter Waters ; Bach Jude; Jon Beamer ; Emery Jacobs
cc: Temple Austin ; Joshua Jude ; Leroy Luther ; Byron Stark; Cary Murdock ; Al Taylor; Amos Blair ; Bill Baker ; Julian Petros ; Deo Trophy ; Archie Stark ; George Taylor; Aaron Adams
Sent: Tuesday, January 06, 2009 8:20 PM
Subject: Letter to Brethren
(PLEASE ACKNOWLEDGE RECEIPT OF THIS LETTER, THANK YOU)

Dear Brothers Tim Mervin, Peter Waters, Bach Jude, Emery Jacobs, and Jon Beamer,

It is a sober responsibility to be one that is called of God to serve the Body of Christ in any position of leadership. Those being led are referred to in scripture as "the flock, over which the Holy Spirit has made you overseers, to shepherd the church of God which He purchased with His own blood." Acts 20:28; I Pet 5:2-3.

We are also told emphatically in scripture that it is a very serious matter in the sight of God to mislead "the flock," misuse a trusted place of authority and responsibility, cause one to stumble, or cause division in the Body. Acts 20:30 vividly describes "and from among your own selves men will arise, speaking perverse things, to draw away the disciples after them." Luke 17:1-2. "And he said unto his disciples, It is impossible but that occasions of stumbling should come; but woe unto him, through whom they come! It were well for him if a millstone were hanged about his neck, and he were thrown into the sea, rather than that he should cause one of these little ones to stumble."

On December 23rd, an email was sent by Byron Stark to leading brethren requesting their presence at a leadership meeting to be held in January 09. At the recent California December camp regional gathering there was a meeting with four of you brethren, going over the purpose of this proposed meeting in Jan '09 and trying to convince you that it would be profitable to attend that meeting at our request. After three hours of discussion the response we got was a "yes" from Bach, "I'll think about it" from Peter, and "not without James" from Tim. That was a grief of heart to think that we could not even agree to simply meet together and continue "endeavoring...." At that time and on the previous weekend in Loomis, Ward and Joshua Jude were assured by Peter that you brethren would not take an independent action in restoring James to ministry. We have registered clearly that such restoration would not be endorsed at this time by many of us. Since December camp Byron's emails stated for many of us a loving entreaty and warning to you of the seriousness of this matter. He pleaded with you "to not disregard your brethren." How could you then possibly conceive of taking this divisive step? Where is your consideration for the flock? Where is your respect for your fellow ministering brethren? Where is your sense of accountability to God? The biblical basis for your action was notably absent in your letter. It is now your stated plan to voice the differences you have with leading brethren to all people from the flock you have been "entrusted with." May God help you to see the severity of your independent action. The scripture calls this "heresy" which is a party spirit or choice that causes division.

Tim, Peter, and Bach, we address you three brethren specifically in that we believe you hold the primary responsibility at this time for the expressions and decisions related in your email letter dated 1/3/09. You three brethren have discredited your testimony among most ministering brethren by your actions over the past year. We believe that Emery and Jon have been drawn into this situation in a different manner, and have not in this same way discredited their testimony. However, signing on to a disorderly action, God will hold one accountable and responsible for his actions.

We have repeatedly complied with your various requests for meetings in the past, including allowing you to have much control of the agenda. This has obviously not helped you, but has only served to prolong the situation and add to the confusion. You have denied, rejected, and ignored the explicitly stated, biblically based concerns for our brother James. It seems there is only one outcome that's acceptable to you and you have continuously demonstrated lack of hearing any reasoning that doesn't fit your conclusions. You have not "esteemed others better than yourselves," you have not respected the collective counsel and judgment of your fellow ministering brethren, and you have not been able to hear your brethren with understanding and keep rank.

We are not asking that you agree with us on all the issues at this juncture, only that you immediately rescind your decision to reinstate our brother James to public ministry and commit to work together with us as we continue to endeavor to be of one mind, as we are commanded by God to do. We have been extremely patient with you, repeatedly endeavoring to be longsuffering and forbearing. It is now time to "warn the unruly." We hope and pray you will accept this intervention on our part as a faithful rebuke motivated by our love for the testimony of Jesus Christ, our love for God's children, and our love for you. Pro 9:8. "....rebuke a wise man and he will love you."

Believing that Christ is the head of His church, the undersigned overseers, deacons, evangelists, pastors, and teachers have soberly, prayerfully, and carefully considered the events of the past few days – indeed of the past months – and with the authority of God's word, we admonish you to:

1. Retract your letter of Jan 3, 2009.
2. Cancel your plans for the proposed CA meeting Jan 11, 2009.
3. Commit to meeting with your fellow ministering brethren in the near future to give account for your actions.

We who send you this letter do so with soberness and heaviness of heart.

This letter of rebuke is the first admonition of Titus 3:10-11, "Reject a factious man after a first and second warning, knowing that such a man is perverted and is sinning being self-condemned." 1 Thess. 5:14, "And we urge you, brethren, admonish the unruly..."

We would expect to hear from you no later than Wednesday Jan 7, regarding this serious matter. Brethren, please be prompt or early in responding for Christ's sake.

In Faithfulness to Christ,
Your fellow ministering Brethren,

Ward Morgan, Joshua Jude, Byron Stark, Deo Trophy, Cary Murdock, Julian Petros, Al Taylor, Bill Baker, Leroy Luther, Aaron Adams, Temple Austin, George Taylor, Amos Blair

P.S. Archie Stark is out of the country but has expressed the following by email "I certainly believe my father should not be restored to ministry at this time and believe that the action that was mentioned in Peter's letter to remove the restrictions was untimely, unfortunate, and disorderly."

The letter rebuked the California ministers for their "independent action" in doing this "wicked and divisive" thing and ended with:

> We would expect to hear from you no later than Wednesday Jan 7, regarding this serious matter. Brethren, please be prompt or early in responding for Christ's sake.

The letter also had the wording at the very bottom:

> This communication is intended for the recipient only. Further distribution without the express written permission of the original author and/or sender is prohibited.

Hoping the California ministers would cave and keep the letter a secret as ordered, Deo was calculating they would retract their attempt at reinstating James under the time pressure of less than twenty-four hours. But instead, the California ministers read it publicly in their own areas; they had learned the hard way not to keep Deo's secrets.

This created the hardest week of their lives for Peter Waters, the minister from Visalia, Tim Mervin, the minister from Southern California, and Bach Jude, the minister from Long Beach. The letter was from a lot of formerly respectable men, and they were threatening to mark them for avoidance.

Depending on how the chips fell, some of these men might have their grown children, relatives, and close friends shun them for the rest of their lives. As word got out, person after person called them from around the country to tell them goodbye, in the gloaming hours of their lifetime friendships.

Most people immediately presumed them guilty; thinking the Iron Curtain of the Marking Doctrine would slam shut soon, believing these men and their supporters would soon need to be shunned.

All three men and their wives left town after several days to recuperate from extreme stress, lack of sleep, and frayed nerves. It was by far the worst week of their lives.

Ward Morgan didn't know that the "Letter of First Admonishment" had been read publicly in Southern California. Thinking the letter he had sent out from his own computer was still a secret, he went to a local Loomis leadership meeting, not knowing others there knew of the monumental letter.

As Ward lead out in the meeting, he told them, "Peter and those guys don't want to minister anymore. Peter's really getting paranoid about this whole deal! He sent an e-mail out to Joshua Jude by mistake that really blows his cover."

A local person asked Ward during the meeting: "Is there information you have that you're not sharing with us, Ward?"

Ward responded, "No, there's no new information."

"Are you sure there aren't any letters you sent out recently?" the man asked again.

Ward said, "There's no new information."

This caused more bewilderment. Why had Ward dramatically changed from his normal caring and honest self?

Ward had just sent a letter from his computer attacking and threatening to mark lifetime close friends and ministers, including Peter Waters. Leaders he had known for most of his life as he grew up in Southern California, yet he would not confirm sending it, and accused Peter of having unexplainable and unreasonable fear! Why was his conscious benighted?

Finally Ward admitted, "There was a letter sent out from my computer," as if Ward's computer had automatically generated and sent it out on its' own.

Deo strategically asked some older respected ministers, including Bill Baker and Aaron Adams (both were retired and living in Texas), to sign the letter, which they unwittingly did, believing in Orderly Following.

This letter, especially with all the signatures, greatly strengthened Deo's hand as he successfully used people's fear and respect of the Marking Doctrine to influence most of them against the California ministers.

This letter is a type of extortion, like the verse about not to keep company with anybody called a brother who is an extortionist, somebody who motivates other people by fear with threats and intimidation. Deo and his followers are using coercion to make people conform. It should be the Love of Christ that compels Christians, not the fear of other humans that are using coercion by threatening to shun and mark them, thought Rhett, after he read it.

As Ward Morgan said, Peter Waters did write an e-mail privately to the local California ministers. His frayed nerves were pushed a bit past the threshold of human tolerance levels. It is a rough thing to likely lose a lifetime of relationships and family within a few days, his wife was completely losing all of her relationships with her large extended family and siblings.

The e-mail Peter accidentally copied the Atascadero minister Joshua Jude - one of Deo's Bishops, is below:

Jan 7, 2009 09:32:02 PM

To Brethren:
- Do we believe and are we ready to stand on what we wrote???

- It may have been better to have held the letter to restore James for a few more days after we sent the response to Byron. But we can't undo it. And it shouldn't change what we believe.
- The curtain is going to drop on information very rapidly. And misinformation is spreading faster and faster.
- If we believe we are on the side of truth on this shouldn't we have a responsibility and aggressiveness to get the information out as quickly as we can to salvage as many of the saints as we can. Get going on our meeting and let it be known we are still willing to get together and resolve the issues. Being marked shouldn't stop it our ability to get meet with them. I am ready to move forward with our meeting. Tim are you, Bach are you, others???

- We are not going to change these men, we are 180 degrees out of sync with them.
- Which of the three demands can we meet with a clear conscience.

1. Retract your letter of Jan 3, 2009.
Do we believe in what we did.

2. Cancel your plans for the proposed CA meeting Jan 11, 2009.
This would gain us nothing and only put off getting much needed information to as many as we can.

3. Commit to meeting with your fellow ministering brethren in the near future to give account for your actions. We who send you this letter do so with soberness and heaviness of heart.

BRIAN, TIM, MYSELF: We are never going to minister again among this group of saints as we know. As they are expressing themselves.

- Guys the reports coming back from the reports being given seem to be spreading mis-information rapidly. The sooner we can stop this the better.
- The best defense is a good offense.

- Guy's we need to be solid and firm to move ahead or we are not going to have much left.
- If we are ever going to have an opportunity to get them to blink I think we need to do it from a perspective of confidence in what we are doing.

Others are looking to us. Lets don't keep sounding such an uncertain sound and confusing those that are looking to us and I believe would be willing to submit and follow our lead.
Please respond ASAP

We have a local leadership meetings tonight, we need to know where each are going to stand. This will give us more confidence.

> In Christ,
>
> Peter Waters

Joshua Jude lost no time in forwarding on Peter's e-mail.

The local Richmond leadership meeting the next day on Thursday, January 8th, in a local couple's living room had more inaccurate accounts. Most of the information was being withheld. Some of it was technically true, but since most of the people didn't know all the other things that were also true, they came to a completely different conclusion based on limited information. Rhett had decided to put a recorder in his shirt pocket in case things were disputed later in the meeting. Rhett didn't say anything or ask any questions during the meeting.

Mark Shifflett (Rhett and Sabrina's neighbor) asked Cary Murdock, "Cary, did you talk to these California ministers?"

Cary responded, "No, I haven't been talking to them. Deo Trophy has been the one talking to them. You see, we each do different things."

Cary was practicing what he preached; he was trusting in and believing what Deo was telling him without looking into it for himself, believing Deo was ultimately accountable. In turn, Cary laid claim to the Orderly Following doctrine and asked his followers in the Richmond Assembly to trust him, and believe what he was doing.

Cary instructed them in the leadership meeting:

> ...if you see someone who is independent as these men have chosen to be, that is sin!...that helps, you know, you don't follow sin, it does not matter who is doing it, when you have other leaders that are pointing that out and make it clear, then that relieves you at that time having to traipse off into sin following somebody because they are ahead of you in the Lord. You don't follow their bad example. Does not mean that all of us are not going to stumble at some point, what I'm saying here, is that this is a significant thing. This was meditated, was determined, a little different deal you might say. If you are grounded you will follow those that aren't heading off into independent action, you'll be safe. That's sad, to put, you know, younger men and their families in a place where they have to choose like that.

Virtually all of the people in Virginia and Texas in the Assemblies saw the California ministers as independent, exactly as the Bishops who supported Deo painted them. The information was being withheld, the Virginians and Texans were told to be orderly, and obey their leaders to not look into it further.

Rhett e-mailed his detailed notes back to his dad, who then distributed them to the California leaders. Other reports of what Deo and his league of Bishops had done in the public meetings came in from Texas, Oklahoma, and Virginia.

Meanwhile, in Richmond Virginia, as in Texas, Oklahoma, and Newfoundland, the messages over the next few weeks continued to be directed against the California ministers, casting them in a terrible light.

George Taylor spoke on witnesses in the Richmond Assembly. "There are three witnesses to James Stark's behavior in the February 2008 meeting," George said in his deep authoritative salesman's voice, "The Bible says if the witnesses are false, then it is God who will judge them."

Cary Murdock spoke up from the audience, adding, "Scorners don't find wisdom, they find dirt on the witnesses. You shouldn't need a defense attorney defending you."

"It's like Deo Trophy is playing a game of chess," Rhett told his dad the next week, "except the chess pieces are people and lifetime relationships."

"I know, I have thought that myself," Mycroft Stuart responded, "I'm losing many lifetime friends from the last fifty years in Atascadero, California, and also Texas."

Some people like to play games just for the game's sake, dreading the monotony of their existence. And the stakes were high in this game, lifetime friendships people were willing to throw away to follow Deo and his Bishops.

The First Admonishment Letter was successful in swaying people in Virginia, Texas, and one California Assembly in Atascadero, California. The minister in Atascadero, Joshua Jude, was Cary Murdock's brother-in-law and had years of close communication with Deo Trophy. His Assembly, he referred the people there as "my flock", obediently walked in Deo's Orderly Following, shunning lifetime friends and close relatives from California and around the country as they obeyed their local leader, Joshua Jude.

The California ministers and elders agreed to have another country wide meeting at the end of January, 2009 in California with Deo and his Bishops.

It is much safer for a prince to be feared than loved, because men are generally ungrateful, fickle, false, cowardly and covetous. As long as a prince offers them benefits, ruling with a noble mind, he will earn their faithful service, but that alone cannot be relied on. Because when it cost them something to support the prince, they will break an obligation out of love due to ignobleness for their own advantage, having more scruples in not offending someone who is feared. Fear therefore, will preserve a prince, because a dread of punishment never fails.

– Niccolo Machiavelli from The Prince, 1513 –
(paraphrased)

12·

Mind Control = Modern Deception

Not wanting to wind up being pointed out publicly for being divisive, Rhett was mindful not to let out the information he gleaned from his dad and leaders from California to people in Virginia.

Also, Rhett wanted to privately observe how the Richmond leaders handled things, knowing probably nobody else in Richmond had their suspicions keenly aroused like he had, because of the additional information he knew of.

He suspected Deo's disease of not telling the truth had spread to two of the local leaders, Cary and Julian. George Taylor hadn't gotten the same disease, but then George hadn't been to some of the influential meetings in which Deo and Byron had so successfully infected many others.

Rhett's belief that it was very wrong to leave the Assemblies was heavily reinforced by a lifetime of messages, and made him want to be crystal clear these leaders really were dishonest before leaving.

There were a few exceptions Rhett made in talking to people in Virginia; he would tell what he thought when some asked him directly about it. It was a few close friends who specifically asked Rhett what he thought.

One was Calvin Hobkins. Calvin had also lived in Loomis, California for most of the twelve years Rhett lived there. He had moved back to Virginia in 1998, two years before Rhett did, living in Deo's Fredericksburg Assembly.

Rhett and Calvin met for a lunch one afternoon, as they occasionally did to enjoy their twenty year friendship.

Calvin said, "You know the Euesters, the family that came around for a few months in Fredericksburg? She told me she noticed the broken baby-changing table in the ladies restroom, and said to another woman who has gone to our meetings for a long time, "I have a better baby-changing table at home, I'll bring it." The woman responded, "Uh, you ought to ask Deo about that first..." I think that's odd, don't you? Seems like we ought to be able to do some things on our own!"

"Seems like the women could make the call about getting a new diaper changing table in their restroom," said Rhett, in between bites of a chicken sandwich on sage and onion bread. They had their own private table by the fireplace. The wind blew snowflakes past the window, salting the ground white. Calvin began to ask a few questions, and Rhett cautiously answered.

Toby Tait was another close friend in the Richmond Assembly who asked Rhett to go out for a lunch.

"Rhett, I'm sort'n thru this James Stark deal. Wha'du you make of it?"

Rhett said, "You really want to know what I think?"

"Yeah, I do!"

So Rhett briefly told him, and Toby looked into it.

But after a month, Toby said, "It was really troubl'n my mind, heavy on it you know, and I was gett'n preoccupied and not pay'n attention to my kids, so I just decid'd to forget about it and move on and focus on my family. Things'll work out after a while; I can't do anything about it."

It was troubling Rhett's mind also, but he figured he ought to find out what was happening for the sake of his families' future.

Something was nagging at the back of Rhett's mind as he left the office and hit Interstate 95 one cold winter day in mid-January. It may have been a book he had read a long time ago, or something said in a college class. Rhett still doesn't know what prompted him to surf the internet, buying some books on Cult Mind Control in the middle of January, 2009.

Brainwashing, Rhett found out, involves physical torture and is against the law. But there are no laws against Mind Control, the art of using modern psychological techniques to deceive people by presumptuous leaders.

Rhett was intrigued in reading how the military uses Mind Control, like in boot camp. Rhett's nephew in the Army, stationed in Afghanistan, wrote when he was in boot camp he snuck out in the middle of the night to eat out of the garbage dumpster due to his extreme hunger. The soldiers are run hard, given a few hours of sleep, and a few minutes to gulp down a few bites of food, with constantly present strong authority figures demanding instant obedience. The soldiers, deprived of food and sleep, learn they should never question authority. It was a war they would be in, and it wouldn't do to have soldiers acting independently. Mind Control took men slated for prison who couldn't make their own beds, and turned them into compliant soldiers who would instantly obey their leader to their possible deaths.

The war in Afghanistan and Iraq was difficult, against an unseen enemy in disguise. It was the battle for the mind of the people; the physical weapons of American soldiers were at times useless external objects that just reinforced preconceived perceptions, so the soldiers needed to closely follow orders and sometimes not their own instincts, just as in any war.

One of the Army's expert Mind Controllers went on to start a cult. Since there was no abuse, the Army and courts could do nothing about it. It is a free country and people can choose to believe and do what they want, whether mind control is involved or not.

However, young people who sign up for the Army know what they are in for, sort of. People going to church aren't expecting similar, but much more subtle, mental manipulation tactics.

Deo Trophy was a computer scientist in secret weapon development in the Navy. What Deo worked on was so classified he could not talk of it. Everybody knew Deo was highly intelligent. Rhett wondered what exactly Deo did there, and why did he say so little about his employment?

Rhett learned in his quest that Mind Control is a very subtle process. It usually starts with long indoctrination speeches that last hours and hours. The critical thinking defenses of the human mind breaks down after several hours of confusing speech and the subconscious is opened up. A person can only run for so long before eventually tiring. The human body ultimately tires from physical exertion.

The human mind can only stay critically alert for so long until it finally gives up resisting. After the mind stops resisting, the critical judgment is suspended and the mind readily receives what is said, accepting it into the subconscious mind. **After this takes place, the person defends what they accepted into their subconscious mind when they are later questioned or criticized for what they now consciously think.**

They have been subconsciously convinced, and will intellectually defend themselves with their conscious mind.

The human mind, despite all of its strength and ability, has weaknesses. It is dependent on a stream of coherent information for it to function properly. When people are deprived of this, they become incredibly suggestible in the confusion. Like a ten hour leadership meeting in a small curtained room with a single lecturer dominating the entire time.

The evidence was purely circumstantial, but some pieces of the puzzle fell into place as he recalled many events that had happened over the last year or so.

Rhett remembered Deo's "Mind of Humility" message he directed for ten to twelve hours one day at a country wide leadership meeting with no time for questions until the next day, Deo's other long presentations, and Byron Stark's five hour emotional appeal that had temporarily swayed the leaders in California.

Rhett learned that confusing statements are made to disorient the listener, and he remembered all the long confusing messages Deo had given that he never really did understand. Rhett remembered one of Deo's opening statements on August 3rd, 2008: "I am trying to describe something I have never seen to people who have never seen it."

Deo was characterized by being so smart that people had a hard time comprehending what he said. Had Deo been confusing people on purpose over the last several years in order to manipulate and control them? Did the emperor not have any clothes? Many others certainly thought he did, but Rhett had a niggling doubt about it for several years.

Another mind control technique is to say simple phrases over and over to emphasize points, as a mantra. Rhett remembered, among many other instances, Deo speaking on "Making a Choice," and also repeated the phrase: "Byron was trying to help his father become more effective" in his August 3rd, 2008 lecture, over and over again.

After hours of uninterrupted lecture, lack of food and not much sleep, an emotional high is attempted to try and connect. This too, had been done by Deo at times during weekend long camps. The pattern was having hours and hours spent convincing people in boring rooms with little to distract. Most people were tired, having stayed up late for the meetings and talking until late the night before, and hungry. This had been going on for years in the Assemblies, but Deo seemed to be exploiting the tired condition of people during camps.

Jar had a gag order to keep him from interrupting. Rhett remembered all too well the hours Deo used on his captive audiences. I Corinthians 14 says to let two or three prophets speak and let the others judge. But if something is revealed to another, let the first keep silent. This would prevent a Mind Controller from taking control for hours. In California people were free to ask questions or make comments during messages; in fact several people usually did.

Mind Control uses cunningly devised subtle and subconscious influences used in combination to create a new social structure and thought process for controlling people; one that is of the Mind Controller's choosing, a perilously false premise that serves the Mind Controller. Together, these influences create a strong delusion.

The Six Key Elements of a Mind Control Environment:

1. Idolatry – Create excessive, and sometimes blind, admiration and devotion to a person or group, and their beliefs.

2. Systematically using subtle techniques for changing the way people think, what they think, and keep existing member's thoughts and hearts loyal to the Mind Controller and his cause. The goal is to have the Mind Controller as the parent, and the adult subjects functioning as his children.

3. Almost total dependence on a leader, leaders, and the group, combined with cutting off most of the outside world. Especially close friends and relatives.

4. Teaching that the group has all the answers; it has everything good in life and there is nothing else.

5. Creating an environment of fear in leaving. Any deserters are punished by shunning, and are vilified and marginalized by ridicule before and/or after they leave. This creates a profoundly deep subconscious fear in the existing members to never leave, so this won't happen to them. Anything outside of the group is inferior and of Satan. It is evil. There is no rule or doctrine more pure, or better, than the group's. Outside is failure and disaster.

6. There is a well developed, and often unstated, system of rules and codes for behavior. Teaching God will approve of the members who follow the leader and are loyal to him is of utmost importance. God is not acting out of grace, or mercy. God is a strict judge of justice who is working directly with and through the leaders who alone know what God really wants. The Mind Controller becomes their parent, and his followers are treated like children. They do not need to know everything, but just what the leaders think they need to know.

There is a lust for power that burns deep inside a lot of men, and some women. Most people suppress it, or are never in a position to use it. Some people are just not smart enough to figure out how to control others. Some just dominate their own families in wrong ways. Christian leaders are not much different; they still have an old nature that lusts for power and control.

Satan tried to tempt Jesus with this, with his offer to make Him king over the entire earth. It is a temptation common to all humans.

When a leader has deep insecurities coupled with a licentious lust for control over others, layered thick with deep welling pride, then a wolf, an abusive and divisive leader, emerges. Like a vortex that begins swirling and sucking everything into themselves, they become incrementally worse and worse, sucking people inward and downward.

This was a common expected problem to deal with for Jesus. He warned his disciples right after the mother of James and John asked for a place of honor for her sons in the Kingdom. Jesus said, "You know the rulers of the Gentiles lord it over them, and their high officials exercise authority over them. Not so with you. Instead, whoever wants to become great among you must be your servant, and whoever wants to be first must be your slave – just like the Son of Man did not come to be served but to serve and to give his life a ransom for many."

Godly leaders need to lead by example, serving others. Peter was inspired by the Holy Spirit to write: "Do not lord it over those entrusted to you but rather be examples."

John strongly rebuked Diotrephes for his wicked words and lengthy malicious speech, and for casting others out of the church for unbiblical reasons.

The Bible warns against Satan disguising himself as an angel of light, and his servants as ministers of righteousness. An abusive control is deceptive, and the doctrines of demons. "What, you don't want any authority in your life? Ahh, you're a sinful rebel, rejecting accountability to your leader!" People often just "put up with it", and allow themselves to be motivated by satanically inspired guilt and fear.

When the abusive authority ridicules others, marginalizes, and puts opponents who threaten their control out of their association, then followers just 'put up with it'. The more the followers 'put up with it', the stronger the control becomes, and it spirals inward into an increasingly abusive vortex of control. The abusive authority takes full advantage of the common trait most people have in wanting to appease leaders.

Christians are especially vulnerable to manipulation by perceived spiritual authority figures, and easily intimidated in large groups by their desire for living quiet and peaceful lives, and respect of authority.

Christians meeting together in a living room can start out with integrity and fine motivations. Gradually, after a few generations of meeting together regularly, formality and legalism invasively penetrates and infects some. Former 'judgment calls' become rules. The most aggressive and the most assertive people rise up and gain control. Hopefully these new leaders fear God. Most people are complacent and passively content to let them be in charge. It takes energy and effort to make things happen. This sets up a new opportunity for a false and abusive leadership to rise up and scatter Christians. The pattern keeps repeating itself, just as the Bible warns many times.

A successful Mind Controller will have an elevated, superior, intellectual 'guru' mentality toward others, surrounding himself with smart people who will protect and defend him. The foundation of his success is gaining strong-minded and intelligent loyal followers who are willing to convert others for him. Getting more subjects later on is much easier when this groundwork has been made. Weak minded people have hang-ups, and cause time consuming problems later, so are avoided.

Some clues to help tell if it's a Mind Control environment:

Deception is heavily used with mind control. If it's the truth then it's not mind control, so the Mind Controller claims it's the truth and so it's not Mind Control. Once the victims pass through the gate of deception, and they accept the way they were deceived as rational for 'the cause,' then they are set up to deceive others the same way. A lie that leads to many other lies to cover the first lie. They become a slave to the deception themselves by believing the end justifies the means. The lying isn't looked upon as real lying, since the lying is done for a good purpose, for 'the cause' or 'the truth.' These people unwittingly become

Mind Controllers themselves by straying from the truth, and are exploited by the Master Mind Controller.

By buying into deceiving others, the converts become deceived themselves by not letting the truth control what they say. The expression 'just trust us' was used liberally by Deo and his Bishops.

Mind controllers seek out strong-minded people who are intelligent, talented, and successful. These assistants are made to feel they are the elite. These leaders feel driven to perform, and with a seared conscience they exalt the authority figure who gave them their own power. These followers become the foundation as powerful and persuasive assistants helping win new converts. Deo did tell the audience when some of his messages were for a few elite leaders who were present in the audience. Most people think they will never get sucked into something like that, and even after they leave they tend to defend their own actions.

Mind Controllers hone in on a person's weaknesses by first making their target comfortable, then get personal and confidential information to exploit the person later. What the participants unwittingly give out is used later to incorporate them into a new belief system, and an identity that serves the Mind Controller.

The Mind Controller reveals little of himself. A lot of pressure is leveraged to make a commitment right then, under pressure, as soon as possible while they are under the influence of the 'ether.' This makes it hard for the people who sign on, to back out later. They tend to defend their agreement made under time demands. Reflective thinking is discouraged, and they are kept busy.

Successful Mind Controllers size up people, categorizing them into one of Four Groups: Thinkers (intellects), Feelers (emotional), Doers (action oriented), and Believers (looking for a spiritual experience). They ask subtle questions to feel the person out, and then present arguments the people will fall for depending on what motivates them.

People are easier to control by a Mind Controller after a vulnerable time of stress in their lives, making them easy targets. Defense mechanisms are broken down or overloaded, and people are easily controlled.

Some successful cult leaders project themselves with false humility, as spiritual men. They take the place of the person's physical father and successfully use this emotional leverage for all human's deep seated need for approval in order to motivate and control them. The goal is to make the adult followers as much like their own children as possible. When people accept this, then they accept human authority in their lives to the point where they are hopelessly dependent on the authority, as children are with their parents. One technique used to obtain this type of parental control is to keep them off balance to foster dependency, making it hard for them to make their own decisions.

When cunning craftiness is plotted to deceive the followers into functioning like children, they become much more manageable, being easily influenced by false doctrines and other tricks of deception.

There can be a 'love bombardment' to initially control people, flattering people to take advantage of them. If mind control is not initially working, then the effort goes back to swelling words of flattery, overly nice and complimentary. A person likes to be treated like royalty, and will often put up with being manipulated and lied to under the right circumstances.

These Mind Controlling imposters use friendships and peers to leverage control over others. People tend to doubt themselves and defer to their group. This is why it is so important for a Mind Controller to first establish several leaders who are loyal followers, convincing them first, before moving forward with a larger group.

A new doctrine needs to be presented which becomes a focal point for those controlled, filling them with a sense of purpose and meaning to follow the leader. The interesting thing is, the new doctrine needs to be vague and not definable, nobody really knows exactly what it is. Carson Frund had produced the e-mail in which Deo referred to a 'new order' he wanted to put in place when James was taken out of the way. Nobody really knew what Deo had in mind for the Assemblies future, or what he meant by 'The New Order' which he had referred to a few times. Deo dismissed the idea he was trying to do this when asked.

Creating confusion controls a person's behavior because they will change their thoughts and feelings to minimize the dissonance, their confusion. Humans don't like confusion, so they will accept what the Mind Controller is telling them to do or think to avoid continuing being confused. Hypnotic techniques include a double bind: "If you are having confusion, I am the one creating the confusion, so you will see I am the true Teacher." Whether one believes or doubts, both bases are covered.

The Mind Controller strives to get all the bases covered first, so the only alternative is to come to his fabricated conclusion. This was Deo's Modus Operandi in his messages, covering all his bases first before delivering his main point. Not Mind Control of itself, but together with everything else, it started to smell of it.

After most people are bombarded with hours of confusing talk, their mind goes numb due to mental exhaustion. It gets confused and overwhelmed, and the ability to think critically becomes difficult. It is in this weakened state people become suggestible to the speaker. Their opinions formed while in this state can last a long time, especially when they continue to be exposed to the same reiterated and repeated points. Group hypnosis works well in these situations. When the speaker notices blinking rates are slower and swallow reflexes slow down, the mind is open to receive information without much conscious critical thinking involved. People lose their frame of reference and accept what is being said to them without objection. Faces relax into a blank neutral stare. Repetitive, monotony, rhythmical, droning, lulling, hypnotic cadences repeated over and over. The talk is varied to keep interest but the message is always the same. The personal opinions of the audience are put down, they don't understand what is given, and they accept, in time, the truth, the truth of the Mind Controller's choosing.

The objective is to have people surrender, to let go, have faith, and trust the deceiver. Conveying that their rational mind is holding them back from great things begins subtly, then more forcefully. The Mind Controller seeks to mimic and mix in the truth as closely as possible, but the motive is to control others with deception, not help them. The goal is for people to trust them, not God.

As Christians put their trust in God by testing to see if what they hear is true, refraining from every form of evil, and embracing what is good and true, the Mind Controller loses control over them because the Holy Spirit is no longer quenched; God is able to purify them from the wickedness.

The audience will likely feel guilty for falling asleep. The speaker may even tell the audience they are dozing off to make them feel guiltier. Rhett remembered Byron Stark's five hour emotional appeal in California, how some people were very convinced afterwards and appealed to James. Later, when the hypnosis wore off over the next few weeks, they reconsidered. Rhett asked Cary Murdock, the minister from Richmond, what Byron had said in those five hours. Cary answered that Byron gave very good information during that emotional appeal and he was going on the information, not the emotion of it. But he couldn't give Rhett much information to consider. Rhett also recalled Calvin Hobkins from Fredericksburg telling of many hours of lengthy 'personal counseling' sessions with Deo at his home, and how confused he had been for days afterwards.

"But the power which has always started the greatest religious and political avalanches in history rolling has from time to immemorial been the magic of power of the spoken word, and that alone. Particularly the broad masses of the people can be moved only by the power of speech." said Adolf Hitler (Mein Kampf). Speeches can have the power to move small or large groups, regardless of it being true or false.

During the long meetings, new converts are surrounded with many people who express, feel, and act the way the mind controller wants them to also act. New converts will usually have doubts but feel they are the only ones and conform to the majority. Any negative comments are squelched, and told to wait until 'after the meeting is over,' but the question is never answered later. The other perspective, the other side, is never presented. Just those thoughts and feelings in favor of the new agenda are allowed. Rhett recalled the meeting in March of 2008. Only things against James were allowed, and when Carson Frund said, "There is another side to that," Deo responded, "This is not the time for that now Carson." It was never time later since the goal was to stop critical thinking permanently.

Deo had lied to Tim and Peter, the older ministers from California who were left out of the secret March meeting, to get them to sign onto the California agreement in July by assuring them James would soon tell his side of it. But Deo never let it happen, until he was virtually forced to later in the year during the November Texas meeting.

Byron performed another public emotional appeal in Texas, just prior to the First Admonition Letter being signed in January, 2009, in spite of being criticized for months for trying to convince others with emotional speeches. He was successful in convincing many. The Texas leaders were asked to sign on after the strong persuasive arguments were given, with little time allowed for reflective or critical thought.

Mind controllers are shrewd manipulators and effective communicators. Followers are taught to follow orders without hesitation or question, like soldiers in the Army. The TRUTH becomes perfect and absolute; any flaw pointed out is associated with that person's flaw, not the TRUTH. Follow the TRUTH even if you don't understand it. The living and true God becomes smaller and smaller.

Information is tightly controlled. When the information is controlled it restricts the ability to think critically and make sound judgments. This was done extensively. Rhett thought of the gag order made on James. Also, the California ministers and elders were requested by Deo to not talk about James' situation to others. Rhett recalled the

Orderly Following doctrine Deo had preached for so many years, since at least 1985.

Fear of the outside world, and all the bad things that will happen if one leaves, is firmly and methodically embedded in the mind of the followers by creating an 'us vs. them'. The 'them' or 'other side' or the 'outside' is associated with Satan.

Phobias are created to systematically create a fear of deserting the Mind Controller. The thought they need the Mind Controller or group to grow spiritually, intellectually, and emotionally is drilled in. George Taylor, in response to the California ministers wanting to 'independently' put James back in ministry had told the Richmond Assembly, "Satan is moving again," and, "there are troubling times ahead for us among the Assemblies." George was not thinking independently when he said these things. He was keeping rank with Deo.

The Master Mind Controller only has so much time available, so he needs Underling Mind Controllers to control people, with the Master Mind Controller at the central headquarter controls of his cell phone and computer over his Underlying Mind Controllers. Common followers slowly lose access to him. Keep them busy doing things; they will forget past concerns after about a year.

Constant reinforcement and interaction with the Mind Controller or his underlying Mind Controllers is needed. The more personal time people can be persuaded to give up the better. People are ridiculed who want "family time" or "personal time."

The Mind Controller stresses followers have to 'keep rank' and 'stick together'. There is a feeling of power from the single-mindedness.

Mind Controllers manipulate so the followers can't make decisions without going to the Mind Controller. They are encouraged to not think independently or make their own decisions. They become dependent on the Mind Controller as their parent. The more dependent they are, the more controlled they are. It would be a terrible thing to be accused of being 'independent' like the California leaders were accused of. But what is wrong with thinking independently of a leader? Does the hand say to the foot "You are independent?" Were the Virginia leaders independently trying to run the California Assemblies?

Who really are the independent ones?

Personal problems are blown way out of proportion to keep the focus on the person being controlled, so they don't challenge the Mind Controller. James Stark's personal problems certainly were leveraged and blown way out of proportion by Deo and Byron.

Mind controllers exploit the natural tendency people have to obey authority. They exploit the fear people have of ridicule, rebuke, and losing relationships. This fear is a very deep subconscious fear that profoundly motivates them to defend what they are doing, and condemn others that do not obey the leaders. Even the thought of people who left the association, or disobeyed the mind controller, conjures up defenses in the minds of those controlled to discount or think poorly of those who have "gone to Satan" and the evil outside world, outside of their association. Their mind is ensnared, and captivated by fear to automatically think evil of anybody who leaves their group.

Getting away with public ridicule, sarcasm, and rebuking automatically lets the Mind Controller gain more control over an audience, because the audience fears the same thing happening to them. Pointing people out publicly creates fear in others to behave so the Mind Controller won't do this to them, so they want to be nice to the Mind Controller and get on his good side and please their parent. And they might tell on their friends to gain temporary favor.

Private slander creates fear in the followers by naturally not wanting the Mind Controller to do this to them. Creative slander can be used to create bitterness and walls against those who could help the followers. Slander against the Mind Controller is a very, very bad sin, and divisive. Slander against followers is not nearly as bad an offense, and acceptable if the leader is doing it. As Rhett read this, he regretted not standing up to Deo when he had done this, except to stare him down. But that didn't accomplish much.

Behavior is publicly or privately rewarded with praise, or ridiculed. Humans don't like the sarcasm and ridicule, and will behave to avoid this, but do things to gain the praise, like tattle telling on others after they themselves have gotten in trouble. Bad comments and thoughts are immediately reported to the Mind Controller, the person reporting them thinking it will gain them approval. Appropriate action is taken against the person making the comments.

Using guilt and fear to manipulate and control keeps them off balance. Confession of past wrongs is a powerful device for controlling emotions. But rarely is the confessed sin forgotten, but brought up later to manipulate.

People are not allowed to talk to each other about anything critical of the leader, doctrine or organization. Tim Mervin's grown kids respectfully talked freely of their dad's flaws with no fear of retaliation. It didn't matter if he was a minister in Southern California. There shouldn't be fear associated with politely and appropriately talking about leaders shortcomings. Proper Christian leaders normally talk openly of their own shortcomings, setting an example of humility.

Followers strive to be obedient and loyal to the leader, hoping to get their approval, just as children seek the approval of their parents. Followers who attain leadership status love the feeling of getting in front of many people and have members look up to them as a wonderful and spiritual person. The Mind Controller holds the keys for this privilege.

Teach people to manipulate their own thoughts so they won't think impure thoughts, but stick to the truth, which is defined as loyalty to the Mind Controller. Give them excuses to justify their fears in leaving or disloyalty, like: 'don't break rank' or 'we need to stay together' or 'there is no reason for us to divide' or 'do not think independently'.

Fear of shunning for leaving the group is very effective at making people manipulate their own thoughts subconsciously. Ridicule others who are independent so nobody would want to do such an 'evil thing'.

It becomes obvious the ones controlled cannot make important decisions without first asking permission from superiors. The ones controlled say they 'will see', and then check with their superior.

Controlling words and their definitions provides the language symbols used for thinking, and consequently controls thoughts. Condensing complex situations by putting a word label on them and reducing them to cliché controls the thoughts of the human mind. Like 'independent'.

Teach people the worst thing is to act like yourself. Rhett remembered Byron Stark had said he does not like the way he was, he was like his father, and Byron wanted to be different now.

When people are being excessively controlled by fears, their sense of humor is blunted.

Mind Controllers often have an inferiority complex and somewhat antisocial behavior. What they require is attention and power. They learn to crave it, and develop a need for more and more power. Some cult leaders are in it for the personal power, not the money. They operate under the belief that people are too stupid and unspiritual to know what is best for them. They begin to believe their own propaganda.

Things can start out good, and be good, for a long time, then deteriorate little by little. When control is exerted a little bit over people they don't complain and get used to it. There eventually comes a point where it becomes really damaging. People like Jim Jones, the infamous cult leader who convinced his followers to drink a poisoned purple punch. Jim began as a minister with a long history of helping poor people. As his power grew he became more and more deranged.

Systematic use of these time proven modern psychological techniques reduces a person's will and gains control over their thoughts, feelings, and behavior. Self-esteem is destroyed so the followers don't complain.

All humans need love, friendship, attention, approval and a feeling they are in control of their lives. There is a common dislike for feeling events are out of control, so reality is put into an order that makes sense. The reality is the one placed there by the Mind Controller's manipulations after his subjects have been properly confused.

Decontrol a person entangled in Mind Control by gently building rapport, being friendly but not critical. Patiently get them to think from another perspective, about their past, what they liked, what their parents thought of them. Get the person to get in contact with their identity before they were controlled. Then get them to think about it from that perspective. To break the control over a deceived mind, it is important to try and get the person to see from his old perspective before this happened, and from others' perspectives, especially his parent's perspective.

Give them information in an indirect way so they can get the information without being defensive. Avoid quarrels; correct them with humility. Talk about other people and other situations, not theirs. Have them visualize being out of the mind controlled environment and still happy. Then talk to them about mind control and its effects. Be supportive and talk it out. It may take a few or several days. Give them space to think it over and make a decision. People need to make their own decision, after thinking critically for themselves.

When they come to their senses, and escape the snare their minds were captured in, it causes a lot of pain, and it can take a few years to heal. Like a pear that loses all of its flesh to the core, leaving just an ever so fragile skinny core.

The fruit has to be rebuilt back around the core, and it takes a long time. Deep depression is common.

It was the middle of January, 2009 when Rhett read the Mind Control techniques and information. After concluding there were implications of Mind Control involved, although the evidence was by no means complete, Rhett thought the leaders in California ought to be warned.

Rhett wrote an eight page document and sent it out to his dad, who forwarded it to several ministers and elders in California, to expose these sterile works of darkness.

The document went over in detail techniques Deo had used to sway people, and warned them with this comment: "I think it would be a very bad idea to allow Deo, Byron, or Cary to dominate the time for hours at the meeting at the end of this month. It is okay to interrupt an emotional appeal with comments like "Byron, this is the third time you have tried to sway others with your emotions" or "Byron, why don't you take a break and let others talk until you can regain control of yourself." We should be as wise as serpents, but harmless as doves. Truth always prevails in the end, and is stronger than lies. Love is stronger than fear."

Keep your heart with all diligence,
For out of it spring the issues of life.
Put away from you a deceitful mouth,
And put perverse lips far from you.
Solomon – Proverbs 4

13·

Love is Stronger than Fear

Calvin, talkative, energetic and athletic, loved to talk
to people about the Lord.   His dark hair and youthful
features made him look much younger than forty-eight.

His father was a NASA engineer, and although Calvin
was also intelligent, he chose a much different occupation,
outside office supply sales. He helped bring many of his
friends to Christ, and consequently to the Assemblies, in
his early twenties.

Calvin was saved in his late teens after he experienced
an exquisitely beautiful vision while on an LSD trip. The
vision profoundly impacted him, and he started thinking
maybe there was a God, as he looked up at the stars. He
was saved a short time later, and it dramatically changed
his life.   He applied his sharp mind to the Bible,
memorizing portions of it, becoming a master of
remembering and locating verses.

Right after Calvin was saved, he starting meeting at a
local home which was connected to the Assemblies in
Virginia.   At first, the Assembly meetings in Maryland

were low key. The three or four families that got together enjoyed open and honest Bible studies for several years. Then there was progressively more organization by James Stark, and later by Deo, who lived in Fredericksburg.

Calvin grew up in Silver Springs, Maryland, and fell in love with a California girl. Calvin was so overcome with love while sitting by Barbara on the front steps that he didn't notice his friend Simon Roland eating all the cookies Barbara had just made for Calvin until they were all gone. Calvin moved out to California and married Barbara, settling near Loomis for about ten years.

Calvin was the caring sort of guy who didn't mind helping other people. One late afternoon he saw a woman changing her tire in heavy rain on the side of a busy freeway in Sacramento, California. Calvin stopped, changed the tire for her and left. The next day the woman's boss called, thanking him. Calvin had helped the administrative assistant of a man who owned a large company, a company Calvin had unsuccessfully pursued for years for a contract. The administrative assistant recognized Calvin and told her boss about it. He got the contract, which proved to be lucrative.

Calvin possessed a tender conscious, liking to get guidance in his life to assure himself he was doing the right things. Rhett knew this and sometimes used this insight to mischievously tease Calvin. One Sunday morning Calvin drove up to the meeting in the Loomis Assembly in a nice new car. Rhett decided to kid him about being materialistic.

"THAT is a really nice car, Calvin."

"It's for my work," Calvin offered as justification.

Rhett said, "I haven't seen that new model before - it really looks sharp."

"I need to have a nice car to sell things, Rhett."

"I sure wish I could afford a nice car like that..."

"It should last me a long time and gets good gas mileage," explained Calvin.

"I like how the headlights are shaped!"

Calvin finally caught on and laughed with Rhett.

Calvin's brother Michie Hobkins was from a different mold, much different. Rhett once tried to tease Michie while visiting him in Charlottesville about being materialist by complimenting him on his nice new riding lawn mower.

Michie immediately saw through Rhett's motivation and simply responded, "Rhett, you work hard and save your money, and you too can have nice things like this."

Calvin and his wife Barbara decided to move back to Northern Virginia in the late 90's.

"I think Deo Trophy's ministry will benefit our family, and there is more stability there," Calvin explained, "Archie Stark is the minister in Northern Virginia where we are moving, but Deo has a lot of good influence in Virginia. The Assemblies in Virginia are Orderly Followers, and peaceful; they have more unity and aren't contentious over standards of dress and lifestyle choices, like many are here in California."

In 2003, Calvin decided Fredericksburg would be a good place to move since he would be able to hear directly from Deo Trophy and get personal counsel from him on a regular basis. Calvin soon realized he was having a hard time understanding Deo, and wondered what exactly Deo wanted him to do. It was confusing, and he wanted to understand why he was so bewildered. He ended up spending a lot of time counseling with Deo, time he could have spent in his commission only sales job.

His wife Barbara related later, "Calvin was totally disoriented when he got home, for days afterwards. You do not know what it is like to have your husband confused and dysfunctional for several days after one of Deo's hours long counseling sessions!"

After several years, Calvin began to consider just checking out of the whole Assembly thing gradually. He could get a coffee shop going in between Fredericksburg and Richmond, and talk to customers about the Lord when the opportunity arose.

Several things happened to make Calvin doubt Deo's sincerity. One of them was going to Deo for counsel regarding a work related sales commission problem with his employer.

Deo told Calvin, "I want you to just come to me for counsel regarding your job, Calvin. Don't talk to anybody else about it."

Since Ernest Showden was a salesman himself, Calvin had already confided in his brother-in-law about the commission problem, and showed him the documents that he was going to send to a boss who was over 25,000 employees, so the corporation would have the opportunity to make things right.

Later, Calvin's wife found out from her sister, who is married to Ernest Showden, that Ernest was secretly called by Deo, who asked Ernest's advice on how to counsel Calvin about his commission problem with his job. Ernest said nothing about Deo's call to Calvin, who was a close friend as well as his brother-in-law.

"Why didn't Deo allow me to talk directly to others about a personal matter like my employment?" Calvin asked Rhett later, "I was forty-four years old at the time!

Deo is a government worker, he doesn't even know much about sales!"

Calvin also related, "I began to suspect Deo had a terrible insecurity complex, so I decided to ask Deo about who was over us in the Lord and had helped us. I've got plenty of men over me! But when I turned the conversation to Deo, there was nobody I could bring up that was over him. I finally thought to ask Deo about his salvation, that person surely would have had a role in helping him. Deo related he had been saved after hearing a song. I thought that was odd because Deo had told me before that it was from hearing the gospel when he was a teenager in Louisiana at his family's church."

"Another thing that made me question Deo's integrity was this recent James Stark situation. I heard Deo going on and on in the Fredericksburg Assembly, meeting after meeting, about how bad James Stark was. He gave a bunch of messages about King Saul and King David, with these little allusive innuendos. My family got the message that Deo thought he was like King David and James was like King Saul, but he didn't come right out and say it. I was really getting tired of so many negative meetings, so I went over to a meeting at Happy Hill to get away from it all on August 3rd, 2008. But Deo went there too, and spoke for two and a half hours about it, which to me was pure psychological bombardment! I started to think there must be another side to the story because he spent so much time trying to convince us James had problems."

Calvin also told Rhett about his family's trip out to California to get the other side of the story in December, 2008.

"Was I ever glad our family made the trip!" Calvin enthusiastically related to Rhett over another lunch, then glancing longingly at his large black coffee and quaffing it. "Tim is about the most humble man I know. He has several grown kids who are all married to Christian spouses who want to serve the Lord, and about twenty-six grandkids, many of them teenagers, who also want to serve the Lord. Tim's commitment to serve the Lord shows through the lives of his children and grandchildren. Tim and his wife really are loving and humble, Rhett!"

Calvin's unselfish and chivalrously talkative nature was fueled by three strong black coffees a day.

The trip opened Calvin's eyes. Suddenly he could see that Deo was perverting the truth to make the California ministers look as bad as possible. By the time Calvin got into some deeper conversations with Rhett, Calvin had been doing some thinking. Rhett on the other hand, didn't really know where Calvin was coming from. Rhett had studied Mind Control techniques by then, but didn't have personal counseling experience to tell to what extent Deo was using them.

"It was like I had a pair of binoculars and was studying this temple in the middle of a dense jungle from a distant mountain side," Rhett reminisced later, "and I met Calvin fighting his way out of the jungle, leaving it. I asked Calvin what it was like and he confirmed my suspicions. It was all I had suspected, and then some."

Rhett gave a book on mind control for Calvin to read, and it greatly impacted him.

"There is absolutely no doubt in my mind that Deo used mind control techniques to control me," Calvin said afterwards, "I am guessing Deo took about five years off my life that could have been used in reaching others for Christ, instead I was being manipulated and controlled. It got me thinking more about our singing. On Friday nights at our sing practice we almost always sang the same songs, about five or six. We started each sing practice with the song – "I'm so glad I'm a part of the Family of God," and always ended with this same song, for years."

Calvin was understandably upset and so was his wife. It took them over a year, through deep depression, anxiety, and nightmares, to feel like they were starting to recover from all the coercion, manipulation by fear, and disorienting counseling.

"Deo told me he wanted to help me with my ministry," Calvin said, "Deo told me, "I'd like to help you with your ministry, let me know what is going on out there and report back to me." But now, thinking back on it, Deo was just inserting himself into my life to gain more control. The more he knew of my affairs with others, the more control he had, and the more prone I was to fear him."

Deo could do a lot of damage with what he claimed he knew. One camp he about destroyed Toby Tait's parents reputation permanently. It was done publicly in front of about four hundred people. Toby's dad stood up afterwards, and with a throwing out of both hands out, said, "Deo, that is not the way I remember it!" Of course, nobody believed him at the time since Deo was a well respected minister and Toby's dad's reputation had just been destroyed.

There was an especially disturbing incident that happened to Calvin with his daughter Georgia. Calvin didn't know it, but Deo, in his personal counseling with Calvin's daughters, was undermining him. "Your father is brain damaged," Deo confidently confided privately to Georgia when she was fifteen, "I don't know if it was the drugs your dad took as a teenager, or just the way he is, or maybe something else. Your home is not a normal home, it's — dysfunctional."

Georgia believed the 'credible' older minister's slander of her father, and 'knowing' her dad had some kind of mental problem disturbed her for several months. Calvin noticed his daughter's distance from him and fortunately found out what had happened. Deo had told her if she told anybody what he had said, he would deny saying it.

Georgia quickly saw through the manipulation, and it was a great relief for her and her parents. When Rhett found out about it he comforted his friend, "Calvin, I don't think a guy who has lead many people to the Lord, paid off his house in his forties, held down some good jobs, and raised a family and three kids to want to serve the Lord, to be brain damaged. It just isn't true."

"One thing that really disturbed me about Deo," Calvin told Rhett, "was when Georgia thought it would be really neat to find out how Deo Trophy was saved. I told Georgia, "of course, go ahead and ask him!" Deo came over to counsel me about my job, and Georgia asked Deo what had led him to the Lord. Deo told Georgia, "Now is not the time for that," and then Deo told me afterwards, "Satan moved Georgia to ask me that question." He never did answer the question!"

What better way to start a counseling session with a young person then with a personal testimony of one's salvation?

Calvin decided to talk to a man he thought was a sincere Christian in the Fredericksburg Assembly, an older farmer, a few weeks before Calvin left the Fredericksburg Assembly. The farmer was upset that Calvin had called him to ask what he thought about the James Stark situation.

Ten minutes after Calvin got off the phone, Deo Trophy called Calvin on his cell phone, and yelled, "What do YOU know BOY-AH! Huh? What do YOU KNOW!?" and Deo also authoritatively said, "Calvin, I'm ordering you to stop being divisive immediately!"

For the first time Calvin found out about Deo's wrathful intimidation tactics. Calvin told Deo, "I am only trying to prove all things and hold fast to that which is good. I'd like to meet with you as soon as possible!"

They agreed to meet the next day. Calvin confronted him with the truth and scripture, pleading with him to stop causing the division. Calvin maintained his respect as he confronted Deo's sins but Deo just stared back when he had no answer for Calvin's reasoning from scripture.

It was becoming obvious to Calvin that Deo was dishonest. This was hard to reconcile in Calvin's mind, as he reflected back on Deo's ministry for over twenty years. Although Calvin had thought something was a bit disturbing about Deo, Calvin wanted to honor the Lord in upholding His 'strong leader.'

Calvin quietly withdrew with his family. Fortunately, his oldest daughter was already married, with Deo officiating, to Mars Thomas' son, a young man who wanted to serve the Lord. They quickly understood the problem, telling how Deo had undermined and discredited Calvin to both of them also.

Calvin's father videoed the wedding of his oldest daughter and accidently caught Deo clearly mocking the man praying during the wedding ceremony. Calvin had seen Deo do this many times before, but this time it was caught on video. The man Deo was mocking was one who strongly supported Deo.

Calvin's youngest daughter Georgia was nearly engaged, and her bright soon-to-be fiancé quickly understood Deo manipulating to gain his allegiance. He had been bothered by some things himself.

Calvin was soon reunited with his younger brother Michie Hobkins who had left a few years prior with his family, also being disturbed by Deo Trophy.

"I thought Michie was really wrong and divisive for leaving, so I shunned him," said Calvin, "But now I can see I was just legalistic, and for some reason, Michie was able to see through Deo easier than I could."

Maybe it was because Michie had married one of Jar's daughters and had seen an up front and hidden side of Deo in the meetings with Jar than what some had experienced. Deo had not spent any time personally counseling Michie for over twenty years.

Deo also tried to turn other grown children against their parents. It is hard to tell what a man is really like by his performance behind a podium.

I will love You, O Lord, my strength
The Lord is my rock and my fortress and my deliverer
My God, my strength, in whom I will trust
My shield and the power that saves me, my stronghold
- David, when he escaped from Saul - Psalms 18

14·

Attempted Checkmate

Byron Stark planned to present: "The reasons why daddy should not be in ministry," with questions from the audience afterwards, time allowing.

The California and Virginia leaders agreed the meeting would be at the end of January, 2009, and held in Long Beach, California.

Byron Stark, with Deo's assistance, would attempt to sway the California leaders there yet again with the support from Deo's league of bishops flying in from out of state. Deo had pulled it off before; he might be able to do it again, permanently. Then they would be working for him, not against him. If they changed their minds later, they would be even weaker, with more flip flopping, and easier to discredit.

The battle was for the mind, the strongest opponents were also prized potential prey for becoming the strongest proponents.

When Byron Stark was in his late teens, James Stark told his son, "Deo will be around longer then I will be since he is younger, so you ought to be getting counsel from him. You boys shouldn't be so dependent on me, it's not healthy for you."

Deo had flattered Byron and Archie since their mid-twenties, telling others in front of them, "Byron and Archie are very well trained, and perceptive to problems before they even start, due to the close interaction they have had with their father around the dinner table as they grew up."

Some think, from e-mails Carson Frund of Newfoundland had gotten hold of, that Deo's inserted comments cutting down James, comments inserted into responses to Byron's e-mails, were indicative of a lot of phone conversation of Deo running down Byron's father to him, like Deo had undermined other grown children against their parents. Most people didn't know Byron was closer to Deo than his father for the last several years, thinking it odd Byron Stark was so against his dad and resented the very things about himself that reminded him of his own biological father. Most of the leaders under Deo didn't have much of a spiritual or personal relationship with their own physical fathers.

The prior meetings followed the pattern of Deo or one of his Bishops making a false statement and then spend hours building a case on it. There was never time to unravel it, and in the meantime others had bought into it. The California leaders assumed there was credibility with the speaker, looked into it afterwards, and then disproved it a few months later. Then they were accused of flip flopping after they changed their minds.

The leaders in California agreed Friday night every false statement should be dealt with immediately. Many people from their own area were coming to the meeting, the future of their own local relationships was unpredictable.

The leadership meeting started with Peter Waters, "I'm not sure if you all want to pray with us, since you publicly called us heretics in your own areas a few weeks ago."

After an awkward joint prayer, the battle for the minds began with Byron Stark making his presentation on a large screen from his computer.

Byron took the first ten hours or so on Saturday, but he only got through a small portion of his presentation. Everything was critiqued and the error of it pointed out right after he made it before he could build on it. None of his points had been made. His dream of convincing everybody his father wanted to minister so he could use that power and influence as an opportunity to persuade with smooth words and cause utter chaos and departure from the truth, was thrown down and trampled on.

A man from Atascadero, California objected to the interruptions, saying, "Let's just let Byron finish and we will ask questions later."

Several men quickly responded: "No, we are not going to do that."

Byron's magic of persuasion was not working anymore. Part of the audience was now informed.

Deo was scheduled to speak on Sunday but since Bryon had gotten through so little of his own presentation he was going to continue. Byron called for a leadership meeting outside with Deo's Bishops and leaders Sunday morning. There were sixteen leaders out in the parking lot, buzzing like wasps around their knocked over hive, with forty or so others inside the building.

As they talked, some that were inside, not with Deo and his followers in their parking lot meeting, went for a walk around the neighborhood. A police officer slowed in his patrol car, asking why one of them was openly weeping.

After hearing the explanation, he responded, "The guy walking around the next block over was crying and told me the same thing! I was wondering what was going on!"

Of the cluster of sixteen in the parking lot, eight leaders were for marking the California ministers immediately, and eight were against any markings at that time. Joshua Jude, the minister from the Atascadero Assembly, was the only minister from California on Deo's side.

Since it was starting to look like the eight leaders for the markings were in the minority and the independent ones, and they couldn't pull off the markings without the support of the other eight against the forty people inside from California, they came back in and said they would submit to the California ministers and allow James Stark back in ministry. The meeting ended, and a letter was drafted and signed announcing their decision.

Meanwhile, Rhett was in Richmond, Virginia, fully expecting a marking of the California men, and consequently a mass marking of most of the California Assemblies. George Taylor had not gone to the California meeting either; he was over at Sunday's Sing Practice at Rhett and Sabrina's home. Deo had told George and Lyle Cooper to stay home, so they did.

Rhett figured it would likely be the last time they were with everybody in Richmond before they were shunned, so they might as well go out with a bang and have everybody over one last time, taking advantage of the ignorance Deo and Cary had created.

Around 9 pm Rhett's cell phone finally went off. He stepped out on his back porch.

"They all agreed to have James go into ministry Rhett! Everybody is in agreement!" said Mycroft.

"I can't believe it! Are you serious!" said Rhett, his brain trying to readjust to things going back to normal, "that is such good news!" He debated making an announcement to the one hundred and twenty or so guests in his home and decided to just talk to George, telling him, "I'm not going to say anything about it, so it's up to you to make any announcement."

George had just gotten off his own phone call. He got everybody's attention in the crowded living room, and announced: "There has been a good report from the meeting!" George didn't give any details.

When Cary Murdock got back, he gave his report as if he was the Martyr on the Altar of Unity at the next Wednesday night meeting.

Cary said, "We still are very concerned about our brother James Stark. We submitted to those leaders for the sake of Unity."

Cary gave no explanation why he and Deo signed a letter accusing the California leaders as heretics and divisive men, rebuking them publicly behind their backs as a tiny subset, not having a sound mind, warped, sinning, wicked and divisive, yet a month later submitted to these same California ministers. Nobody in the Richmond Assembly thought much of it either, which puzzled Rhett even more. Surely some would start questioning the hypocrisy and confusion.

Shortly afterwards, James Stark headed up to Newfoundland to give his support and help, as he had done a few times a year for the last thirty years, since he was finally back in ministry.

This time it was much different. The Newfoundland Assembly was split in half over the issue, and also there were long standing unresolved issues with Al Taylor, the

Bishop there who strongly supported Deo. James had tried to cover for and back Al over the years, trying to help him see how some judgment calls were poor, helping to keep the peace.

This time James didn't go to be on Al's side. The half who had concerns for Al Taylor insisted Al have a meeting with them. They were puzzled over Al's lack of honesty in reporting publicly what was happening with the James Stark situation. Al had faithfully followed Deo's orders, giving partial truths in public reports.

James was forwarded some recent letters from Al, showing Al disliked James coming to Newfoundland over the years and had just ignored his advice. Al denied this when James asked him about it, but Al's own recently written letters showed he was not telling the truth. Al had professed a lot of respect for James for years.

Al refused to meet with them, and the situation escalated when the four men and James Stark did not go to the Sunday meeting. James returned to California, with Al obstinately breathing threats and complaints against him.

Shortly after James left, Al Taylor sent out a twenty-eight page letter, filled full of accusations against James, to the California leaders and Deo's league of Bishops. There were eight families in the Newfoundland Assembly. The four households who were for James and had concerns about Al, including Carson Frund, were never contacted for their side of the story by any of Deo's Bishops and leaders. Three men sent out their own individual multipage response to Al's, but they were ignored.

As the Newfoundland situation heated up, Deo Trophy spoke at the next monthly regional gathering of all the Assemblies at Happy Hill in Charlottesville, Virginia, on February 15th, 2009.

Deo announced he would speak on "The Gospel."

Standing at the podium, looking across the audience in his dark suit and infamous red tie, breathing heavily into the mic, he warned the audience:

And uh, as most of you that know me fairly well, I can lay some things out and paint a picture, but you might have to go with me for an hour or an hour and a half painting that picture and it might not come together in your mind. You may get weary on the travel through.

A little later, Deo made another point:

It almost might seem, why could you, why would you put the principals, why would you put the body of Christ in with the principals, it almost seemed like it, is that, is that a good thing? It's a good thing. It's a good thing, and I'll hopefully elaborate on why that's a good thing. But when you look at God the Father, God the Son and God the Spirit and then you put Christ's body. Does that seem appropriate? Well if you understand the truth of the gospel, it's very appropriate - very appropriate. It's very appropriate if we understand who we are in Christ. It's very appropriate. So anyway, I'd just ask you to forbear on that one if it looks like I am putting believers, uh, in with, uh, - God. Well, that's the truth of the gospel. We are put into Christ, and we have Christ in us.

Later, Deo hammered his point home:

Okay, this can take you somewhere. What if somebody says, "The only important relationship for me as a Christian, or well not the only but, the most important relationship for me as a Christian, is the vertical relationship with God." On a horizontal level you got people, on a horizontal level you got people, people can let you down. God won't let you down, right? Is there truth in what I just said? Yes. Will God let you down? No. Is a vertical relationship between you and God important? Absolutely. And the horizontal is secondary. Let's look at that. Let's look at that. It's true that every individual needs

236 The Bishop Maker

a relationship between God the Father and himself. That can be what's referred to as a vertical relationship. The vertical aspect is representative, as I would understand it, in that sense, of a relationship between an earthly creature, like me, and a heavenly creator, God. That's essential. That's essential to have that relationship between me as a creature, and God, the creator. That is essential.

A horizontal relationship with fellow members is essential according to the word of God. A horizontal relationship with Christ, in Christ, is what we are called to by the gospel. Those who respond in belief to the gospel of Christ, have fellowship with Christ on a horizontal plain. This is manifested by the unity of the body to unbelievers. To exhibit division is to misrepresent that Christ is divided. That's sin in the scripture. It's sin because it misrepresents who we actually are in Christ, by belief in the gospel and by walking in the faith once delivered unto the saints.

If someone is persuading you that the vertical's it, what happened to the truth of the gospel about the horizontal? Subtle shifts in your mind. Think about these things. I am giving you some heavy stuff to think about. And it is worth meditating on. It is worth reading the scriptures and going back over them, to look at this.

He lectured for two and a half hours. Some branded it the "Gospel of Unity", or "Unity at all Cost". Although partially in denial, Deo was distinctly raising the 'Body of Christ' to the same level as the trinity, making it a 'Quadity', and Deo put himself as the leader of the 'Body of Christ'. "There are no valid reasons for Christians to divide," Deo kept repeating, as if he was trying to justify submitting to the California leaders he had just run down in his own area as heretics, then lied back home and said he had submitted to them because they had done a lot of apologizing.

Deo also exalted unity over truth:

Deo: Another thought, another notion. What's most important? Truth or Unity? Which one's the most important?

George Taylor's brother from the audience answered: The One who was truth prayed for unity.

Deo: Uh, right. The one who said, "I am the truth," prayed for unity..... What's most important? Truth or unity? Framing a discussion determines outcomes, many times of discussions. Framing a discussion can determine an outcome of a discussion. Is that a scripturally sound, biblically based question to ask, according to the gospel of Jesus Christ? Right. That notion doesn't come from scripture. That notion doesn't come from the scripture. Where does it come from? Well, it doesn't come from the scripture, okay. When we think, or somehow being persuaded that "standing in the truth" is somehow in competition with the walk in unity, it's time to pause and think and go back to the scriptures and say, "what?"

If a so-called stand for truth will potentially divide the body, then that is not the gospel truth.

To have, quote, truth at the expense of unity is to promote another gospel, which is not the gospel of Jesus Christ.

A so-called stand for truth that can lead to a division of the body, typically exalts the individual making this stand. Others may be easily swept up in this personal exaltation benefit. Maybe we want to be identified with it. It truly does bring good feelings. To truly understand what you are doing is courageous, and appears to be godly, oh, wow, this is, I am going to stand for truth. That appeal can actually be a very subtle device.

Deo ended by stating:

If the love we say we have that we're implementing by standing in the truth, divides the body - that's a sterile love. That's not the life-giving love shed abroad in the heart of every believer. We know that Satan uses scripture with those who love God and are informed by the truth. <u>So as a warning, as a warning, we know our enemy uses truth. We have scriptural examples of that. So, it won't be the absence of truth, it will be the twisting of truth, the misuse of truth. That is the deception. Think about that — it's not the absence of truth, but it is the misuse or the twisting of truth that is deceptive to a child of God.</u>

I love the Lord so much that I am going to divide the body. That. No. That's contrary to the gospel truth. A love or a stand for truth that is a splitting force of the body. No, No. A love for Christ and a stand for the truth of the gospel is a unifying love.

Rhett took extensive notes, including Deo's ending comment "It takes faith to trust in Christ, and in another human being who has Christ," and sent his notes back to California, including a link on how to download the MP3 recording off the Happy Hill computer server.

Harley, the sound tech from Charlottesville, heard Rhett still had access to the MP3 messages on the server, and blocked him from getting other messages in the future, but not before many had downloaded it. A legalistic older man in Charlottesville thought the message was great and sent videos to people all over the country.

So a lot of people on both sides of the issue listened to "The Gospel" within a few weeks, and it created a lot of controversy. People on Deo's side said it was just about unity and the gospel, there was nothing new about what he gave, and it was wonderful truth.

People on the other side said Deo was teaching false doctrine and preaching another gospel. Only by first having fellowship with Christ could they have fellowship with others, the vertical relationship with God through

Christ is way ahead of the horizontal with other human Christians. There *is* no horizontal relationship with Christ.

Deo left himself plenty of outs as he presented the gospel in a way that he claimed would take ninety minutes to figure out. Most never figured out what Deo's definition of the gospel was after two and a half hours.

Earlier in the year Calvin Hobkins had discreetly recorded a local Fredericksburg leadership meeting, in February, at the urging of Rhett. Rhett had also recorded a similar meeting in Richmond before he left, and felt it was morally justifiable, although technically a potential betrayal of a few long standing friends in Richmond. Self respect and reputations are important, but sometimes judicially settling disputes later on with high stakes are worth taking the reputational risk of espionage when dishonesty is anticipated. Local leadership meetings were almost always openly and privately recorded in California with no objections. Rhett had seen the pattern of blowing things out of proportion, and knew what they would likely criticize him for if he had to produce it later.

James Stark wanted everything recorded to document what was said in case there were any disputes later. James had severely regretted not recording the February 2008 meeting in which Deo had so grossly exaggerated his behavior. James had encouraged all the Assemblies to record all their meetings for years, both public and leadership meetings, and said he would never again go into a meeting that wasn't recorded.

Local leadership meetings in Virginia were never recorded, including Fredericksburg. The public meetings were recorded, except when Deo had requested the public recording of him talking so poorly of the California ministers just prior to his 'First Admonishment Letter' the first week in January of 2009, to be destroyed. At Deo's order, the fifteen year old boy who recorded the MP3 CD broke it up with his hands before trashing it.

Lyle Cooper wound up with the recording from the November Texas 2008 meeting and, not getting permission from Deo or Cary to give it up, refused to give a copy to the California leaders who wanted it to settle the dispute that they were right in putting James back into ministry, and that Deo had apologized to James.

Rhett and Sabrina went out to visit California late in February.

"Sabrina, we will go out to visit, our kids will know there are many children and adults who see this the same as I do, and when we return we will not go back," Rhett told his wife. Sabrina hoped it wasn't true and things would change.

While driving through the central valley of California to visit friends and family, they passed a dairy.

"Looks like there's 2,168 cows in that corral, Dad," said Dawson.

"How did you do that? Seems like a lot of cows to count as we drove by," said Rhett.

"I counted their legs and divided by four," Dawson answered, a smile lurking at the corners of his mouth.

A few days later, Rhett and his dad Mycroft Stuart were invited to a small California leadership meeting. They drove down to Long Beach, California for the day from Visalia, a four hour drive each way, just as Mycroft had done many times over the last year.

In the meeting, Bach Jude from Long Beach asked, "Why do Deo and his followers have so much authority?"

James Stark answered, "Because you guys keep GIVING it to them!"

Luke Alastair, who lived in Long Beach near Bach, had changed careers from the prescription drug industry to work at his father's business. A quiet intellectual, he was graciously soft spoken in a precisely articulate manner. He was hesitant to pass judgments on anybody, and had carefully investigated the James Stark situation. Although he really liked and preferred Deo's carefully calculated delivery and speaking style of years past, he found evidence pointing to Deo's dishonesty.

Luke had asked Calvin if there was a recording of the local Fredericksburg leadership meeting, so Calvin gave him his private copy of it. In the recording, Luke was surprised to hear Deo telling the uninformed Fredericksburg people the reasons Deo had agreed to put James back in ministry during the California leadership meeting at the end of January. Deo's exact quote explaining why he had submitted was because the California leaders had given:

> ...lots of acknowledgments, apologies, etc, so there has been a long list of things that have been going on and so at any instance in time when you report out where things are at that instance in time, that's an instance in time and so subsequent to that there may be apologies made and so you address that, you accept that, there may be asking forgiveness, you accept that and you move on and try to recover from that. <u>There has been a lot of that done.</u>

Rhett listened as Luke played the recording for the California ministers who all sat around in Bach's upstairs room; the same one Byron Stark had given his five hour emotional presentation in several months prior. There were twelve men in all, including Rhett.

They were astonished, what Deo was telling his local congregation was quite a big lie! There had been no apologies or asking for forgiveness by the California leaders at the January meeting a few weeks prior. And Deo was forbidding his local Fredericksburg congregation to check into things for themselves!

Before Luke played the recording, he said, "Deo went on for about twenty minutes without answering the question, and then he made this excuse as to why he submitted to the California ministers."

What really interested Rhett was, when he checked on it later, none of the five Fredericksburg men who by now knew of Deo's problems, remembered the lie during the actual meeting. Even though they were familiar with what was happening. Was the first twenty minutes of not answering the question part of the magic of Deo's confusing mind control at work, to "disorient them" before he lied to them?

The California leaders planned some public communication meetings to finally go over it publicly and let people know what was going on. The meetings would have to be done quickly without giving Deo Trophy time to out-strategize them again. Although the communications weren't put together or motivated by James Stark, he was asked to speak Sunday morning and be available for questions. They would have the first meeting in Southern California on Sunday, the next one in Visalia in Central California on Wednesday night, and they offered to open up all the letters and e-mails for whoever wanted to review them for themselves.

As they traveled to their third and last one in Northern California the following Sunday, the e-mail marking James Stark for avoidance came storming out of Deo's angry hornets' nest from the East coast on Wednesday. It gave James ten hours to submit to them, or be marked.

George Taylor from Richmond explained: "The house was on fire, and we needed to put it out. We needed to stop James' communication meetings."

The Biblical basis for the marking of James was never provided later when asked for. It suddenly became okay to just do things without any Biblical basis. Two of Deo's supporters in Northern California got into the rented Assembly building in Loomis, California, and took the sound equipment out in an attempt to sabotage the communication meeting the next morning. New sound equipment was quickly rounded up and the meeting went forward. Several families left the Loomis Assembly, most of them legalistically minded people in support of their former minister, Aaron Adams, who had bought into Deo's Orderly Following and had since retired to Texas. The communication meetings generally went well, and most people could see what the issues really were.

Meanwhile, Calvin was following up on Deo's claim that he, Deo, had been mentioned publicly in Southern California, to the hurt of Deo's family. Calvin called several people in Southern California to see if Deo had been run down or mentioned publicly at all, especially negatively, in the Southern California Assemblies. What Deo had told Calvin wasn't true; in fact the Californians had been very careful to say little to nothing of the situation. One person Calvin asked was Luke Alastair. Luke was surprised to hear Deo had claimed this, it was not true, and confronted Deo with the false claim in an e-mail.

Deo responded back to Luke a few days before Deo and Company marked James Stark:

I did not say nor attempt to imply that there had been any public mention of my name in Southern California. This is another error on your part. What I said was that I had been reported on with negative information.

This does not demand that the report be public mention of my name. It may have been private one on one discussions or in small settings. But the reports get around. Most of what I was referring to I have heard directly from those in that area in meetings I have been in personally. I am told, at various times, what is "known" about me or what I have "said about me" by those on the receiving end of reports. I am asked to confirm these reports and many times am completely amazed at what is "understood" about me. A question you might ponder is what is being said about me in private that you hear? Is it negative? Does it get passed around? Can it be prevented from being passed around? When there is public expression of "those" on the east coast or such expressions then people in the audience plug in names. These are usually the same names they hear about in private. This is how these things work. Those plugging in names may be right or wrong in their choices. But the implicit mention usually winds up in time as an explicit reference whether stated in public or not. Let us understand how the enemy of our souls works against us.

Now Calvin was now looking foolish for getting mixed up and asking several in California if it was true.

Luke suspected Calvin *had* heard Deo correctly, and went back to Calvin's personal recording of the Fredericksburg meeting from February. Luke then sent Deo another e-mail a few days after Deo and Company marked James Stark to try and sabotage the California leader's communication meetings.

Luke inserted the actual transcript of the recording, hoping to refresh Deo's memory, explaining there <u>was</u> cause to be concerned about Deo's honesty:

Deo: Do you think anyone has mentioned my name out there?

Calvin: Not sure, I don't live out there but I understand they have been careful in the public meetings: that's what I have been told: I don't know: that's up to being shot down.

Deo: Maybe you ought to find out.

Calvin: Okay.

Deo: Does it impact my family if my name is mentioned -publicly out there?

Calvin: I would think so.

Deo: And I appreciate the impact that it has on my family.

Calvin: I would hope so.

Deo: Ten months worth Calvin.

Calvin: Okay, I don't know. I will find out.

Deo: I'm telling you, ten months worth.

Calvin: Publicly, like family meetings?

Deo: Yeah! Just say you go check it out.

Calvin: Okay.

Deo never responded to Luke, except to locally accuse Calvin behind his back of a "secret recording," as if the personal recording was to be blamed for Deo's falsehood. But there was no need for Deo to respond. Calvin had already left the Fredericksburg Assembly and was no longer available to locally confront Deo with his dishonesty. Also, Calvin had already been discredited by Deo so local people were unlikely to believe anything Calvin said.

Evidence of Deo's dishonesty was stacking up, but as it did, the people who could make the case against him were being knocked off by discrediting, defaming, or marking by Deo and his followers. There were now many examples of Deo fabricating events to win arguments. But most people just believed him and didn't follow up to see if they were true. Unity behind Deo was primary, and truth secondary. Deception was a small price to pay for unity and control over others.

The Californians planned another large leadership meeting six weeks later. Everyone was invited to discuss the issues. George Taylor flew out from Richmond, Virginia, and publicly took on the leaders there, with their permission. Archie Stark, who had also been turned against his father by Deo, was there but kept quiet.

Blair Warren from San Diego asked, "George, why don't you guys give up the recording of the November 2008 Texas meeting in which you agreed to reinstate James Stark?"

Lyle Cooper had the recording of the Texas meeting, but Deo and Cary had forbidden Lyle to release it to the California leaders.

"We don't think it would be helpful to give the recording up," explained George with his deep authoritive politician's voice.

George did more to convince the people in Southern California that the problem was caused by self-willed leaders who were not easily entreated than any other single event.

The California ministers wrote Deo and his Bishops a letter a few weeks later with their concerns regarding his "Gospel of Unity" message of February 15th, 2009, and also a letter stating many examples of unbiblical conduct over the last year.

Deo and his Bishops never responded. After three or four weeks, the California ministers sent the letter to every household in the country, including Newfoundland, Mexico, and Peru, all who were associated with the Assemblies, warning them of many specific examples of unbiblical conduct with Deo Trophy and his Bishops.

The letter had been tweaked until it was virtually perfect, carefully gone over, concise, with many well documented points and proof of unbiblical conduct.

It didn't matter; the California ministers were quickly marked by Deo and his Bishops for sowing discord.

Deo never did respond to it.

Incredibly to Rhett, most of the people in Texas and Virginia went along with the California markings, not even wondering or thinking about why there was no response to the letter. Quite an impressive achievement for Deo, considering most people had considered their Assemblies a fundamental Bible believing group, champion and pillar of Bible based truth, trying to function as the early Christians did...

The apathetic conformity resulting from years of Orderly Following indoctrination won over real truth and unity for the day. Deo had divided this body of believers within seven weeks of saying, "I love the Lord so much that I am going to divide the body. That. No. That's contrary to the gospel truth. <u>A love or a stand for truth that</u>

is a splitting force of the body. No, No. A love for Christ
and a stand for the truth of the gospel is a unifying love."

Right after the California ministers were marked, Deo
Trophy and his followers had their own "Communication
Meeting" in Atascadero, California. Since the California
ministers were now marked, they could not speak up in the
meeting or present their side.   The information was
restricted.

Several of Deo's Bishops took the meeting, their
leadership personage well presented in a friendly sales-
manship fashion as they authoritatively continued their
marauding endeavor to supersede the leaders in California,
giving partial truths. They aggressively proceeded, as they
had since January, audaciously assuming the California
leaders would disembark from their leadership roles.

Peter Waters and Mycroft went to the meeting anyways.
Mycroft wasn't marked and he asked a few questions, but
nobody paid much attention. Peter had been marked so he
couldn't ask questions or make comments. He knew the
rules.

Deo sat near the wall in the front of the Atascadero
meetings, rarely speaking.   He didn't need to; his hard
work had already been completed behind the scenes. His
league of Bishops and close supporters were promoting his
agenda from the front.   The meeting worked well in
swaying the Atascadero Assembly, along with a few
others. A few older people that came up from Southern
California were convinced, but the bewitching wore off
after a day.   Several families from Southern California
were solidly on Deo's side, but the majority wasn't.

One of the swayed men, who stayed swayed, was
Rhett's other brother-in-law, Randy Greens from Visalia,
California.

Randy had a lot of problems with the local minister in Visalia, Peter Waters, who believed deep down people needed to be motivated by their own convictions and the Holy Spirit, and should not be forced to follow rules. Randy spent a lot of time telling Rhett and Byron Stark over the years about Peter's inability to deal with things. Rhett and Byron didn't get Peter involved to work it out. Rhett just sympathized with Randy and sided with him, and advised him on how to work around Peter's lack of dealing with problems. Randy, Byron, and Rhett had heavy buy-in with Orderly Following. Rhett regretted his part later, and had apologized to Peter earlier that year.

Randy at first believed Mycroft, but was then persuaded by Byron and Temple from Texas. Randy had been helped as a young man in Texas by Temple Austin and Byron Stark, and it was hard for him to see how they could possibly be wrong.

Randy and Rhett both agreed shortly afterwards that they disagreed about the James Stark situation and didn't talk together anymore. It was sad for Rhett, but it seemed the more he tried to convince Randy, the more Randy became convinced he was right and Rhett was wrong.

The real issue was their now different views of Orderly Following.

Randy's father had polio since childhood and could barely walk with the help of two permanent crutches. Most people, pitying his physical condition, respected his ability to follow the Assembly's rules. But Randy's father was secretly very abusive at home to his six children, including Randy, yet at the same time very legalistic, putting on a plausible pharisaical front, even speaking publicly on proper Christian conduct at times in Texas where he lived. Randy was saved in his late teens and held no bitterness towards his father.

The day after the Atascadero Communication Meeting ended, Cary Murdock, the minister from Richmond, and Leroy Luther, the minister from Oklahoma, finally following through on their public defaming messages from January, went on a depredatory sheep raid together to Visalia, to convince as many as they could that the local minister Peter Waters should be marked, shunned, and not followed. Julian Petros also played a large part in trying to convince those in California to abandon their ministers and follow after himself and Deo's band of bishops. They didn't need to do much talking there, the talking had already been done. They relied on their position in "the church".

Peter Waters and Mycroft Stuart held a meeting the Tuesday after the Atascadero meeting to answer questions in Visalia. Cary Murdock told Peter he wanted to be there with Leroy. Since Cary had marked Peter and was obviously there to gain followers, Peter declined.

So Cary and Leroy met at a cooperative local man's home and waited for Peter Waters' meeting to end. Afterwards, several legalistically minded young adults, including Randy Greens, went over to meet with Cary and Leroy. They stayed up until 2:30 in the morning talking.

Randy and his friends followed Cary's advice. Their concerns about Peter's lack of trying to control things over the years, of wanting dress, lifestyle standards, and meeting attendance tightened up, were exploited and used to gain their allegiance to Deo. Some of the men had married women from Texas and the women's families, fearing a severance in their relationships, had also influenced them.

Deo's Bishops flying out to California from Virginia and Texas to run out the local California ministers to take control reminded Rhett of Matthew 23, "Woe to you, scribes and Pharisees, hypocrites! For you travel land and sea to win one a convert, and when he is won, you make him twice as much a son of hell as yourselves."

The California ministers' markings threw the whole country wide group into a state of confusion. The congregations under Deo's headship wondered: Should everybody associating with these marked California ministers be marked or shunned also?

Rhett had enough by then, having withdrawn from the Richmond Assembly after returning from California in March, 2009.

It was really hard for those who got married in the summer of 2009. Some couples were from each side, and some had friends in the weddings from each side.

One young girl grew up in Atascadero, California and was getting married to a boy from Southern California who thought Deo was wrong. Hardly any of her friends in her own area went to the wedding; she was almost completely shunned by the Atascadero Assembly at the order of her long standing minister Joshua Jude. They shunned her, even though the wedding was in their town, being conducted by a man who was not marked, and they had been her friends for many years. Joshua Jude being the cousin of Bach Jude, the minister of Long Beach; they were also on opposite sides.

Others had friends canceling out of their weddings, or saying they would walk down the aisle but leave when the 'marked minister' spoke. Bridesmaids cancelling out needed to be replaced, hearts tearing as tears came easily. The wrenching heartaches were widespread and obvious.

Young people being separated from good friends they had grown up with and had been close to all their lives grieved over their losses. Some young children couldn't see their cousins and friends on Deo's side, even though they lived near each other.

Fathers and mothers were separated from their grown daughters who had moved out of state and wound up on Deo's side. Some courting couples broke off newly made relationships when their parents were on opposing sides.

One set of parents had the misfortune of sending their eighteen year old son off to visit in Texas. Deo's ministers in Texas convinced him to leave his parents. When he flew back to Loomis, there were two groups of people waiting to greet him from both sides. He went over to his parents and hugged them goodbye, then joined the other group of people to be with them permanently.

At another wedding in Southern California, the Atascadero Assembly came down to give their support, since their minister Joshua Jude was going to speak.

People from both sides were there, some with tears streaming, some shunning others, some crying and hugging forty-eight year old cousins and close lifetime friends they knew they would likely never see again in their lifetimes. Bach Jude, the minister from Long Beach, California, went to a side courtyard and openly wept, deeply grieved over the enormity of what was happening. Some of his cousins and lifetime friends would not even shake his hand. The devastation to close personal relationships was widespread, terrible, and permanent.

> My flesh and my heart fail
> But God is the strength of my heart
> and my portion Forever
> - Asaph, from Psalms 73 -

15·

The Shunning

In less than a week after leaving, Rhett and Sabrina were deleted from the list of getting the automated phone reminders of Richmond Assembly activities.

Most of the people in the Richmond Assembly immediately shunned them, and only a few bothered to call them after nine years of friendships. Close friendships with regular contact two or three times a week.

Sabrina noticed a good friend's birthday was coming up on her calendar, a friend since childhood who had also moved from California. She wanted to give her a present, as she had done for many years. Sabrina offered to give it to her at her home, or have her stop by Sabrina's, or Sabrina could meet her at a park. The friend said it wouldn't work out. Sabrina was able to get the present over to her house with another friend and received a short thank you note back.

The fort the Shifflett kids made with Rhett's children in the woods between their adjacent properties was in full view every time he came home from work, with the little cups and deserted jars dangling from the trees in the imaginary kitchen. There were small stacks of bricks for stoves, branches sticking up for Indian teepees, and worn paths meandering to raked out rooms. Rhett wondered what the future held; the Shifflett's were still willing to have their kids play together for now.

Rhett and Mark's sons, they had one son each, still played down by the creek, catching fish and crawdads (which they brought home to have their mothers cook up but it never did seem to work out). The kids picked black berries, the boys tore out poison ivy and other plants to make surprise forts for the girls, and rode bikes along the many mountain bike paths in the woods Mark and Rhett had worked together to create. Often the boys just kicked back and played with the dogs.

The girls still swam together, baking cookies, picking wild flowers or just hanging out visiting. As always, there were never any fights or disagreements afterwards. Mark and Rhoda were arguably the world's best neighbors. Rhoda's chatty, friendly, witty, and un-judgmental personality was still a perfect match for Sabrina's. Mark's laid back attitude, noticing the small things in nature, normally blended well with Rhett's focus on just getting things done as efficiently as possible. But things were different now, strained.

At first, Rhett and Sabrina's withdrawal didn't make much of a difference. Mark probably had a hard time realizing what had actually happened, and how serious Rhett was in leaving. Their kids still played together in the woods. Rhoda came over to visit when Rhett was at work. As the next few months went by, Mark got pressure from Cary Murdock and his neighbors, so he finally cut off all contact with Rhett's family. The Shifflett and Stuart kids could not play together anymore, at all. The wives could not visit.

Rhett and Sabrina's kids looked forward to seeing them through the van windows as they left to go to town, frantically waiving if they spotted them out in the yard.

At first Mark explained to Rhett, "It's confusing my kids, since the others aren't doing anything with you now, except us. I need to give it a break." But after several months Mark boldly told Rhett, "I am having my family shun your family, so you will feel the pain and realize you were wrong in leaving."

Rhett suspected it was some public ministry that was influencing Mark; he knew from long experience that people were discredited after they left the Assembly, usually publicly, always privately. Rhett also learned he was publically pointed out as one of four men who were considered "Dangerous". Dangerous meant being a threat to the control the leaders had over their flocks, and was worse than being shunned, but not as bad as being marked.

"Daaangerrroussss," Rhett told Calvin over a lunch, "They say I'm veeery dangerous!"

"Uh, you don't look too dangerous Rhett," said Calvin, "sorry."

It *was* painful. But the shunning by all their old friends didn't work, it backfired. It wasn't Biblical; Rhett and his friends hadn't sinned. Rhett had nothing to confess. The leaders had misled to gain a following. They had publicly railed on other ministers behind their backs, marking them, even flying across the country to give partial truths to gain a following. They attempted coercion on the California ministers to pressure them into submitting to them, and divided hundreds of close, personal, lifetime relationships with adults of all ages, teenagers, and children.

Yet, it still felt so wrong to be shunned.

Rhett and Sabrina were shunned for no longer going to the Richmond Assembly meetings. They were considered divisive for leaving. They did the Lord's will and were suffering for it; they needed to be patient to be commended by God.

The shunning had the effect on them that Deo and his Bishops wanted it to have: Rhett and Sabrina and others like them would never come back and risk the pain of having to go through an unbiblical shunning again. Once in a lifetime is too much. Deo now had virtually uncontested control over what remained, including many of Sabrina's close personal friends she grieved for.

Sabrina felt wounded and bleeding, bloodied by the shunning wounds of her close friends in Richmond. Sabrina was often haunted by the image of many knives plunged into her heart, the handle of each dagger bearing the name of a dear friend.

There were several families in Virginia who were in the same position as Rhett and Sabrina but unfortunately they did not have children the same ages as Rhett and Sabrina's. As the spring and summer wore on, the emotional pain became more and more difficult.

Rhett and Sabrina had been raised in this close knit community that was closed off socially from the rest of the world, even though Rhett worked and lived with the outside world. It was an exclusive group, an elite group, with many who felt they had the inside track on Biblical knowledge and pleasing God. Rhett and Sabrina had moved from California to raise their family with other committed young families, spending the last nine years investing hundreds of hours in their friendships. Suddenly it was terminated by the marking and shunning doctrine and the Orderly Following Doctrine.

The leaders, as it turned out, controlled the relationships.

Sabrina said, "I feel like I've been eating a delicious pie over the last several years, and the last bite was poison, ruining the whole experience."

There were suddenly no Wednesday night meetings to go to, or Friday night sings, no bi-monthly get-togethers for the kids. Rhett instinctively felt guilty not going. Sabrina deeply missed her friends: Rhoda, Cary Murdock's wife, and George Taylor's wife. Rhett and Sabrina had their own meetings with the several other families who had withdrawn too, on Sundays, driving a few hours to get there, staying all day to visit. But there were no children for all his kids to play with anymore. Their kids just listlessly floated around all Sunday afternoon, waiting for the monotonous day to end so they could go home and go to sleep.

When Rhett's eight year old daughter Ruth found out Mark Shifflett cut off all her contact with his children, she was thrown into the depths of despair. Normally a sweet natured, easy going girl with a funny sense of humor, Ruth disappeared when she found out she couldn't play with her best friend and next door neighbor anymore. Sabrina looked all over and finally found her down in the spare basement bedroom, lying on the bed, sobbing as she tightly clutched her teddy bear. Ruth could not be consoled or comforted; she deeply missed her best friend, Mark Shifflett's spunky daughter.

On a third Sunday when the Assemblies got together for their regional monthly meeting at Happy Hill, Rhett and Sabrina were at a friend's home, having their twenty person meeting. Sabrina whispered to Rhett she wanted to check on their fourteen year old daughter, Julia. The adults all sat inside at the dining room table.

Sabrina came back after a few minutes, "She is outside by herself at the picnic table."

Rhett felt sick. He knew that Julia knew there were about fifty young people visiting over their meals about an hour away at Happy Hill, and she sat alone. Rhett went outside.

"There wasn't enough room for me at your table, Daddy."

Rhett wept.

Sabrina grieved over the loss of her friends, and fell into a deep depression. Rhett's kids would suddenly cry for a few hours and could not be consoled. They all went on some week long vacations and cheered up when they were away. But as they rolled up their small country road at the end of the trip, the neighbors' homes on each side reminded them their closest friendships were lost, and they fell back into the same depression.

Fortunately for Sabrina, Lacy Beth was one friend who kept in much needed contact with Sabrina, which helped.

Sometimes his neighbors invited the Richmond Assembly over to their home. Rhett's kids looked out the van windows as they drove by, watching their old friends playing together.

Rhett considered selling, and would have, but his kids all talked him out of it. "We like it here Dad, we don't want to move," they tenderly pleaded.

"I don't think it's healthy for you to drive by and see your old friends and not be able to play with them."

"That's why we want to stay, in case we see them, and then we can wave to them," they responded.

Rhett consented to stay there longer, but thought they might move when his kids were more used to the idea and had time to adjust. His kids loved playing under the huge hardwood trees, riding their bikes and four wheeler, each having their own garden to care for, their two black lab-hound dogs steady companions at their sides. Fortunately the dense woods of Virginia shielded them from their neighbor's homes.

After getting over the guilt of a slower pace, Rhett and Sabrina fell into a relaxed family life during the week, getting away from the intense schedule of Wednesday night meetings, Thursday night leadership meetings once a month, Friday night sing practices, occasional work party Saturdays, and three day holiday weekend regional camp meetings. All on top of the all-day Sunday events.

Rhett and Calvin met for a lunch to exchange their woes and encourage each other.

"You know Calvin, does the hand ever tell the foot – 'You are independent?'" asked Rhett.

"I agree," said Calvin, "all Christians need each other and can be used in their unique way with the talents the Lord gives. It is not up to an individual to coordinate the movements of the body, but Christ. We need to be led of the Holy Spirit."

Out of the fifteen families in the Fredericksburg Assembly, five had left fellowship about the same time as Rhett. Fredericksburg was where Deo ministered, and many had uneasiness about Deo for years. Deo blamed all the concerns on Charlie Cooper for sowing discord long ago. Charlie is Lyle Cooper's father.

A few of them had gone to James Stark to protest years ago when James lived there, but James Stark saw them as disgruntled troublemakers with a poor sense of judgment.

"That is just the way Deo Trophy sees things," James responded to complaints regarding Deo's dishonesty and exaggerations. Deo always had a plausible explanation for everything.

James Stark's son, Archie, had also told his father that Deo was dishonest long ago, but James didn't believe him. Now James couldn't believe Archie would be on Deo's side of this.

Although Cary Murdock was Deo's closest supporter and defender, Cary's father Albert Murdock was not. Albert kept quiet about his beliefs. He didn't want to lose contact with his entire family, but really Albert didn't think the Orderly Following and the Marking Doctrines were Biblical. He kept quiet, having learned the hard way not to get in the cross hairs of leadership. He was eyed with suspicion by Deo's followers and held off at a distance. Albert and his wife traveled to Europe during the summer, then on to their beach apartment in Florida in the early winter.

"I was thinking of Megan Carnigan," Rhett commented to Sabrina during another evening walk around their property.

"What about her?"

"Well, she either got murdered or committed suicide soon after she left the Richmond Assembly."

"Yeah?"

"The police concluded it was suicide. I'll bet she got really depressed because everybody she knew was shunning her when she was only eighteen years old. I know there were other problems, but that sure didn't help her!" said Rhett.

"Didn't you tell me Deo was counseling her?"

"He came down and met her at a karate studio, her mom told me about it when I saw them. I don't know how often, but I doubt it helped. I mean, if Deo was doing the same thing to Megan he tried to do to Georgia Hobkins, you know, isolate her from everybody else, her friends and relatives, and turn her against her parents," said Rhett.

"But we didn't really graciously love her. A few did, like Julian's mom," said Sabrina.

"I was thinking the same thing. We'll never know, it's just speculation. There were a lot of problems in the family," said Rhett.

A few couples in their fifties were shunned by all of their young married children and grandchildren with Deo's group. These young married couples unwittingly set a bad example to their own young children; they set the stage to be shunned themselves, when their own children became young married adults and grew mature enough to know they could not stay in this ungodly system and still honor the Lord.

There is a tremendous fear in being shunned and losing friends, so shunning parents is sometimes worth it so they can keep their friends. James Stark was shunned by all three of his kids and nine grandkids, with the exception of one granddaughter.

Garth Hughes was one of those who left when Rhett and Sabrina did.

About thirty years prior, Garth Hughes agreed as a young man to stand against his own father for avoidance in the Texas Assembly in order to keep his engagement intact. Garth's dad was having a doctrinal dispute in 1981 with Dudley Franklin, the distinguished intellectual minister who produced deep doctrinal studies. Dudley was the only minister who had gone to a four year seminary before he had joined the Assemblies, which may have helped him develop his sophisticated and intellectual way of making people feel stupid for disagreeing with him. As Dudley Franklin took the Marking Doctrine to a new level with lengthy indoctrination speeches in the mid 1970's, Garth Hughes' father became one of his victims, nine months after Garth got married.

Garth never did completely agree with his dad's marking in 1982, and it really bothered him. Garth convinced himself, "If you agree with somebody, you have to submit intellectually." So Garth submitted intellectually with his father's marking, even though he didn't agree with it deep down. Garth didn't want to lose all his friends. This caused a lot of subconscious turmoil in his heart, and to add to his troubles, he tried to raise his three children the same way. If his children or wife disagreed with him, he felt he needed to 'discuss' it until they thoroughly agreed with him. It wasn't okay for them to just submit and do what he asked, even though they didn't agree with his opinion. They had to believe his opinions really were the truth.

This belief caused a lot of turmoil in Garth's home. But around 2000, he came to the place in his life where he realized God truly loved him, and his family didn't have to intellectually submit to him. Garth sought the approval of God, allowing him to grow in his faith, Christian walk and his relationship with the Lord. His growth was evident over the next several years, and he was well respected in Fredericksburg, Virginia in 2008.

As Deo Trophy put it - "Garth, I haven't discussed the concerns you have for me, because you have been doing so well. I didn't think you needed my time and attention."

Garth started doing so well he saw through Deo and his conscience wouldn't let him stay under Deo's ministry. Also, his wife was stressed over the controversy and it bothered her too.

As Garth and his wife Lucia left he was at a strategic disadvantage. Garth's kids had some legitimately poor memories of their father from their childhood that bothered them. They had gotten along well with their dad over the last several years, but that did not compensate for the bad childhood memories.

Garth's cheerful outlook on life, engaging personality and almost permanently cherubic face helped win them back some over the last several years. But Deo Trophy had quietly undermined Garth's headship over the years, as Deo had done with other parents. Garth's reputation was sabotaged as Deo stole his children's hearts and embezzled their approval.

So when Garth left, his two married daughters stayed in the Assemblies with their husbands, and so did Garth's son, Alex. Alex was remembered for giving testimony at the large regional camp meetings, saying, "I always want to be here in the Assemblies and to be a part, I never want to leave." Mind Controllers love people like Alex.

Alex kept his commitment, and influenced by Deo Trophy, told his dad he considered him divisive for leaving and disagreeing with Deo Trophy. Garth was marked for avoidance by his newly married son, just as Garth had marked his own father when he was Alex's age. Alex likely never considered it might happen to him also, years later.

Garth and his wife Lucia had one grandson from their daughter who lived in Virginia, with another grandchild on the way. They were devoted grandparents, eagerly anticipating visits from their young grandson, with a box of toys all ready for him when he came over, and were ardently awaiting more grandkids during the coming years. But when their children were quickly turned against them, the loss of relationships created deep wounds. Deep wounds causing intense emotional pain, because now they could no longer see their children or grandson.

Garth said to his friends on a Sunday afternoon while lamenting their state of affairs: "I wish I had gone to my kids first, quietly, and let them know what was going on. I tried to work it out with Deo but within a few days Deo and his followers had talked to my kids and turned them against me."

In spite of Garth's hardships, he was able to maintain a cheerful outlook on life most of the time. Lucia sadly put the box of toys away in storage, and they continued to have guests over, doing what they could to help others. But sometimes her pain was overwhelming.

The Lord is a refuge for the oppressed
A refuge in times of trouble
And those who know Your name will put their trust in You
For You, Lord, have not forsaken those who seek You

- King David in Psalms 9 -

16·

Reunited with old friends

After twenty years of ministry and officiating for many weddings and markings, the Texas minister Dudley Franklin was disqualified in 1991. Then Dudley's own turn at the Marking chopping block came via Byron Stark a few years later.

In 2009, Dudley was still very marked and having Bible studies with two other men. People who cause the upright to go astray in an evil way fall into their own pit later on.

Although friendly and kindly at times, Dudley had extensively preached and practiced that people who disagreed with him doctrinally and continued to talk to others about it, should be pointed out, rebuked and marked if needed to stop 'division'. Those who dared not walk in his authorized markings from the pulpit were also marked for associating with the marked men, like Garth Hughes' father. As a young married man, Garth couldn't visit his father. He risked being marked himself and losing his young friends, so he just went along with Dudley.

Long ago, back in 1985, Dudley Franklin got involved in the affairs of the California Assemblies, and through his preaching and intellectually intimidating ministry, helped generate a massive marking wave. This included the marking of his own older brother, Dan Franklin, who he thought was primarily at fault for some local problems in the Atascadero Assembly. Dudley and some others had an interpersonal conflict with Dan. Dan thought it was okay to spend time with Christians who went to denominations, and sometimes listened to preachers outside their group.

Dudley decided to use the pulpit as the epicenter to turn as many people as he could against his brother at the California December regional Assembly camp in 1985, and it worked well, with the drawback of losing a lot of the Californians in the resulting mass markings fissure. Dan and those who would not stand in his marking were marked for being divisive and sectarian.

Dan Franklin was lucky enough to wind up with his entire family, except for his oldest son. In contrast, most of Dudley's children were not with him fifteen years later.

The magnitude of the California Assemblies' seismic loss was one third. Some were marked directly, and some indirectly, for simply not walking in those initial markings in 1986. Some were just shunned but not marked. All ten of Rhett's good friends were lost in the rupturing of so many relationships and families. He lost his best friend Duke, one of Dan Franklin's sons.

So families had been split up for the last twenty-four years, young women who had just gotten married and had the misfortune of being on the opposite side of the divide from their parents lost contact with them almost completely for years. Consequently their grandchildren grew up from babyhood into their late teens and early twenties without ever knowing their grandparents, some of them living only fifteen miles away for the last twenty years.

The markings that took place on the California ministers in 2009 made most people re-think how the Marking Doctrine was wrongly expanded and implemented; so many families were very happily reunited with their families and friends after twenty-four years of separation. The grandchildren were now grown, in their late teens, and there was a lot of heartache associated with the lost time, but it was good a renewal of relationships was happening now!

After seeing the fallacy of past markings during the last year, most were bewildered and wondered why it took them so long to realize the Marking Doctrine was wrong, including Rhett and Garth.

"I think it was the fear of it," said Garth, assessing his past.

"Yeah, like we were talking earlier, the fear creates a subconscious motivation to go along with markings and shunnings," said Rhett, "otherwise, we'd get the same treatment. So we intellectually defend markings because we know subconsciously we'd really suffer otherwise."

Garth was a really deep thinker. Rhett had learned to pay close attention to what he talked about, because after looking into things for himself he realized Garth was often right, and not afraid to challenge long held beliefs that most people just conformed to. Garth had long been labeled as somebody who 'had a problem with leadership'.

Bach Jude, the minister in Long Beach, was overjoyed to be reunited with his siblings and parents who had all been marked for the last twenty-four years. Bach was so excited, and ever so delighted and happy to have the markings of his family be a thing of the past. Life had been difficult, losing his oldest child in an auto accident years ago, his wife was told she would never walk, but she did recover. God was good, and walking in his Word was putting things back the way they should be. Bach's siblings had grown in the Lord, one of them becoming a successful personal Christian counselor.

Dan Franklin grew bitter over the years since 1986, about never holding the granddaughters of his oldest son in his arms, not ever; even being forbidden by his oldest son to go a few miles to the hospital to see his new granddaughters when they were born. This bitterness eventually spilled out into the internet. Dan and his younger son Duke made some comments on the internet running down the 'James Stark Cult' around 2000.

Duke had been Rhett's best friend as teenagers, and it really bothered Rhett that they made these comments, running down some leaders Rhett respected with Dan's "colorful adjectives."

Shortly after he left, his mind began to clear and Rhett soon came to believe that there was no Biblical basis for 'marking those who would not go along with a marking' or 'domino markings' or 'marking by association' or even 'marking over unclear doctrinal disputes to protect the leaders'. The truth should decide doctrinal issues and stand on its own.

He decided to make an effort in getting to know Duke again. Maybe Duke had changed; maybe Duke Franklin knew more than Rhett knew. This recent situation opened Rhett's eyes; other people might have some truth in their perspectives, things in the past may not all be as he had thought. After all, it was the same Atascadero Assembly with Dudley's influence that marked Duke years ago that had just marked the California ministers with Deo's influence.

Rhett sent an e-mail through Duke's photography website, and Duke was ecstatic about finally being in contact with Rhett again! They had several long conversations and exchanged many e-mails. Both of them loved photography, and both of them had their own photography websites. After a few months of debating the past, their friendship was rekindled. Duke said he regretted the way he made some comments on the internet that were harsh and was sorry about it. This helped relieve Rhett's mind.

"Pleasant words promote instruction; the Lord does not want us to be harsh and bitter against each other. Remember that Stephen prayed for those who had stoned him, we need to use gracious words," Rhett preached. Duke took it okay, but said Rhett might feel differently after twenty-four years worth of shunning. Duke and his dad had been painted as "being of Satan."

Rhett finally apologized to Duke for what had happened. Although, looking back on it, Rhett likely would have done the same thing if he had to do it over. He had stayed with his parents and siblings, married the sweet girl in his Assembly, and been helped by James Stark's ministry on marriage and child training. The Marking Doctrine forced him to choose sides, when he didn't really want to.

Unfortunately, most of his Virginia friends were now history. Just as Rhett walked in Duke's marking out of fear of being marked himself, so they were walking in Rhett's marking.

During one conversation, Duke, after joking about keeping his demon horns trimmed, said, "Well, Bach Jude apologized to me last week, so there are only one-hundred and sixty-eight people to go now."

Rhett responded, "I'm not wanting everybody to apologize to me."

Duke said, "You don't know what it is like to be marked for twenty-four years!"

"You don't know what it's like to be under the fear of being marked if I didn't walk in other people's markings for twenty-four years," Rhett said, "but you're right, I don't know what it's been like for you."

It must have been rough having a bunch of lifetime relationships ripped away from a twenty-one year old young man.

Duke and Rhett talked together about the best way to reach Duke's brother who still had his mind locked by Orderly Following and the Marking Doctrine. Rhett told Duke he and his dad were painted as angry and bitter, and suggested appealing to his older brother's new nature. Duke sent a contrite, polite letter to his brother, asking for his marking to be lifted, and he wanted to work things out.

Duke's brother response - "Why would you want your marking lifted after all these years?!" grieved Duke.

Duke left a few messages for his brother asking to get together to resolve things, and after no response sent a text message to his cell phone. Duke's brother sent an e-mail back - "Don't text me, it cost me money when you do that."

Rhett figured it was about twenty-five cents down the drain for Duke's brother, who was wealthy. Duke guessed it was more like fifteen cents. Duke sent a few more e-mails and his older brother put him off a few more times. After several months of waiting, Duke finally gave up trying to reconcile their differences.

Rhett called up his brother-in-law Jarvo and apologized for shunning him. Jarvo invited them over for dinner.

Rhett and Sabrina greatly anticipated their reunion with Jarvo and Laura after three years of separation. Jarvo stood in the driveway as they pulled in, and they gave each other a big warm embrace.

"You had a point Jarvo, Deo WAS dishonest!" Rhett said with an approving grin over a delicious Mexican dinner Laura had made for them, sitting on the patio outside their restored vintage farmhouse on seventy acres near Charlottesville, Virginia. Jarvo's trial had helped him grow spiritually over the last few years. He was also chosen as the local 'Joe the Plumber' in 2008 for the local TV station interview in Charlottesville.

Rhett's sister Laura had grown too, but being shunned by her family and friends had been very hard on her emotionally and physically. She met several local Christian ladies who helped her through her trial. Laura had lost a lot of weight and was unhealthy. Some days she hadn't even gotten out of bed, due to severe depression over her own personal shunning.

This emotional pain left Laura with a deep seated phobia of anybody from the Assemblies. She felt queasy and faint if she saw any old friends from the Assemblies in town, to the point of needing something to hold onto for stability. Associating great emotional pain with former close friends makes it very difficult to be friends again. The shunning device was very destructive to her, burning the bridges down on eighteen years of friendships after she left.

To Rhett's surprise Jarvo was well aware of Deo's mind control tactics. Rhett was reminiscing about Deo Trophy's long awkward hug when Jonathan was on life support, and laughed, "I had to stick one leg waaay out to balance myself!"

Jarvo said, "Oh, that's Deo's power hug. He tries to pull people off balance, onto his chest, especially when they are stressed, to send a subtle mental message that he is in control and can support you."

A mutual friend was there, and said, "Deo tried to do the same thing to me!"

Deo was using the same principle as being safe in the arms of Jesus, but different. Much different.

They all recollected how Deo would ask them all how their fathers were doing, as if he wanted to talk about it more. He had even done this to Sabrina.

Rhett quickly reassured his sister that he really had changed, and he now understood some things were not doctrinally sound. One of them was the Marking Doctrine, which had caused so many problems for Laura.

Rhett explained his new understanding to Jarvo and Laura: "Biblical markings are always **reactive**, never proactive. They shouldn't be in **anticipation** of sin, but reacting to a sin already committed. Romans 16:17 says to avoid those who cause Divisions and Offenses, so there are two elements. Offenses are things that **cause** people to stumble. Things are being taught and preached using smooth speech which are causing Division with false doctrine, and making people stumble (Offenses) in their Christian walk and faith. The stumbling could be people who need stability in their lives see the falsehoods and leave, then stumble with the lack of positive influence from the marital and child raising stability in other families as their own relationships fall apart."

"There is a perfect example of Romans 16:17 in Second Timothy 2, which speaks of men who preach things that spread like cancer. Hymenaeus and Philetus strayed from the truth, preaching the resurrection had already past, and they overthrew the faith of some. This false doctrine caused some to stumble in their faith, their faith being ship-wrecked."

"Hymenaeus and Philetus were perfect examples of Romans 16:17 in causing Division and Offenses, but nowhere is there any instruction on also marking or noting those who associated with these men. First and Second Timothy, First and Second Thessalonians, and Titus all discuss the false doctrine of the resurrection being past, but nowhere does it instruct marking by association, domino markings or shunnings of those who associated with Hymenaeus and Philetus, or marking simply over doctrinal disagreements," Rhett finished, a little out of breath.

"Do you think it's wrong to be divisive?" asked Laura.

"It depends on what the division is over, is it over the truth? What Jesus did caused division over the truth as people chose to not follow Him. It depends on the reason and motivation. Diotrephes clearly caused an ungodly division for his own benefit. It could be to protect their position and control over people, like the Pharisees did in expelling those out of the temple who confessed Christ, because they loved the approval of men rather than God. Or like King Saul who was motivated to protect his power. This marking and shunning doctrine puts a lot of fear into people, and puts the control of our relationships into the hands of the leaders over us."

"These markings have been going on for a long time," said Laura, wanting nothing to do with any such markings at all whatsoever in the future.

"Dudley Franklin caused division and some to stumble in their faith I think, after those marked were banned from

274 · The Bishop Maker

fellowshipping with those stable Christian families who remained. Many just followed along with his teachings, long after 1990 when it became obvious his own family had severe personal issues, when he was disqualified as a minister twenty years ago. We just stupidly and unquestionly followed along with his teachings. Now Dudley is meeting with just two other men, and is threatening to mark one of them! And we kept walking in his doctrinal teachings for twenty years! The Lord was so right when he called us sheep! We naturally follow other sheep, subconsciously following the same paths without seeking the Lord's will and love in our lives by truly reading the Bible for ourselves, with the Holy Spirit's influence," said Rhett. He wanted to make it perfectly clear to Laura she had nothing to fear of another shunning.

Jarvo said, "The two most listed reasons people are turned off on Christ is legalism and hypocrisy. Seems to me that a minister who promotes these has some accountability for making Christians stumble in their faith."

Rhett met with Michie Hobkins and apologized for avoiding him. Michie was unsure of Rhett, but after visiting a few times they renewed their same warm friendship they had before this whole thing started. Except now, the friendship had more depth and understanding, no longer was the fear – 'follow your leader regardless of what they say' a wedge in their relationship.

Rhett was disappointed Aaron Adams signed onto the letter marking James Stark. Ten years ago James had flown out to Loomis, California, spending two weeks investigating some accusations against Aaron. After interviewing all the people involved, he cleared Aaron of the accusations. James had even stood up against his own brother-in-law Kevin, to back Aaron. This was on top of James spending many weeks a year living in a camper on Aaron's property to back him up in his ministry in Loomis, as James' wife was left behind in Virginia.

In stark contrast to James' efforts, Aaron had done no investigation with the accusations against James, but just took Al Taylor's word that James was the problem up in Newfoundland. Aaron didn't even talk by phone to the half of the people up in Newfoundland who disagreed with Al.

Rhett e-mailed Aaron a few times about signing the letter without looking into it, but Aaron just ignored him. *Aaron never ignored me when I had been so supportive of him and the Orderly Following he tried to implement years before,* thought Rhett.

Rhett was able to talk to two couples who had left the Fredericksburg Assembly many years before this. Deo spoke poorly of them after they had left, and Rhett assumed they had a lot of problems. They were well aware of Deo's mind control manipulations and Deo's habit of giving partial truths to distort what had actually happened. All of them went on to walk with the Lord, helping others as they could, taking in foster kids.

Rhett's dad reminisced about trying to resolve the conflict between Deo and Jar years ago. Jar had told Mycroft that Deo was ignoring him. Deo explained to Mycroft that Jar followed him around after the meetings, trying to engage him in provocative debates. This agitated him, so he was trying to avoid Jar. Mycroft suggested writing Jar instead. Deo agreed to this and copied Mycroft on the letters. Mycroft was shocked at Deo's inflammatory wording. Deo suggested Mycroft screen and edit them first. Mycroft agreed, and toned them way down before Deo sent them on to Jar.

Deo had given a series of messages on Abigail over the last several years, how Abigail had been right to go around her husband Nabal. Although Deo didn't come out and say it, Deo set the stage for making it okay for women to complain to Deo about their husbands behind their husband's backs, and some women did. Deo also counseled young couples individually to go to him if they had a problem in their marriage. He said it to each one without their spouse there, as if he wanted married men and women to confide in him about their spouses' problems.

Deo had quite a track history of isolating people he counseled from everybody else, encouraging them to cut off contact with friendships and relatives, leaving only Deo to go to.

Rhett wondered where it would all go. Years ago, in the 1960's, Julius Shacknow was a minister who started counseling women in the Fredericksburg Assembly while their husbands were away at work. The men put a stop to it so Julius left, moving up north. Julius started his own group, being a dynamic speaker with a vast knowledge of the Bible, and eventually proclaimed himself as "Julius Christ" and his wife as the "Holy Spirit." There was alleged severe abuse to some of his followers. Rhett was able to find out more about Julius on an internet search under "brother Julius cult."

Rhett asked Mycroft what he remembered of Julius in California, and he related, "We were on this men and boys trip in Central California in the 50's, and it was sweltering hot. Cars didn't have air conditioning back then. We all stopped to swim in the cold water of an irrigation canal by the side of a rural highway. We all changed into our swimming trunks, some just wearing their underwear. We were just beginning to swim and a car with two young ladies stopped to ask directions. Julius was embarrassed to be seen, and peering around the tree, gave the girls directions."

The result of the Orderly Following and Marking Doctrine had redefined unity as submitting to the authorities controlling the podium, and the resulting conformity exalted over God's Holiness and Grace. Followers are now discouraged from setting their hope fully on the Grace of God. Individual faith in God as a foundation was discouraged. Deo considers the teaching of the Holy Spirit to individuals a selfish freedom of choice, rather proclaiming that he, Deo, and other leaders are being used by the Holy Spirit to inhibit and direct followers. Deo and his leaders took the responsibility on themselves for holding back a lot of works of the flesh that they thought would otherwise occur with their flocks. When human authority becomes the mediator between God and Christians, it evolves into worship of the creature rather than the Creator. This was the actual practice and fruit of his preaching.

Deo Trophy had exploited and taken advantage of the imbalance of two doctrines to lure two thirds of the people into unquestionly following him. He used the Marking Doctrine to get rid of those who wouldn't 'put up' with him, and the Orderly Following Doctrine to control those who were left. Those who stayed with Deo stoutly believed it was wrong to leave under any circumstances and they needed to work it out. Working it out meant hearing Deo's long and confusing explanations, but nothing changed as a result. It was just wrong to leave, and there were no alternatives.

Sociopaths love people like that.

Nothing teaches like experience, and the California minister's own markings taught most to see the doctrine from both sides of the issue. Unfortunately, James Stark was still defensive about it. The same doctrines he had preached and walked in had been expanded on and turned against him by Deo with dishonesty, yet he still believed past doctrines and markings to be entirely Biblical. He slowly lost credibility, although he still counseled with a few who saw the value in his ability to think critically, and his perception of human relationships.

First Timothy 4 states the Holy Spirit warns in the latter times some will depart from the faith, listening to and obeying deceiving spirits and doctrines of demons. These spirits and demons don't need books or media. They supernaturally use leaders to impose more control and manmade rules over people than the Bible authorizes. This works well to keep things Orderly for awhile, but has disastrous fruit over the long run.

"I think I can safely say that we had some rules that went way beyond what the Lord authorizes in the Bible," Rhett Stuart said to Calvin Hobkins over a sandwich during a mid week lunch.

Calvin took a swig of coffee, and said, "Yep, those spirits and demons certainly are alive and kick'n in 2009!"

It really is good, and peaceful, to know and believe the truth, serving the Lord with a clear conscious. Better a meal of vegetables with peace, than feasting with strife.

Kevin Banks' wife Louise, also James Stark's sister, was against James Stark for not obeying Deo and his band. She sent Sabrina a short hand written note ending with:

I'm so sorry how the Devil has gotten in but it doesn't have to stay that way. A humble heart and letting folks know you don't like it this way and then endeavor to keep the unity of the spirit and work things out, and it could all be resolved. I pray this will happen to all those who have been marked. The children are going to be the ones who suffer and in turn, the parents. Also as they see their children turn to the World and the heartaches begin. We love you and pray for a restoration.

Christian Love, Kevin and Louise

"Well Sabrina, worldly can mean self-righteous, or getting drunk and stuff like that. But I think she means our kids will be turned away from Christ for leaving their Assemblies and be physically immoral, rather than turning from Christ to religion and self-righteousness," said Rhett.

Kevin's sharp mind started thinking something wasn't quite right during 2009. After covering his bases with Byron Stark, not wanting to be publicly rebuked, he got a nod that he took as a yes and sent out letters to all the men over fifty-five years old on both sides, requesting a meeting to discuss if they would be interested to discuss peacefully resolving the issue.

Kevin found out virtually all the people who opposed Deo in the West were in favor, but those who were still with Deo's group in Texas and Virginia declined having any meeting. A few on Deo's side did express an interest, but quickly retracted it.

When Kevin realized his efforts were futile, he sent out his study on "Elders" to the same group, concluding:

1. Biblical history concerning elders, with few exceptions, has elders as the ones who have the responsibility to do or at least being a part of, ruling, making decisions, making judgments, and etc.

2. We, as a group of older people, have not done a good job in taking our positions, of being good examples, of making decisions and judgments as we are supposed to do.

3. We have let a very, very small and select group of bishops and deacons do a lot of what is our responsibility along with them to do. In other words, elders should be a part of most of the decisions made.

4. A bishop or deacon, as individuals, has more authority in the church than an individual elder who does not hold an office, but a group of elders, as a group, should have authority in the church, including authority over bishops and deacons as individuals. I am not referring to the kind of responsibilities given to husbands as individuals and etc.

5. This arrangement gets rid of the "dominant man" theory and gives support and guidance to our bishops and deacons. They are not lone Rangers, but have a body of elders as support, guidance and council.

The above mode of operation is, as I remember it, the way it used to be. In my mind there has been a slow shift from what used to be, to what is now, but that doesn't prove which way is more correct. The way it is now in the East and Midwest, but perhaps not so much in the West, does go along closer to the "dominant man" theory. It is my understanding that in some places in the West, men operate more as I have stated above (assemblies run more under the authority of groups of older men rather than by bishops and deacons).

Again, I want to run this study past various ones of you for your input (both ways) before I would want to say that this is the truth on this subject, I could be wrong in my thinking, so if I am, please show me where.

Your brother in Christ, Kevin Banks

Kevin carefully pointed out Deo was guilty of what Deo had accused James, of being the dominant man. Deo and his band of Bishops just ignored him, and Kevin's comments went away after about three weeks. Deo and Byron owned the top of the hill and there was no reason to relinquish any of their authority.

Power is hard for people to give up, and it is rarely given up willingly.

The Orderly Following doctrine resulted in progressive control, *incrementally*. Small slits in skirts, makeup, shorts or beards for men, pants, and earrings for women, gag orders, trying to forbid sandals, untucked shirts, banning coffee during public meetings, not drinking water during lengthy sing practices, green hats with a tractor company name on them, and especially the enormous disaster of splitting up families and friendships for years.

Strictly enforced rules that had once been recommended standards, and commandments to obey markings the rulers had decided on, all went well beyond what is Biblically authorized. Men living godly lives were banned from leading the children in singing because their wife wore earrings, another was threatened to be pointed out as dangerous if his wife wore pants.

The Marking Doctrine went well beyond avoiding obviously immoral Christians; even to the extreme of splitting up close Christ-centered families and friendships, separating parents from grown children and grandchildren for years. There had been mass shunnings of friends, family, parents, daughters, sons, and grandkids lasting twenty-four years, and now even more mass markings and shunnings in 2009. Yet many people clung onto the past twenty years with Deo and his Bishops, thinking the next twenty would be better, not realizing it was actually getting even worse. The emphasis on the Rock, on a Biblical foundation, slowly decomposed over eighty years, leaving a structure standing on the sands of human wisdom.

The claim of leadership: "We are building Christian lives, Christian homes, and the Church which is Christ's body" became part of the hypocrisy. It was in practice: "Dividing Christian's lives, Christian's homes, and the Church which is Christ's body."

Putting a group ahead of Christ is idolatry, but it is difficult to comprehend that is happening as the group deteriorates. People serving their group claim they are serving the Lord. However, in practice, when people like Deo rise up in their midst, they are unable to leave since they have a conviction it is wrong to leave under any circumstance.

Garth Hughes said, "I still can't believe we didn't see the problems with the Marking and Orderly Following Doctrines long ago, Rhett!"

Rhett said, "I can't believe it either. Like we were talking last Sunday, maybe the fear of being shunned and losing my friends and reputation made me intellectually submit to these doctrines. You know, Dudley Franklin really had a lot of charisma but the marking guillotine he created ended up being used on him when he was marked. He's been separated from many of his kids, grand-children, and friends for years. Yet we continued to walk in his teachings for the next eighteen years after he was marked."

Garth said, "Yep. When I visited my dad last month I found out Dudley had just marked one of the two men he met with for associating with my dad. It got me to thinking more about Dudley, who marked my dad thirty years ago. Now Dudley just has one follower left to have fellowship with! Two of his kids told me they had been marked by their dad, and when their mother was in the hospital they came to Dudley's house to clean it. Dudley told them, "You kids need to leave, you're marked!" His two grown children cleaned the house anyways."

Garth Hughes heard Deo Trophy had given a message, 'The Simple Believe every Word', in Fredericksburg, where two of his children still went. Deo pointed out that simple people doesn't necessarily mean stupid or dumb people, but could also mean uninformed people.

Garth sent Deo a letter, stating, "It is really audacious of you to speak on that. What more unsuspecting could people be of than a minister who is guilty of keeping people simple, and then give a message on it and accuse others of it?"

Deo strongly disagreed with Garth. Deo had virtually perfected the paradoxical art of accusing others of what he was guilty of.

Maybe the hand of the Lord was in it, Rhett can't say for sure. But he came across three people who had worked with Deo Trophy at the Navy weapons development center within the Aegis Combat System.

One person said, "Deo had gotten some mind control training, and had a reputation of being one of the best mind control people the center had. Deo's ability to manipulate and control other intelligent people earned him the nickname of 'The Puppet Master'."

Rhett wanted to confirm this with another prior coworker of Deos', but unfortunately he was a technician, and didn't know much of what Deo had been intimately involved in. He said the Naval center would pay for training, almost anything remotely related to their work, but as he remembered Deo studied mind control on his own, technical papers that anybody there had access to.

The third person who had worked with Deo knew nothing about it.

One of Deo's superiors was known for saying: "You know what it takes for us to succeed? Staying Power, Determination! That's what I tell my people. It's such a messed up process that six people who know what they are doing can get the job done! Remember, you're building the means to defend your country, children, and grand-children! Well into the 21st century!"

Deo might have thought he was doing that with the Assemblies, but good intentions don't change the consequences, or make it okay to deceive other humans.

Rhett gave James Stark a call to talk about the mind control stuff. James hadn't studied it much, but thought Deo just did a really good job of convincing people.

"Deo is a very good salesman," James said, "He really knows how to convince an audience."

Rhett disagreed, he thought something more was involved, and also James Stark once defended Deo's dishonesty against Archie Stark, Sean Lane, and Lyle Cooper. If James had been wrong about Deo before, he might be wrong about the mind control tactics.

James had always done the best he could to help others using credible information, to judge carefully based on established facts with a servant's heart, giving both time and money. James assumed Deo shared these motivations in the past, since he thought they had shared the same convictions on Orderly Following and the Marking Doctrine of shunning and avoiding.

James didn't have solid proof of Deo's dishonesty predating more than two years, and it was too late to go back after all those years to establish the facts with two or three witnesses to support each claim from the long list of people over the years who told of Deo twisting the facts. Even though Deo's dishonesty had recently been exposed, James wouldn't allow facts that were not established with two or three witnesses to carry weight in his mind.

James would not agree with others how his support and backing of Deo over the years was a mistake, and didn't think he had a reason to apologize. The imbalance of the Orderly Following had born bad fruit, and the Marking Doctrine's extremely damaging effects were exposed and obvious to many people, but he didn't agree with many others who thought he had made a mistake in strongly backing and preaching these things himself. His credibility suffered as he kept contending for them.

Rhett thought if he was in James place he would have apologized. David in First Samuel 22 said, "I knew that day, when Doeg the Edomite was there, that he would tell Saul about me being there. I have caused all the deaths of your father's house. Stay with me and do not fear. Saul wants to kill both of us, but you will be safe with me."

No court would have justly convicted David of those deaths, but David openly accepted responsibility for his part.

Do not put your trust in princes or in any other human
The fatality rate is one per person, and someday -
The prince's spirit will depart and all his plans will perish

You will be happy if you make the Lord God your hope!
While I live I will praise the Lord
I will sing praises to my God while I have my being
Because it is the Lord who raises those who are bowed down
But the Lord turns the way of the wicked upside down
So Praise the Lord, O my soul!

King David, paraphrased from Psalms 146 and 150

17·

Preserve me, O God, for in You I put my trust
- King David in Psalms 16 -

The Wolf -
A Religious Sociopath

Life goes on as young people, impacted by the past, expectantly forge their futures, hoping to avoid repeating the errors they know of.

Calvin Hobkins' daughter Georgia got married September of 2009, several months after Calvin and Barbara had left the Assemblies.

Although Calvin was careful not to talk to anyone, Deo Trophy and Cary Murdock discouraged people from going to the wedding. Georgia invited the California ministers who were marked, along with any who dared defy the control Deo and his followers had over the people of the Assemblies.

The prime roast feast prepared by James Stark and his wife Marie helped make it a special time in Southern Maryland. Marie was an experienced professional wedding caterer, catering for people outside the Assemblies to send money to relatives in Peru, a superb cook in her own right. The events over the last few years had given her a twitch in her face at times, a form of palsy, likely due to the stress of having her husband dishonestly accused, the focal point of Deo's take-over.

Since the wedding was three hours away, Rhett and Sabrina decided to stay at a hotel the night before the wedding with several from California who were out for the wedding. At the continental hotel breakfast, Rhett sat next to a lady from California.

Cindy had learned of Rhett's mind control document he had sent to the California leaders mid-January, 2009. She explained to Rhett as he ate a few hardboiled eggs with salt and pepper, "A few years ago I was out for your regional camp retreat at Happy Hill, and I heard some men talking behind me. Somebody said, "I got some training at work on mind control, and boy, does that stuff work! You would not believe what you can get people to tell you!" I was pretty curious to see who was saying this, and turned around. Do you know, it was Deo!"

"Are you sure he said that?" asked Rhett.

"I'm very sure! He was talking to another man, I don't know who it was but I wish I could remember. Anyways, Deo noticed me turning around and eyeing him, so he kept quiet 'til I moved out of earshot."

"Did you hear anything else?"

"No, that was it."

It was weird to be at a wedding in which most of the guests were being shunned or marked by Rhett's previous

288 · The Bishop Maker

religious organization. Peter Waters commented, "I know marking us was wrong, but it just affects you psychologically. All our lives we have been taught that wicked, sinful, and divisive people are marked. Now we are the ones marked."

Being on the other side of a marking allowed Peter to see how erroneous the Marking Doctrine was that had been ramped up by Dudley in the mid 70's.

In addition to Dan Franklin opposing his brother's Marking Doctrine, he too disputed with Dudley and James Stark over the Moses Doctrine.

Dudley believed and emphatically preached that Moses was a type of church leader. In practice, whoever had control over the podium was in control and should be obeyed. Questions could be asked for clarification, but any who talked to others of their disagreements were hunted down and silenced like Korah, Dathan and Abiram were when the earth swallowed them up. People who persisted in disagreements with the Moses type leader, like Dudley Franklin's physical brother Dan, were marked for avoidance, along with any who would not go along with the marking.

Dan believed that Moses was appointed by God to represent Him to the people; so Moses was a type of Christ and the head of a new nation. He insisted that church leaders today didn't have the same authority as Moses, but should function as servants – not lords or apostles. A leader's doctrine and conduct should be questioned when concerns arose. The ultimate decision maker was the Word of God, rightly divided and understood in context.

Dudley Franklin, and then Deo Trophy with the backing of James Stark, taught it was wicked for a congregation to hire a minister or fire him. That would put control in the hand of the audience, which is sin. They argued the audience wouldn't want to hear any speaker who was faithful and get rid of them. The right way they taught was for the leader to have control, so he could eventually get rid of any in the Assemblies that opposed him, those who continued to verbalize alleged false doctrines.

Anything taken to an extreme becomes evil: A congregation firing a teacher for faithful and convicting messages; or a self-willed teacher obtaining unchallengeable control and abusing a complacent congregation willing to put up with it. True ministry is edifying, it is not controlling and it is not contentious or disruptive. A true minister has the heart of a father, not the heart of an instructor. All should minister, pastors, and teachers should help teach the saints for ministry to edify others. When everybody is doing their part, this causes healthy growth.

James Stark strongly supported and preached Dudley and Deo's controlling doctrines, but wasn't an instigator of them. James had avoided both the mass markings of Dudley, and the extreme controlling of Deo, by counseling regularly with elders. He encouraged many elders and deacons to be involved, seeking advice from them regularly. He strongly backed the few local leaders in the Assemblies who controlled the podiums, but some complained he should have expanded his view of leadership by including more than just a few.

Deo slowly got rid of a lot of savvy older men and women who were not going to put up with him. These older people were consulted heavily by James Stark, but cast out as worthless by Deo Trophy because he wanted only the younger leaders who controlled the podiums, who he in turn controlled. The small footprint of Deo's

290 · The Bishop Maker

foundational control had been carefully crafted over many years in extensive communication with these younger men. Crafted to gain their full trust and stick with him at all costs, and not break rank when adversity came. And it was working, for now.

Charlie Cooper was one of two men who introduced Deo to the Assemblies around 1974. The other man who introduced Deo to the Assemblies was marked by Deo in 1985.

For over twenty-five years Deo accused Charlie Cooper, Lyle Cooper's father, of influencing a lot of older people in Fredericksburg Assembly against him and "sowing discord we will likely never recover from." Charlie became the scapegoat for any concerns other people had of Deo.

Charlie disliked conflict and caved in after his public rebuking, and the letter about him that was sent across the country. He decided to keep quiet while living in Fredericksburg, he enjoyed being able to socialize with his kids and grandkids. Charlie's youngest daughter was Rhoda Shifflet, the other daughter married James Stark's son, Byron. Charlie's son was Lyle Cooper, the Charlottesville minister.

Deo said in a meeting in 1990, "As many of you know, Charlie Cooper has caused a lot of leaven for a lot of years, lots of years. We will probably never recover from the discord he sowed, of accusing leadership of exclusiveness, claiming he was left out. Well, Charlie is just envious of leaders. As many of you know, Charlie has had immorality in his life for a long time, a long time ago. I'm glad he confessed to that. Really glad. But Charlie has sowed discord and influenced several older men here in Fredericksburg. He has caused serious serious serious serious problems. We will probably never recover from the discord Charlie sowed among us, and I am sorry he is here this morning, but I really think he needs to hear this. He caused many many many many problems. Big, big, big, big unbelievable problems, by his attack on Orderly Following and accusing ministry of just wanting to have it their way. Does ministry 'just want to have it their way?' No, of course not! We don't feel that way!"

Some other older people had concerns with Deo's Orderly Following doctrine he had helped implement within several years, thinking there was too much authority being given to those who controlled the podium.

Deo blamed their concerns on Charlie's discord, of course.

BJ was one of the older men concerned with the older men being excluded. But Deo hotly denied excluding the older people, blaming BJ's confusion on Charlie Cooper, and accused BJ of ignorance. However, time proved BJ right. Deo threatened another man having increasing concerns for Deo, that if he talked to BJ about them, Deo told him, "I'll have to — point BJ out." This man caved in under the pressure of Deo lecturing him for many hours in front of his friends, and the public rebuking at Happy Hill for his sin in daring to stand up against Deo's authority. He complained to James Stark about Deo's twisting of the facts, but Deo offered a plausible explanation.

Most of the older people in Fredericksburg decided to keep quiet after observing the public rebukings. Deo continued flattering Byron and Archie Stark since their mid twenties, claiming they had above average ability to detect problems. Both became pillars in his control over others.

Deo warned his followers, insinuating other leaders might cause problems, as he was doing it. Deo became skilled with the art of accusing others of what he himself was guilty of, but once Rhett and his friends caught on, it was quite revealing when Deo accused others of something: It exposed what he was up to. Like in 2009 when Deo falsely accused several people in the Fredericksburg Assembly, behind their backs, of trying to entrap him with questions to frame him, and playing politics.

Proverbs 26 provides a good example of why no preacher today should have unchallengeable control, and get away with slander of others:

> The words of a talebearer are like tasty trifles that go deep into the body; they go deep into the subconscious mind. Fervent lips with a wicked heart are like clay pots covered with a cheap silver coating, he deceives himself by disguising with his lips who he hates.
>
> When he says kind things, do not believe him, because there are seven abominations in his heart; Though his hatred is concealed by deceit, his wickedness will be revealed before the assembly. Whoever digs a pit will fall into it, and he who rolls a stone will have it roll back on him.
>
> A lying tongue hates those who are crushed by it, and a flattering mouth works ruin.

It is hard for a Jesus loving Christian to honestly believe a kindly speaking leader with a great knowledge and understanding of the Bible, who talks fervently about the Lord, can be motivated by a sinister and wicked heart, whose seared conscience is carefully concealed from almost all of them. A sincere Christian naturally won't suspect the minister, preacher, teacher, pastor, or reverend is unscrupulously lying and flattering in utter hypocrisy to harm innocent people, and secretly hates those who are crushed by the lies and flattery. Some leaders really do prefer others to fear them, rather than love them.

Just like any organization, Christian associations have always drawn leaders who want to selfishly control. Christians, especially those with struggles, make a good target: they are more cooperative, want to please leaders they think are godly, and many have tender consciences. "Right' becomes obeying the leader, regardless if they deserve it or not. Leaders couldn't get away with this type of abuse in a large corporation or government without some repercussions or accountability. But in a Church they might be able to get away with it for a long time, if they surround themselves with a strong support group who protects their control over the podium.

What better group to control than a Christian group? The person who lusts for control over others has to learn how to act, learn the lingo and scripture, and be a good talker. He doesn't have to actually be a Christian himself. This man will propel himself towards the podium, the perceived place of authority and control over others, and by trickery and false doctrine deceive the hearts of the simple, 'the unsuspecting', those who, as the Religious Sociopath sees them, are disabled with tender consciences.

The best way to control the podium is to gain the wholehearted support and trust of current authorities, using them to develop even stronger positions of authority, and then get rid of them later on when the time is ripe, inserting themselves into their place of power.

"Worst of all, however, is the devastation wrought by the misuse of religious conviction for political ends. In truth, we cannot sharply enough attack those wretched crooks who would like to make religion an implement to perform political or rather business services for them," said

Adolf Hitler (Mein Kampf).   In hypocrisy, Adolf also quoted scripture, weaving it through his speeches. Religion has long been used to manipulate others to buy in.

Religious Sociopaths relate to true Christians as wolves relate to sheep. The Bible warns of this, wolves <u>will</u> come to divide and scatter sheep. The apostle Paul warned Christians in his day for three years, day and night with tears, knowing wolves would come, and leaders will rise up within their midst, twisting the truth to mislead so they can get their own following. The apostle Peter also warned of this happening.

It's not if, but when.

What better disguise for a wolf than as a shepherd of the flock? The sheep tend to think the pastor is there to herd them, guard them, take care of them, and minister to their needs as a shepherd does over his flock. The wolf knows this and conveys it, he exudes it, he radiates love and concern, and he projects humility, of wanting to help others, and preaches with charisma that as their Shepherd he needs to be submitted to, trusted, and pitied when others are against him. The Shepherd's costume is his disguise. He is a false shepherd, a deceitful worker, turning them away from the true Shepherd.

"Parallel to the training of the body a struggle against the poisoning of the soul must begin. Our whole public life today is like a hothouse for sexual ideas and simulations. Just look at the bill of fare served up in our movies, vaudeville and theaters, and you will hardly be able to deny that this is not the right kind of food, particularly for the youth... Theater, art, literature, cinema, press, posters, and window displays must be cleansed of all manifestations of our rotting world and placed in the service of a moral, political, and cultural idea," said Adolf

Hitler (Mein Kampf). And people who agreed and backed Adolf also bought into some other things Adolf believed.

A Religious *Sociopath is a highly intelligent person who is manipulative and cunning with superficial charm. Justifying his selfish motivations as permissible because "God wants me to do it for the good of the group," he does not recognize the rights of others. His motivation is sometimes revealed in the indecent ridicule of humiliating victims, justifying it by saying he needs to "keep order." If he can get away with the ridicule, he gains more control.

A Religious Sociopath enjoys the opportunities to intimidate and ridicule, relishing the fear followers have of him as a powerful leader with secret delight. When wrongdoing is committed by devoted followers, it is just another opportunity to humiliate them, but he needs to mask his secret pleasure of it.

Religious Sociopaths feel they are entitled to have their way, since it is their right to abuse people. Being extremely sophisticated liars, they decide to believe their own lies at will. They are extremely refined in their quickly thought out persuasive answers, knowing to whom, and when, they can lie and get away with it. Friends and other people are just opportunities to exploit and control. They do have friends for many years, but the friends all end up as victims because a Religious Sociopath does not truly love others. The love, friendliness, and compassion is feigned, it is actually hatred. There is no remorse for those who are hurt or crushed by them. They don't truly empathize, but have contempt, distain, and scorn for others, and for God. The sympathy is feigned.

When a Religious Sociopath has control over a group, he quickly claims a very dominant style of leadership, claiming his authority cannot be challenged or questioned, just as God can't be challenged or questioned. In time he comes to believe he is a powerful person who knows so much more than his followers. His followers simply have to obey; he is entitled to their obedience.

There is no personal respect for the lives of others, their dreams, their relationships. He is indifferent to the damage caused to others, and as needed, blames them for the carnage he, the Religious Sociopath, caused. He preaches and believes the Holy Spirit is using only him, and the Holy Spirit in practice cannot teach others, motivate others, or comfort them. Only the Religious Sociopath can teach and provide comfort; all others need to go through him or the leaders who follow him. He loves deception and is intimately familiar with mind control techniques.

A Religious Sociopath says what it takes to satisfy people for the moment, but does not follow through or deliver on promises. He conceals his deep contempt for sincere Christians as he politely helps them understand what he wants them to do. A Religious Sociopath is deeply insecure, having his own deep seated fears. He is highly intelligent and only puts himself in situations where his dictator type behavior will be tolerated or even admired. When he is caught he mildly apologizes to diffuse the concerns as he embezzles pity to escape accountability, and then tries to continue on, to cause more damage.

A Religious Sociopath seeks to look as normal as possible, fitting in with his lingo and clothing to deceive, charm, and disarm with his charisma. His true goal is to serve the seven abominations in his heart: A proud look, a lying tongue, hands that shed innocent blood, a heart that devises wicked plans, feet that are swift in running to evil, a false witness who speaks lies, and sowing discord within Christian groups. And he will accuse those who oppose him of what he is guilty of, to avoid detection. If he portrays this himself, he won't last. To get away with it, he needs a disguise, he needs to deceive. Shepherd's clothing is an excellent camouflage, a miry pit disguised as a watering hole.

A Religious Sociopath wants to control every aspect of his victim's lives for his own self gratification, concealing it within lengthy messages, scripture woven with truth and lies to conceal the true motivations. This brew of truth and perversion allows him to gain the confidence of sincere Christians who know the Bible, and then slowly deceive them with false doctrine over time.

Religious Sociopaths crave the admiration and approval of others, but at the same time hate those who they control with their deception. Their doctrine is motivated by their licentious lust for control, for the need to have even more naïve victims who will willingly do what they ask. They feel no remorse for the devastation in people's lives and relationships, just as Proverbs 26 states.

*Some of the Sociopath traits are based on the psychopathy checklists of Dr. Hervey M. Cleckley and Dr. Robert Hare. The Hare Psychopathy Checklist-Revised (PCL) is a psycho-diagnostic tool devised by Robert Hare to assess the main characteristics of psychopathic behavior, and based in part on Dr. Cleckley's work.

I know what you are doing, your labor with patience,
and that you can't bear those who are evil.
And you have tested those
who say they are apostles
and are not,
and have found them to be liars;
and you have persevered with patience, laboring
for My name's sake
and have not become weary.
Jesus – in Revelations 2

18·

Appealing to Diotrephes

It was a last ditch effort to try and fix a very damaging situation. Since the House of Chloe appealed to Paul, Rhett figured he could do the same.

He had nothing to lose, except valuable time he could be spending with his family, by sending out some e-mails to get Deo's followers to think. He and Sabrina had been shunned for a few months by nearly all the Richmond Assembly, James Stark and the California ministers had been marked, and everybody associating with them had been shunned. It was a last ditch effort to deflect the anticipated lifetime severance of hundreds of relationships. The short-term damage was bad enough.

Rhett's first appeal quoted Kit Jude, Bach Jude and Joshua Jude's grandfather from Riverside, California. Joshua's parents had moved from Riverside to Atascadero, California, where Joshua became the pastor. Bach Jude moved to Long Beach, also becoming the pastor.

Kit was a highly respected full time Riverside pastor in the 1950's. He led by the strength of his example. One

Sunday he ran out of gas going to the Assembly meeting. Lacking the money to buy more, he simply walked home. Meanwhile, the Riverside Assembly was waiting for him to get there and speak. But there was no Kit, so they drove to his home and found out he needed more money to live on. After fifty years young people who had grown up under his ministry helped form the backbone of the Assemblies in California, and maintained close knit relationships until Deo's split. Kit believed everybody should be studying the Bible, making things their own – not force others to obey, and to go to the Bible to resolve any disputes. The Riverside Assembly thrived, and bore fruit for many years from his ministry.

Kit's comments from a study he did:

> The Holy Spirit provides elders, or ministers, who are to be recognized as such when they have the qualifications of this office as described in I Tim. 3 and Titus 1. So-called "presiding elders" are not mentioned. The word "bishop" simply designates the office of an elder (Titus 1:5,7), not higher rank as commonly believed. <u>This error of rank, from early times has hurtfully divided an equal brotherhood, giving rise to a priestly order, or "clergy" over "laity" and finally, a "ruling clergy" over all.</u> Condemnation of this evil is found in Matt. 23:8-12 and I Pet. 5:3.

Rhett compared Kit Jude's comments with Deo Trophy's Orderly Following which made these points:

> Our duty is to obey those that God has placed in positions of authority. They are to be obeyed because that is pleasing to Him, not because the individual merits it. This is very important to understand and truly believe.
>
> But <u>God puts them in and takes them out</u>. Those under authority <u>do not</u> have the privilege <u>to install or remove</u>. They only have the privilege to recognize either what God

has done and is doing or that an individual has misunderstood what God wishes to do with them. <u>This is an essential difference between man-made "hire and fire" mechanisms of sectarianism and the divinely ordered Body of Christ.</u>

It is undeniably clear in the scriptures that God chooses to direct the lives of those that are His through the agency of men in positions of authority.

If we can obediently do what one in authority directs us to do, then the one in authority is responsible before God for what was done.

In contrast to Kit, Deo Trophy referred to himself as a "ruling elder," and functioned as an Apostle.

Rhett concluded:

Has the concept that there is 'laity' and that 'laity' has no duty or responsibility to do 'diligent inquiry', and to 'search the scriptures daily' to check up on, and if necessary stop submitting to 'clergy' ordained for religious service who have been guilty of unbiblical conduct headed us back to a 14th century religious system? Is this a Biblical system of leadership in the body of Christ?

Does Deo Trophy and those who espouse his theology as we have seen by their recent conduct truly believe that those who disagree should truly submit regardless? If so, then there would be no need to answer the many questions that have come up. There really is no right to be asking questions other than to clarify activity of ministry. Motivation and action should not be questioned. All that can be done is to find out why, regardless if it was Biblical (not question the rightness or wrongness, but merely clarify why it is right, trust and believe it, and submit to it). This is a major departure from how we have functioned in the past. Should the judgment against James and others just be submitted to, or should it be based on what facts and truth can be established?

Does "laity" really just have two options:

1) have the <u>privilege to recognize</u> what God has done and is doing; or
2) just <u>recognize we misunderstood</u> what God wishes?"

The only response was from leaders who already agreed with Rhett. Rhett sent out the same appeal five weeks later to every friend he had across the USA and Canada. To his lifetime friends in Texas, Oklahoma, California, Newfoundland, and Virginia, about two hundred households, including people he had gotten to know at regional camp gatherings, weddings and family vacations.

Again, the only responses came from some who already agreed with Rhett. Deo and Company ignored him. Archie Stark, James Stark's oldest son who was fully under Deo Trophy's influence, called Rhett to disapprove after the second e-mail but declined to put anything in writing.

Rhett's final appeal provided the witness statements and transcribed notes detailing Deo Trophy's greatly exaggerated August 3rd, 2008 account of James Stark's conduct during the February meeting of 2008. There was still no response, and Rhett finally gave up trying to help, praying that the Lord's will be done. There was nothing more Rhett could do to reach his friends, it was in the Lord's hands.

The ear cannot hear what the subconscious mind is not prepared to receive.

"I can't complain, Sabrina," said Rhett, walking around the trail through the woods on their property. They decided to give up the evening walks on their gravel road, there was too much emotional pain from seeing the neighbor kids playing together and waving from a distance.

"Complain about what?" said Sabrina.

"About us being shunned. We did it to Jarvo and Laura for a few years."

"Well, hopefully they change. If there is hope for us realizing Jarvo and Laura's shunning was wrong, then there is hope for them," said Sabrina.

"Yeah, but that deep seated fear of shunning and public ridicule causes them to buy into it intellectually. They truly believe they are right, to the core of their heart. It could be years."

"We can only pray and hope," said Sabrina, "but we need to find some friends for our children to play with. That's the main thing that worries me. How will our kids turn out after being shunned like this?"

In one of his three appeals Rhett referred to Diotrephes in Third John:

I wrote to the church; but Diotrephes, who loves to have the supremacy among them, does not accept what we say. For this reason, if I come, I will call attention to his deeds which he does, unjustly accusing us at great length with iniquitous words; and not satisfied with just this, he himself does not receive the brethren, and he forbids those who desire to, and puts them out of the church. Loved ones, do not imitate what is evil, but what is good. The one who does good is of God; the one who does evil has not seen God.

Diotrephes was probably a well respected man who controlled the podium of his day and was motivated, like the Pharisees, to have the approval of men rather than God. And Paul had warned for three years, with tears, about Diotrephes and others who he knew would rise up.

This motivation to get approval and control is in direct contrast to the desire to serve and minister, building relationships in love, to genuinely help others grow in their

Christian life and relationship with the Lord. All Christians should grow to the place where they can minister, and help others.

Diotrephes lorded it over a flock, self willed, and not easily entreated. He was intimidating. He prated against John, accusing him at length with empty confusing words. If he was able to put the brethren out of his church who opposed his preeminence, and shun any who associated with those brethren, then he would have free reign to do just about whatever he wanted to do. Diotrephes was practicing domino markings, first marking John the elder for avoidance, and then shun any who would not avoid John. Those who agreed to shun John the elder knew all too well the consequences of resisting Diotrephes.

Diotrephes needed to get rid of those who could refute his teachings with sound Biblical doctrine. He wanted to have his own doctrine and following. So he did a character assassination of those who opposed him Biblically, and probably accused John of character assassination. He had to do this, because he could not rely on the Bible to answer questions. Diotrephes had to be political and do some manipulative mudslinging.

Creating doubts and suspicions, Diotrephes created impressions in the minds of those he wanted to control. Diotrephes attacked, trying to force them to defend themselves. "How selfish, to defend your own integrity," he might have argued. "They are assassinating my character," Diotrephes cunningly could have accused the older brethren when they defended themselves of what he himself was guilty of.

Diotrephes likely told partial truths, mixing in perversions of the truth with it. That way he couldn't be pinned down, since he could claim he told the truth when the perversion was pointed out. Double tongued.

Diotrephes was an accuser of his brethren. He pressured his followers to break off contact with any who associated with the brethren who threatened his power and control, by putting fear into the hearts and subconscious of those left, who Diotrephes controlled and influenced. They had nowhere else to go, and leaving meant losing their friends. After those who opposed him were taken out, there was less need to defend poor doctrine. Just as King Saul didn't justly deal with the facts and truth, but rather relied on the strength and fear of his authority, or like Absalom who slowly stole hearts by secretly slandering his father King David to gain a large following over time.

Those who challenged his leadership were taken out permanently, with no further entreaties or invitations to come back to fellowship if there was a change, unless it was really clear they would never challenge him again and confess their sin of opposing him. Diotrephes would have demanded they apologize for slandering him but likely had no desire to have them back, ever.

True and godly church judgment is not too severe on a Christian, in case the one who sinned is swallowed up in too much sorrow. And not forgiving the one who sinned is a snare of Satan. True church discipline is intended for restoring true fellowship.

Actually, the sinner and accuser was Diotrephes. He couldn't be in control and gain the approval of followers when those who could challenge, refute, and expose his wickedness were in the audience. So Diotrephes painted godly leaders as being what he himself was guilty of, and simple people believed him without checking up on him. His unfruitful works of darkness might not have ever been exposed in his lifetime. When people who left or were kicked out found out how he worked, it was too late to fix the lies told of them, and of others from years earlier. The damage had been done.

The accusations could have been specific, or innuendos, just hinting at faults; or strong, lengthy accusations of weaknesses all Christians have, blown out of proportion, twisted and torqued with exaggerations. If there were any strong reactions to Diotrephes' lies, then Diotrephes could have accused the brethren of a lack of self control, maybe even accusing others of anger, bitterness, or being contentious. "John accuses me of saying wicked words. Does a man of God use ungracious words like that, is this loving? Where is the truth? John is accusing and condemning others! Is John exhibiting self control?"

What better way to get the attention off of himself, and avoid having the true sin detected, than to accuse others of what he was guilty, of dividing Christian families and the Church? The truth does divide; Jesus caused division but based on the truth and the Word of God. It is Satan who does not stand in the truth. Diotrephes strayed from the truth, and had to resort to poor political tactics to keep his authority.

Most of the true believers, after realizing what happened and were convicted, could no longer stay with a clean conscious towards God. They left on their own or were forced out by being marginalized, shunned, and marked. They likely suffered public rebuke or ridicule, leaving behind friends who were willing to put up with it.

Dead fish float downstream, only living fish can swim against the current. It is easy to cave under peer pressure. Shunning people for things which are not sin destroys relationships, but the Lord devises ways to restore them again.

Princes persecute me without a cause
But my heart stands in awe of Your word

I hate and abhor lying
But I love Your law

Great peace have those who love Your law
And nothing causes them to stumble
Lord, I hope for Your salvation
And I do Your commandments
My soul keeps Your testimonies
And I love them exceedingly
I keep Your precepts and Your testimonies
For all my ways are before You

- King David in Psalm 119 -

19·

Lyle Cooper

He needed to get away from the pain of losing all his best friends in the Dudley Franklin mass markings in California, so Rhett drove out to Virginia in the summer of 1986 to work for Archie and Byron Stark, hoping to save a little money for college while working shoulder to shoulder with Lyle Cooper.

Lyle was only eighteen then, and although Rhett was three years older, he was impressed by Lyle's commitment to serve the Lord. Maybe it was Lyle's commitment to the Assembly, rather than the Lord, but the Lord will have to be the judge of that. Idolatry is putting a person, group, or belief ahead of God, and that is a harsh accusation to casually make of anyone.

A lean, dark skinned go-getter, Lyle started his working life in his early teens as a stocker for a local grocery store in Fredericksburg. He earned his reputation for always being near the center of what was happening, including athletics in the Assemblies. Lyle attended every meeting, getting there early and staying late. He organized a canoe trip that summer in 1986 for the young people. Lyle paid for the twenty rented canoes out of his hard earned wages, asking to be reimbursed later, all before he was nineteen years old.

At the end of the summer, Rhett headed back to California to finish up college, and Lyle Cooper continued in construction for Archie and Byron Stark. But after a few years, things didn't work out between Lyle and Byron, so he moved from Fredericksburg to work in Charlottesville at a tire shop owned by an Assembly member. Lyle started his own shop several years later, and hired his Christian Assembly friends to help him.

Lyle was politely aggressive. He was a leader, naturally coming out on top with people respecting him while managing his company as well as the Charlottesville Assembly. His thirty-five minute messages and sincerity were a welcome change, and in stark contrast, to Deo Trophy's confusing multi-hour messages. His wrestling matches in his office with some workers earned him some respect too, except with his secretary, who had to work around the aftermath.

A few years before Deo toppled James Stark, Lyle set up a meeting to talk about his concerns for Deo's dishonesty. Unsatisfied he was honest, Lyle backed off. He still worked with Deo, but with caution.

Lyle managed Happy Hill for his father-in-law who had donated the property for Assembly regional gatherings and local Charlottesville meetings many years ago. Jarvo criticized Lyle Cooper for allowing Deo to speak there before he left, telling Lyle, "You could stop Deo from speaking there if you wanted to." Lyle never would admit his inner feelings about Deo, and tended to vaguely defend or ignore Deo's actions.

Lyle took it upon himself a year after Jarvo left, in 2006, to pay Jarvo a visit at his home. After an hour or so of talking, Jarvo told Lyle he would still not come back to their Assembly.

"Waall then," said Lyle with a smile, in a chummy customer service friendly voice, "I think I'm gonna need to mark yah, Jars."

Lyle's next stop was at Michie Hobkins, but Michie wouldn't come to the door, knowing the 'marking squad' was there. Michie was hoping to quietly fade out without being marked, and a leader showing up unexpectantly at his front door was not a good sign he could pull it off.

Lyle then unexpectantly announced a week later at the Friday night meeting of a 2006 Happy Hill weekend camp that Jarvo and Michie Hobkins (Calvin's brother) were marked, mainly for leaving the Charlottesville Christian Assembly, and for not avoiding Jar, who was marked.

Rhett himself had avoided Jarvo for his comments about Deo Trophy's dishonesty a year before that, so he fully agreed with Lyle at the time for formally marking Jarvo for shunning and avoidance.

About two years later, in 2008, Lyle felt a burden about Jarvo and Laura, and Michie and Rae Hobkins, that they should not have been marked and shunned. Lyle's main goal as a minister became trying to lift Jarvo, Michie Hobkins, and Jar's markings.

As the Deo vs. James Stark events unfolded, Lyle was in a quandary. His deep respect for James Stark's integrity compelled him to go against the other Virginia leaders, and Deo's exaggerations bothered him. But James was the one who was down, being defamed and publicly ridiculed. Going against Deo probably meant the same public execution would happen to Lyle. Lyle didn't want this; he was a respectable owner of a large business that was staffed by several people from the Assembly. Also, he was the leader of the Charlottesville Assembly, and felt some accountability to look out for them.

Deo Trophy did not control Lyle, but Deo did control Ernest Showden, Calvin Hobkins' brother-in-law.

Ernest fancied himself as a Bishop one day. He was legalistic and deeply loyal to Deo Trophy and his Orderly Following Doctrine. Lyle was concerned Deo might take him out and put Ernest in his place, and worried what might happen to the Charlottesville Assembly if Ernest became in charge. Ernest would be a much better choice for Deo, since Deo could control almost anything Ernest did. Ernest would go to Deo for his personal counseling, and Ernest's wife continued her counseling with Cary Murdock, but she slipped more and more into her depression. Cary had counseled her to cut off her relationships with her parents and siblings.

Lyle kept feeling rising guilt and remorse about marking Jarvo, Michie Hobkins, and Jar, and plotted how he could lift the markings in 2008. Any lifting of those markings was certainly not going to benefit Deo Trophy or his control, so Deo stoutly resisted it when Lyle brought it up. Jar had yet to drag himself up by his fingernails to the front and beg for forgiveness. And if he did, he might have the police called on him again.

Deo told Lyle they would first need to work through the James Stark situation in 2008 before discussing any markings being lifted in Charlottesville. After much deliberation, Lyle decided to "walk in James Stark's marking." Lyle justified it by saying he wanted to do things in the best interest of the Charlottesville Assembly. Some accused Lyle of being political and following orders from the headquarters of his Army Captain Deo Trophy, as a proper soldier should.

But Lyle still had Ernest to deal with. Deo was working closely with Ernest and leaving Lyle out of some selective leadership meetings. This bothered Lyle. His Assembly was the largest and he didn't even know about some of the meetings Deo was having with his loyal Bishops.

The Charlottesville Assembly was a foot out of joint as far as Deo was concerned. They weren't Orderly Following but rather wanted to sort out their own problems, rejecting his control over their local affairs.

So after Lyle finally said he would walk in James' marking, he asked Deo again about lifting the markings, and Deo told him they needed to address local Charlottesville leadership concerns next. So Lyle had a series of local Charlottesville leadership meetings in 2009 to see what others thought of him, Ernest, and four other local leaders who had worked through things in the past.

Ernest made a bad initial strategic mistake by sending a detailed copy of his laptop notes off to Deo Trophy and Cary Murdock within hours after the first leadership meeting. A lot of local people were distressed to have Ernest so quickly get Deo's outside authority involved with their local affairs.

Deo Trophy thought he ought to be controlling the Charlottesville Assembly, but couldn't as long as Lyle was their leader. Moreover, Lyle controlled the Happy Hill building, the place of the regional meetings, so losing Lyle would be a big blow to his cause. Many people might associate who was right with who was going to Happy Hill. Right now it was Deo Trophy and his followers who controlled regional meetings at Happy Hill, so it wouldn't be prudent to rush Lyle out the door.

Deo moved slowly and cautiously during the Charlottesville leadership meetings. He was sitting up front by Ernest during the first meeting. As it became more obvious Ernest was not "commended by his brethren," Deo slowly sat further away from Ernest, and ended up sitting in the back of the room. Deo said hardly anything. Some local people in Charlottesville asked Deo some questions about the past, and doubted Deo's integrity with his answers. It was different now. No longer was there a warm fuzzy crowd looking blankly at him and wondering what he wanted them to do next.

As the series of local Charlottesville Assembly leadership meetings ended, Lyle was well respected and commended by the people of his Assembly.

Lyle asked again if he could lift the markings of Jarvo, Michie, and Jar. By then it was August of 2009. Deo said to wait a few weeks until the countrywide regional Leadership Meeting in Texas, the weekend after the Labor Day camp retreat. Only Deo's league of Bishops would be at the meeting in Texas, along with Deo of course. Deo and Company had already marked or marginalized all of their opponents.

At the 2009 Labor Day retreat at Happy Hill, Deo Trophy and Cary Murdock spent the majority of the weekend giving public, strongly worded, multi-hour rebuking, and marginalizing messages directed towards Lyle Cooper, but they didn't name him. Deo and Cary lectured on keeping rank, sticking together, and condemning those who were independent in front of the three hundred and fifty person or so crowd attending the hours long meetings.

Rhett was in ignorant bliss of all this, he stayed at home that weekend and had a few friends over. They rode four wheelers in the field behind his house. Saturday afternoon Rhett checked the time on his cell phone, it was 2 pm. After spinning a few more doughnuts in a patch of dirt, he pondered if Deo Trophy might be speaking, and if so then the morning meeting was likely to end soon. There were some advantages of standing in the truth. Rhett heard of the long lectures at the Happy Hill "retreat" later. It was one of the reasons he had left. Bad company corrupts good habits.

Those long draining meetings that weekend put a tremendous amount of pressure on Lyle Cooper before his friends, family, and lifelong acquaintances.

At the end of the weekend, Deo told the audience, "There are a few leaders here who are just not getting it!" Not naming any names, but most people knew he was referring to Lyle Cooper and another local man, Noel.

Lyle was urged by Deo to go to the special countrywide Leadership Meeting in Texas the next weekend. It was reduced in size now that Deo controlled it. His Bishops would be there, along with a few others who hoped to be named Bishops by Deo someday, and under his thumb of control.

The next weekend in Texas, Deo and his followers surrounded the stressed out and emotionally drained Lyle with support, concern, and expressed love, explaining to Lyle he needed to be in unity for the sake of his brethren, and for the sake of the local Charlottesville Assembly's future. Lyle knew what the alternative would likely be.

Deo's manipulative mind control magic worked as the cumulative force of his influence surrounded Lyle during the weekend, so he bought in intellectually, somewhat. Lyle came back after the weekend, strongly supporting Deo, saying he finally clearly understood how James Stark was wrong. Lyle knew the consequences of not Orderly Following Deo and Company. His own dad, Charlie Cooper, had been dealt with when Lyle was a teenager.

Lyle's conversion disturbed many local Charlottesville people who did not like the change they saw in Lyle Cooper. Lyle's burden to lift Jarvo, Jar, and Michie's markings were put on the back burner.

Over the next several months in 2010, Lyle's conscience continued to be bothered again by Jar, Michie, and Jarvo's marking. Jar had been allowed to come back to meetings several months after the police were called and was basically behaving. Many local people thought Jar, Michie, and Jarvo's marking should be lifted, it just wasn't Biblical. Lyle thought so too, but Deo would not give his consent or endorsement, and since Lyle wanted Deo's stamp of approval, he didn't do it. Lyle knew the consequences of disobedience. Deo wouldn't stop short of marking several ministers for defying his authority.

Lyle even called Jarvo once, saying he wanted to have a meeting with Jarvo and lift the marking.

Jarvo responded, "Lyle, it's good to hear you realize your mistake in marking me."

Lyle responded, "Well, we changed our doctrine on markings and now we think you shouldn't be marked."

Jarvo still wasn't unmarked. Later, Lyle did call and apologize to Jarvo, after an older man talked to Lyle, saying, "What we did to Jarvo was sin, Jarvo did nothing to deserve a marking! It's wrong to say we just changed our minds."

A few months before Jar was kicked off of Happy Hill permanently, he went uninvited into a informal leadership meeting in the kitchen there, and said he was sorry about his conduct on the stage a few years earlier, of evasively jumping off and on the stage to avoid Ernest, and of standing by Lyle Cooper when Lyle was leading the singing to drown out anything Jar might say.

The Charlottesville people were happy to hear Jar's apology and talked of unmarking him.

One local person told Jar, "We would like to talk to you more about this and get your marking lifted."

Jar responded, "I don't want my mahking lifted."

The person said, "Yes you do Jar! You DO want your marking lifted!"

Jar thought about this for a bit, "Yes, I DO want to have my mahking lifted. Then I could stand at the front door and wahrn every new couple who comes here that their family may get split up and divided yeahrs from now if they keep coming here!"

Jar was referring to himself and what had happened with his grown children. When Jar's family was young, he had walked into the doors of Happy Hill with his young family, and his family had been ripped apart years later.

Some of the Charlottesville people were not pleased with Jar's comment, and quickly signed a letter stating Jar should remain marked.

The leadership in Virginia were hiding any problems and their concerns with Deo Trophy from their "flocks."

Rhett learned Lyle was also one who had concerns about Deo's exaggeration problem for years. In May of 2010, Rhett sent an e-mail to Lyle Cooper, quoting an old e-mail Lyle had sent James Stark in which Lyle said there was:

> concern I and others shared regarding Deo overstating a point when trying to make a point.....when one overstates.....at times it can be not accurate... therefore possibly giving a false or untrue representation of the subject at hand.

Rhett's e-mail ended with:

> It appears to me you had some concerns about Deo's
> honesty a few years ago. This is based in part on some
> conversations I had with you also. Obviously something
> has changed for you, and you currently feel Deo is
> honest.
>
> Could you tell me what it was that convinced you that
> you were wrong about Deo Trophy's exaggerating to the
> point of not telling the truth anymore?

Lyle never responded. Rhett suspected Lyle still had concerns about Deo's honesty and was just compromising.

There were a lot of people who were concerned about Deo's honesty, but he had never been caught in cold blooded dishonesty, always leaving a way out for himself by mixing in some truth. It was in looking at his pattern over time that told the story of his true motivations. Over a few hours time Deo gave the truth, and then perverted it, then he referred back to the truth, and finished by confirming his perversion of the truth. So those on his side argued he gave the truth, but others pointed to his perversion of the truth. The confusion resulting from Deo's formidable debating tactics made it very difficult for Lyle to try and deal with Deo's problem. Lyle was a straight forward likeable kind of guy. Deo was double-tongued and defended himself by also telling the truth in confusing multi-hour lectures, both private and public.

However, the 2009 local Fredericksburg leadership meeting Calvin Hobkins privately recorded, without Deo knowing it, gave concrete evidence of dishonesty.

Luke Alastair from Long Beach, California listened to the recording a few times, and had exchanged a few e-mails with Deo, proving a few fairly large lies with the recording. Rhett knew hardly anybody had gotten the copies of Luke's e-mails, including Deo's response with even more fabrications. Things were closing in on him, so Deo soon marked the California leaders, leaving them with no credibility. The Virginia leaders had no interest in doing anything about Deo's problem.

Deo's underlined comments in the letter were complete lies to make himself look good for first severely condemning the California leaders as independent heretics, then submitting to these same California leaders within a single month, in January of 2009.

The California men had contested every false statement Byron made during the end of January 2009 meeting, and had not apologized. Deo was lying afterwards, back in his home Assembly, to make himself look good for submitting to the California leaders by claiming they had done a lot of apologizing. He also forbid his local followers in Fredericksburg to confirm what he said, but just trust him. So after getting no response, Rhett sent another e-mail to Lyle, quoting Luke Alastair's first e-mail to Deo proving Deo's dishonesty.

To: Lyle Cooper From: Rhett Stuart
Date: Sat, May 22, 2010 at 11:13 AM
Subject: Where do you want to be in your relationship with the Lord 5 years from now?

Lyle,

I am sending this again in case you overlooked my first e-mail. James Stark has told me Archie Stark also had concerns for years about Deo being dishonest, twisting things around. James had told Archie "That is just the way Deo sees it", but now wishes Archie had stuck to his guns. I asked Archie about it late summer of 2009, when he called me. Archie told me "That is just the way Deo sees it." I heard Sean Lane in Fredericksburg has had the same concerns over the years, but now is supporting Deo Trophy.

Here is a document in which Deo fabricates several lies. If you want more details I can give them to you.

This big lie is open and obvious, Lyle!

Deo accused the California leaders behind their backs, publicly in his area, of the California leaders using deception to mislead, they lied when questioned, and if Deo were to tell them some of the things these brethren were saying they would be appalled!

Yet these Fredericksburg people were uninformed, kept in the dark by Deo, and were told not to call any of the California leaders to get their side of it!

Here is an excerpt from the recording in which Deo tries to justify his slander, and then submitting to these same leaders within a month to allow James back in ministry:

> Deo responded: Let me answer that statement - There have been lots of things done, lots of things witnessed, lots of things addressed, lots of acknowledgments, apologies, etc, so there has been a long list of things that have been going on and so at any instance in time when you report out where things are at that instance in time, that's an instance in time and so subsequent to that there may be apologies made and so you address that, you accept that, there may be asking forgiveness, you accept that and you move on and try to recover from that. There has been a lot of that done.

> Someone then asked: Well we do not hear that – we see the battle lines drawn.

> Deo responds: So the question would be one if you don't hear all that do you need all that? Do you want to hear all that?

> The person continued: Well if I'm left with an impression that these brethren are all carnal, I mean that's not for me, I'm not a minister, I'm not a leader, but if I'm left with that impression by Deo who

ministers, what am I to do with it? That's the question... How much confidence should I have in those California leaders if they come out here? With my family? How to interact with them. There is suspicion left in my mind.

Deo responds: Each of us need to realize that the situation we are in and have been in is unprecedented and the struggle that has been going on has been unprecedented and it has involved leadership across the board in all assemblies and so everything that is said and every person that is named in a sense - it is an extremely delicate matter...

Lyle, when Deo said "They are not strong in adversity – they can't take the pressure so they are caving in, and they can't keep rank," it is because the California leaders started to see through Deo's dishonesty. So they are accused of flip flopping and instability when they find out they have been deceived by Deo. "Keeping rank" means "Going along with Deo."

I sent you a document called "Mind Control" on April 18th, 2009 warning you of some techniques Deo uses to manipulate people. I think the September 2009 camp, in which you and Noel (from what I have heard) had some direct pressure put on you both publicly, without naming your names, was a manipulation tactic. Deo knew the following weekend you would be stressed out, and be surrounded by all of his Bishops. Swaying your mind after a time of stress, and surrounding you with his loyal followers is a cliché in mind control techniques. Then, in my opinion, you have stuck to that subconscious decision James Stark was the problem.

James has problems, but he is not the problem. The accuser Deo Trophy is the problem. Are your problems worse or better after James was marked and left the scene there in Charlottesville?

Deo has turned grown children against their parents, and there is little in my mind to doubt the same could happen to you with your son.

We are happy Lyle. Better a dinner of herbs than a feast with strife. Life goes on, and people heal. This letter is an attempt to help you. If there is something you know of that I don't, I certainly would like to hear about it.

    Love in Christ,   Rhett Stuart

Lyle never responded. Lyle put a few calls out to the leaders in California within a week of Rhett's e-mail, asking if they wanted to meet again. They all answered yes, they would be glad to, but nothing changed.

The Charlottesville Assembly continued to fragment.

Lyle kept on attempting to build on his foundation of Christ with placation of humans. Lyle justified his compromise with Deo's leadership by explaining that after Naaman was healed of leprosy he wanted the Lord to pardon him for bowing with his master in the temple of Rimmon.

But Elisha had let Naaman depart, telling him, "Go in peace." ☺

And He gave pastors and teachers
to equip the saints for the work of ministry -
to edify the body of Christ,
until we all come to the unity of the faith and of the
knowledge of the Son of God, to a perfect man,
to the image of Christ;
so we should no longer be children,
tossed all around and carried about with every wind of
doctrine and trickery of men, in the cunning craftiness of
deceitful plotting,
but,
speaking the truth in love,
may grow up in all things into Him who is the head — Christ

- Paul, an apostle of Jesus Christ by the will of God -
(paraphrased from Ephesians 4)

20·

Bill Baker

Hoping to straighten out the Charlottesville Assembly, Bill Baker came to speak at a regional meeting at Happy Hill in April of 2010. He was sure to have a warm reception since there were many loyal Orderly Followers.

Bill was a respected older man who could easily be regarded by the casual observer as an austere retired government clerk. Bill's father was the optometrist who had met up with Maurice Johnson's newly formed group in Southern California in the 1930's, helping support him financially during hard times.

Bill grew up going to Maurice Johnson's street preaching in downtown Los Angeles, and passing out Bible tracts along with James Stark and Mycroft Stuart. As Bill got older, he became convinced passing out Bible tracts was a very good thing, passing out thousands over his lifetime, mostly Spanish ones.

Since Bill and his wife couldn't have children, they moved from their comfortable home in a nice quiet area of

Southern California to Mexico City, so they could evangelize and learn Spanish.

Bill vehemently opposed 'Manmade Religion'. His intense efforts ended up developing a large informal network of Christians in rural areas of Mexico. Bill taught them to think for themselves, and not just go along with religious leaders. He heavily promoted studying their Bibles for themselves.

For thirty years Bill made a weekly circuit in his van, spending the days handing out his Bible tracts, and evenings traveling to rural homes, getting about five hours of sleep every night. Some homes had no electricity and dirt floors. Extreme poverty was prevalent.

At one point, Bill was robbed at gunpoint while trapped in a hi-jacked taxi. Bill attempted to convert the robbers to Christianity. The robbers finally gave up and fled. The local television station caught wind of it and thought it would make a good story. During the television interview, Bill took the opportunity to try and lead the television crew and their Mexico City audience to Christ.

Talking to Bill about doctrine was like talking to a computer with a button for each subject. Asking him a question about the Bible would launch Bill into a very predictable response. For the next five, ten, or twenty minutes, he expounded on the subject as if somebody had pushed the play button. His answers hadn't varied in the thirty years Rhett knew him. Bill was programmed.

His Bible had narrow papers taped in with his studies, telling him when he was younger where to go next in his Bible, and what to say. As he got older, he memorized some of the papers and could successfully recite the verses and arguments from memory.

When the discussion didn't go Bill's way, or it didn't fit into his memorized canned speech, Bill just shut it off with an abrupt comment. It was difficult to have interactive discussions with him.

Bill retired to Texas, mainly for his health, to get out of the bad air in Mexico City. When the James Stark situation came up, Bill was eventually persuaded by Byron Stark, who controlled the large four hundred person Texas Assembly. Bill was convinced Deo, Byron, and Temple were the prosecuting attorneys, judges, jury, parole officers, and witnesses, so there was nothing more to consider, since they were also credible ministers. Bill readily signed onto all the letters Deo and Byron asked him to. He trusted them completely.

Ironically, Bill was deceived by Deo's manmade Orderly Following system, and consequently strongly supported Deo. He didn't practice what he had preached for so many years in Mexico.

Bill was such a stout defender of Deo and his Orderly Following that he requested several families of Mexican ancestry to leave the Southern California Assembly because of Tim Mervin's marking by Deo and Company. The families obeyed Bill out of respect for his ministry in Mexico. Bill was the one who remembered their birthdays.

So Bill decided to do a little tour of the country in the Assemblies, after Tim Mervin and the other California leaders were marked, to give his own version of Orderly Following.

As Bill made his way up to the stage at Happy Hill, Jar sat comfortably against the back wall with his wife Mamie. Jar was still marked but allowed to come back if he behaved himself and obeyed his gag order. Jar basically conformed, with the exception of an occasional thumbs-up.

Jar listened closely as Bill spoke on Christians being soldiers in the Lord's Army and the Christian leaders were like Army sergeants. He spoke of how the Assemblies were a viable representation of the Body of Christ. Bill began to expound on his experience in the Army, making appropriate analogies that Jar knew reflected well on Deo Trophy's Orderly Following.

Bill said, "When I was in the Army boot camp, I knew a man there who could not keep rank and it was pathetic! The man could not follow orders, even while marching! He just kept getting mixed up! He just lacked the ability to follow simple orders and had to leave the Army! As Christians, we need to keep rank, stick together, and obey our leader's orders without challenging!"

Bill's voice beat out an authoritative tempo, his thick glasses expanding his eyes as he stoically turned his head slowly from side to side, peering back at the audience. In automation, he built up his point with obvious zeal and intensity, his rapid distinctly pronounced words coming with the consistency of a metronome.

At the very peak of Bill's crescendo of programmed human logic, Jar stood up in the back of the large 350 person auditorium, and asked in a polite, almost discrete, but stressed voice - "Can I aask a question?"

Bill was caught off guard, and being out of the area, was unsure how to respond. He stammered, "What was the question? What was the question?" and then suspecting it was Jar, asked, "Who is that? Who Who Who is that?"

Bill's recorder was jammed by the perfect timing of Jar's perforatingly disruptive question.

Since Bill was from Texas, and not quite sure what to do in Virginia, he hesitated. Jar didn't accept the cordless mic from the young man who offered it out of concern it would be turned off by the sound tech, he would just ask his question loudly under his own amplification. All of Deo's leaders were caught off guard and kept quiet.

The suspense rose as the tense audience waited with interest, wondering what consequences would befall Jar afterwards this time. Jar took Bill's silence as permission and asked, "Did the maan you spoke of who couldn't keep rank, get an honorable or a dishonorable dischahrge?"

Bill said, "I'm not sure what happened to the man, but as it relates to the Church, it would surely be a dishonorable discharge!"

After the meeting, Jar visited outside for a few minutes with an old friend who dared do it, then walked to the parking lot with his wife Mamie to leave. Lyle Cooper came out, upset, and told Jar: "Look me in the eye, I'm a man! Leave this property and don't come back!"

Jar and his wife left.

Rhett concluded after he saw the video that Jar's question had about the same effect as throwing a pipe wrench into a smoothly ticking grandfather clock. But most people probably just turned off their listening minds when they heard it was Jar again.

Jar told Rhett after they watched it together, "I kneuw something squirrely was going on with what Bill was saying, but that was the only question I could think of to ask him aat the tiime. Deo had claimed I had mental issues, and as an incompetent brother I needed to be mahrked."

Jar thought Lyle might have a hard time keeping him out legally, sizing up the legal aspect of this being a non-profit organization. He explained to a group of family and friends: "I love those people there, I want go back to help them."

However, after some urging by his children and friends, Jar decided to stop going back to Happy Hill for awhile. Jar said it helped to understand other's perception of him when Rhett's wife Sabrina informed him: "People are just not listening to you anymore, it's going against you! They just think you're being divisive!"

Jar now had all his children back with him.

Blessed is everyone who fears the Lord
Who walks in His ways
Your wife shall be like a fruitful vine
In the very heart of your house
Your children like olive plants
All around your table
Behold, thus shall the man be blessed
Who fears the Lord

- Solomon, from Psalms 128 -

21·

The Recovery

The truth began to dawn on Rhett, as the sun rises and casts its light over the dark earth in the early morning. A few months after leaving, Rhett realized how little he really knew and thought, *truly I reeked of arrogance.*

Agur said in Proverbs 30:

> Surely I am more stupid than anyone else, and I do not even have the understanding of a man. I did not learn wisdom, nor know much about the Lord.

Agur was smart enough to be quoted in Proverbs and he called himself stupid? With humility is wisdom.

Rhett began to realize how little he really knew of other Christians and how they fellowshipped. There are problems wherever there are other human, that's just the way it is in this life, even if they are Christians.

Now there was no more busy schedule, no packs of kids for his children to run around with, just their family and a few friends on Sunday to hang out with. It was a big change. Their friends who also left were in the same boat, and with the help of the Great Comforter, the indomitable

Holy Spirit, they all helped each other in their own feeble way. The Lord began to heal their hearts and minds, and they began to get their own identities back.

Some women were hit hard. There was nothing really left, no reason to live. Deep depression, haunting memories and nightmares, doubting their salvation for a time as valued relationships evaporated into thin air; wondering if their beliefs in the Bible really were their own faith, or of Deo Trophy and the group he controlled. One woman's repetitious visualizations of wanting to cast herself down in front of a car so it could run over her head was very real, sickening, and self-tormenting.

It was actually the leaders, as it turned out, that worked the controls of all those close relationships. Rhett and Sabrina didn't have the power to keep their own friendships once they left, and neither did their friends. The friendships were based on an unwritten membership, regular attendance, and their obedience to the leader's judgments, subject to termination by the leaders upon exiting the Assemblies per Matthew 18. But the leaders denied such a shunning system was in place.

Shunnings are a terrible thing, especially when they are done by an isolated and exclusive group. It subconsciously keeps people from wanting to leave, because, when they leave, they lose all the people they really knew. The vanishing relationships are replaced by black depression. Starting new relationships is difficult and takes time. It is like coming out of a divorce mid-life. All the other families in the world have their friends and lives to live. Nobody else is really that interested in starting new relationships when they already have friendships for their families.

It takes years to build relationships, and starting over is not easy, and slow. The Assemblies had been at the core of their existence, dominating their everyday life, defining who they were and what they stood for. What they had valued most highly, their relationships with others, was turned against them, used on them as an example to leverage obedience with those who remained, so those who remained would fear leaving and consequently put up with unbiblical leaders; being held hostage by their own close relationships and family members.

God is stronger than anything else, and nothing can separate us from God's love. Rhett and Sabrina knew that. God also gave humans feelings, emotions, and those take time to work through and heal. God is there to help get people through their trials, and the Holy Spirit is there to comfort, especially when minds have been devastated in the ruins of despair and rejection. Believing in God creates again a pure heart and good conscience toward God in sincere faith.

Feelings of lost time wasted in long useless sermons, time that should have been given to their children, time invested in friendships now destroyed, the bridges burned down to the riverbanks in the shunnings. Rhett had always been a long range thinker and planner. Now there was really nothing to plan for. It was wrong to hate those who were motivated by their own selfish gratifications of coveting leadership and approval.

There were brief times of happiness, then plunges back into depression, and gloomy speculations of what their friends might decide, if they would change their minds about following Deo; some doubting their salvation for a short time since their Christian life had been blended and mixed with standards of dress and lifestyle which had intimately entwined themselves into their lives for so many years.

It was wrong to be bitter. Bitterness would just damage them personally and do nothing to help. Rhett discovered prayer was the key. When he thought of those who had wronged him he immediately prayed for them and then dismissed them from his mind. This habit gave much needed relief.

Having doubts about leaving, questioning again and again if they had left for valid reasons, haunted Rhett and his friends. Some were tormented by nightmares almost every night that they were back in the Assembly, seeing somebody they loved shun them and leave, or sometimes sitting in the back and suffering public ridicule.

There was no turning back. They might gain the small credit of repentance and confession, and then be subjected to being called out as weaker brothers, treated as lepers, and likely be despised by their children and maybe even their wives, as time went on. They would lose control over their families, probably quickly, by going back to a tyrannical leadership and live with a conscience tormented by a bad decision.

Rhett's five year old daughter had regularly scheduled nightmares that people were going to get her. Why would an otherwise well adjusted smart little girl who was loved, and loved her family, have these? One night Sabrina went in to comfort her. She was shaking, and groggily asked Sabrina, "Was my dream fiction or nonfiction?"

There were regrets of influencing others to stay in the past, some who were still in the Assemblies. There was shame in condemning those who had left in the last few years who had seen the same problems. There was distrust for other groups, and what might be the inner motivations of religious leaders, with good reason. It was sometimes hard to relate to other Christians. Some could relate because they had also come out of abusive leadership churches, but for many it was like observing Rhett and Sabrina's Martian Life through a thick opaque glass.

"I'm thinking about going to a local community church and check it out," said Calvin on a Sunday afternoon chat.

"Well, I'll try and remember to pray for you there."

"It just feels so wrong after all that indoctrination about going to some other group, especially one that has a name on the building," said Calvin.

"Yeah, I know the feeling. But just think of what you've been a part of, Calvin. Markings, shunnings, grown adults being shunned by their own married children and grandchildren, godly leaders being publically slandered behind their backs, perverted truth given from up front, the Orderly Following false doctrine, an alternative gospel," said Rhett, "going to a place with a name on the building pales in comparison!"

"Well, religious people are everywhere," said Calvin, "but I am looking forward to meeting some new Christians who genuinely love the Lord. I think the group we left was actually more sectarian from other Christians than any Christian organization I can think of."

"I agree. Worldly can be smoking dope and watching bad movies, or Worldly can be religious, you know, like the Pharisees or the self-righteous older son who looked down on his prodigal brother. What's that verse, relying on the basic principles of the world, do not touch, do not taste?"

Calvin instantly knew the verse, "It's the last part of Colossians 2. Here, read it," he said, pulling out his Bible.

"Therefore, if you died with Christ from the basic principles of the world, why, as though living in the world, do you subject yourselves to regulations — "Do not touch, do not taste, do not handle," which all concern things which perish with the using, according to the commandments and doctrines of men? These things indeed have an appearance of wisdom in self-imposed religion, false humility, and neglect of the body, but are of NO value against the indulgence of the flesh," read Rhett.

"The rules of religion don't sustain us," said Calvin.

"Christ sustains us!"

"Right. Hey, did I tell you a man at my work's warehouse might have accepted the Lord?" said Calvin.

It was hard to keep track of the people Calvin had told about his Savior.

Getting counsel from Mycroft for his work was different than from Deo, who had forbidden Calvin to get counsel from anybody except himself regarding Calvin's employment. Mycroft's extensive sales manager experience was a boon to Calvin's career.

Calvin e-mailed Mycroft:

Hello Commander Stuart,

I hope this finds you doing well, and hoping that your sweet wife is getting around better.

Here is the latest updated plan. Did well in some areas, fell down in others, but am slowly slugging along to new heights of mediocrity.

As always, very grateful for you help and the love you have shown me and my family!

Calvin Hobkins

Hi Calvin,

Congrats and a tip of the hat for being on pace ytd.
CONSIDERABLY BETTER THAN A POKE IN THE
EYE WITH A SHARP STICK.

Here's an idea you may want to consider: Your farm
contact record indicates about four calls per month. What
do you think about raising this to four calls per week?
This way each prospect receives a contact every two
months. I don't know if this would work, but it may be
something you'd want to evaluate considering the amount
of time available to you.

The increased farm contact would give you greater odds
of going over plan for the year and possibly provide
scintillating, oscillating sensations of ecstasy flowing up
and down the grey matter of your spinal cord and medulla
oblongata.

All kidding aside Calvin, nice going for a solid first half.
Let me know if you'd like to discuss.

Your Christian brother,
Commander Mycroft

The Lord created in all people the ability to love and
miss loved ones, and there is pain God provided for in
separation. It wouldn't be love if there was no pain in
separation. Gradually, their pain healed into scars. After
fourteen months, Sabrina began to be glad they left, and
wish they had done it sooner. Rhett and Sabrina read
regularly now with their family, a chapter a night. The
whisperings of the Holy Spirit could be clearly heard.

Rhett could now see the Holy Spirit was being resisted
when he was just following the persuasive dictates of
human wisdom, humans with charisma who claimed God
had revealed to them what their flock should do, whose
mind Satan had control of, and whom the Holy Spirit
wanted involved. There was no thick shell of living his life

334 The Bishop Maker

by a set of rules, by obtuse Christian mechanicalization. Christians tend to evaluate their spiritual life by how closely they follow those rules. Christian Automation had separated him from the Lord.

"You know Sabrina, as we walk in faith and obedience to God's word, then the Holy Spirit comforts and teaches us," Rhett said on one of their evening walks around the property.

"I'd like to have regular teachings from a minister, I miss that," said Sabrina, "but remember what Deo said of women, of how every woman has an overwhelming urge to teach and have authority over a man. How all problems always start with a woman who is trying to tell her husband something she is concerned with, which makes problems go on and on, and then husbands who listen to their wives get bitter with them, and then the wives think their husbands are unspiritual?"

"Yeah, he was exaggerating, wasn't he? He probably gave a disclaimer in the beginning but we just remembered his hour or so of exaggerations. I think a whole lot of problems start with men."

"That really impacted me. I haven't said things a lot of times to you because of that, I didn't want to interfere and be a big problem," said Sabrina.

"Well, feel free to talk to me about your concerns!"

Rhett's eyes were opened little by little on past errors, and what he should do in the future. Before, he had felt distant from the Lord, since the Holy Spirit was being resisted. Now, Rhett and Sabrina felt closer to the Lord as they walked consistent with God's word. God was a comfort and a refuge, rather than a set of rules leaders required obedience to, leaders with an insatiable appetite for human approval.

For eight years Rhett conducted his life trying to please Cary Murdock and follow his advice with lifestyle and the busy Assembly schedule. Sometimes leaving his sick children with his wife as he headed off to a meeting until late at night. In spite of this loyal obedience to Cary, Cary didn't make any effort to contact Rhett after he left. Rhett even asked Cary to meet with him. Cary said he would get back to him when it worked out, but he never called.

Rhett thought, *Now I know how much Cary cares for people. After living my life thinking I needed to follow Cary to follow Christ, Cary doesn't even want to meet with me, or care enough to call to see how I am doing, after eight years of sitting under his ministry and doing what he told me to do.*

Rhett thought he was a strong Christian before, having 'the truth' that hardly anybody else did, but he was actually weak. Now Rhett saw himself for the arrogant fool he was. It wasn't strength; it was just complacently following the leader. The Lord was cut out of the process.

Rhett really felt he was serving the Lord when he went to the Assemblies. It wasn't intentional, a hidden fault, something he couldn't see before. Now the faults were open and obvious; like a painful raw wound that was slowly healing.

They got the kids enrolled in a home school co-op in Charlottesville, and that greatly helped as they began to make new friends. But Sabrina worried about her children losing their close friendships. Would they ever have close friends again?

Pants for women had been banned; it was a cardinal sin to wear them. If any woman had showed up to an Assembly meeting in them she would have caused quite a scandal. Now, Rhett could see the verses on women's modesty were intended to encourage women to not attract attention, to be modest, and not be extravagant. Like a modest income, or a modest house, or modestly concealing.

Time does change clothing standards, and Rhett became fully convinced in his own mind it was okay for women to wear modest pants in 2010 in America. Wearing dresses at times attracted much more attention in public than pants would have.

He wrote a study and sent it out to several friends for their input and advice, then encouraged Sabrina and his daughters to start wearing pants at times.

After leaving the Richmond Assembly, when Rhett saw a group of women wearing dresses, he found himself automatically thinking they were probably just conforming to a controlling leader, and were just a testimony to their own controlling group. What other reason would all those people in unity choose dated clothing styles? The oddness of it can appeal to the carnal nature, the elevated feeling of being persecuted for Christ's sake adds to the close knit relationships within as it creates an even more adverse relationship with Christians outside their group. But their testimony is for their own group and leaders.

It had been promoted at times in the Assemblies for women to dress unattractively, a few people referred to it as — 'The Ugliness Doctrine'.

It was traumatic for Sabrina. Was it really okay? What would their neighbors think? Her first trial run in pants was a discreet moonlit walk with her family late Sunday night down their snow covered gravel road they shared with their neighbors.

A family who had been friends, and had quickly shunned them (the same women who refused to meet Sabrina to receive a birthday gift), was leaving a neighbor's home at the same time. Their headlights brightly illuminated Rhett and Sabrina as they made their way across the ice in front of the van. It was instant advertisement for Sabrina's wearing pants; they would likely be gossiped about and marginalized for 'going back to the world so quickly'.

After four months of wearing pants, Sabrina was upset she hadn't been able to wear them for thirty-seven years of her life. Pants are much warmer than dresses in the winter. Trying to control others beyond what is Biblical is the doctrine of demons. It would be wrong to put a stumbling block out for other Christians, but women's modest pants were not a stumbling block in Rhett's mind in 2010.

Of the five older couples in Fredericksburg who left, not one of the adults left for the same reason. Some left due to seeing the dishonesty with the James Stark situation. Some left because of recordings being destroyed, and it opened their eyes. Some got caught in Deo's crosshairs, challenging his authority over some issue they stumbled across and questioned Deo on. One man wondered why Deo had said nothing publicly about Deo's son's immoral behavior after saying he would give a public report on it. The man was finally intimidated into leaving. Some realized there was doctrinal error being preached. Some discovered a dark secret of dishonesty, or manipulation, or coercion.

Leaving was the first step. But leaving didn't get Deo Trophy and the Assemblies out of them, it was still embedded. All areas of their lives and minds had been deeply entrenched and affected by Deo's doctrine. Since most of them believed it would be wrong to get professional help or Christian counseling, they went to each other, to God in prayer, and to their spouses for help. Having others who can relate, share joy, despair, frustrations, all helped Rhett and his friends. How could they know what they believed now was right, if they had been so deceived and wrong before? Rhett developed a large appetite for reading God's word, to prove all things, to test the spirits and see what was true, and hold fast to what is good. Jesus is the only foundation.

They had known deep down something was wrong for awhile. The healing had actually started before they left. There were concerns about what was happening, thinking some things were wrong, but quickly dispelling those thoughts in guilt. It was okay now to critique, to discuss scripture honestly, and to be real in what they believed and openly talk to others. The ever present threat of public and private humiliation was gone, but the fear and cautiousness of speaking against a leader's obvious wrongdoing was still engraved in their psychic.

Over the first several months, Rhett and his friends told the same stories and concerns to each other until they grew tired of it. But as time went on, so did the healing, and gradually they talked less and less of it. The talking helped them to heal, for the deceiving spirits and poison to be cleansed from their minds, for reaffirming what was true, good and wholesome. It would have been wrong to just be quiet and go on. The stories and sharing had to be spoken aloud, for healing.

As a sexually abused person releases painful memories with trusted people, so spiritually abused people need to download their memories, thoughts, and fears with trusted friends. Speaking aloud about the hurt, the pain, the rejection, the good memories and the bad, are all part of the healing.

Like water washing contamination out of clothing, so was the Bible studying and rehashing with friends. Slowly, the contamination was washed out, no longer was it on the forethought of Rhett and Sabrina's minds. The pain slowly and painfully eased out. Like climbing a mountain one step at a time, each conversation, each prayer, each Bible reading, each mediation were all stepping stones in the recovery.

It was very helpful for Calvin Hobkins to gain an understanding of how mind control was used on him. Cognitive Dissonance became part of his regular vocabulary. Knowing the techniques made him less fearful of being deceived again. Being able to avoid enslavement was a big relief to his mind. Knowing he wasn't going crazy, that he could think clearly and had been confused intentionally was very comforting. No more would he get ensnared under a human's selfish manipulative control, but rather have the Word of God guard and establish him.

As Calvin's old cheerful personality emerged he felt invigorated and enthusiastic about life, sharing his God with others. He identified with Jesus and not with a group, as he cast all his cares on Him.

Timidly reaching out and learning there were good Christian help books and studies made by Christians who were not part of the Assemblies, that others had the Holy Spirit who guides all Christians in truth, was an eye opener and a help.

It was still difficult coming home after a long family vacation. The pain of rejection and lost friendships hit like a twelve gauge blast to his chest. His kids would cry, and Sabrina grieved for her children's pain, and her own. The kids didn't like to hear Christian kid's songs that reminded them of being in the Assembly, so they got new CDs with new Christian songs to listen to. But places they had gone to, and the good times they had with the Richmond Assembly, brought back painful memories.

At first Rhett wanted to recreate a new Virginian style Assembly and go on as before. But after a few months he realized this would be wrong. It would just recreate what they had left. The Lord had something planned for them, Rhett wasn't sure yet what it was, he just had to be patient and see where the Lord led them. The Lord will never leave or forsake us. The Holy Spirit works independently of human wisdom, working individually in Christian's lives in all things as He wills and pleases. The Holy Spirit isn't from the wisdom of man but is like the unseen wind blowing where it wishes, just making a sound as it comes from some unknown place to another.

When the fear of leaving is removed from a group held together by that fear, then that group likely won't stay together after that fear is removed. Jesus said that wolves will come and scatter the sheep, but the Lord can use this for his honor and glory. Those scattered can minister to, and be ministered by, newly met believers.

Rhett was convicted not to follow Deo, Julian, and Cary's examples of talking unfairly or poorly behind others' backs and saying cruel or untrue things, judging another's soul. It was hard to be careful and to control the emotions. It is important to honor the Lord in conduct and be gracious, even in a time of hurt.

The leaven of the Pharisees' began with a slight focus on the external appearance in the Assemblies, with suggested standards. The standards became unstated rules, which in turn bred more rules. This started an avalanche of a seemingly endless supply of rules to keep people in line and protect them from their old natures. Once these Christians put their faith in the rules, they turned away from the Lord and the Spirit of Truth, and embraced a religion organized and designed by mere humans. They sought the leader's approval with their rule following.

This focus on rules breeds legalism and merciless harshness which co-exists with looking religious to other people. Once this structure is allowed to be installed, then new leaders rising up from within their group, following basic instincts of wanting approval from humans rather than God, view the system as a vehicle to control others. With charisma they engineer doctrinal dogmas and leadership positions to satisfy their own needs of control and approval, taking it to the next level.

Unfeigned and refreshing Bible studies in homes openly and honestly seeking the Lord's will, was slowly taken away and replaced by lengthy and repetitious propaganda sessions. The weaker the doctrine, the more it needed to be repeated to strengthen the grip of control over the 'flock'. The consequently larger group over the years called for more organization, more control to keep it together, and more structure, all done in the name of Unity, spiraling inward and downward, producing weak and fearful Christians who no longer were studying for themselves, making them easier to control and manipulate. The more aggressive people took control and others complacently followed along. More and more time was ever so gradually spent in self-absorbing problems within the group.

The frequent problems arising created a need for developing doctrines to end disputes, and a need for slowly increasing the level of authority of a few prominent leaders to keep the peace and the group together. Markings, shunnings, public humiliations, and rebukings were contrived to help prevent fragmenting and loss of relationships by creating fear in leaving so the members would stay and obey.

As the size of the group increases, the inward and downward spiral toward the controlling leaders continues, due to the lack of a personal relationship with Jesus Christ.

The definition of unity changed as the group got more and more structured. Unity started with being one in Christ, and ended in conformity with leaders. Being one in Christ recognizes and approves of all other moral worldwide believers. Conformity just approves of those who agree with the dictates of their group.

Christians who began with personal Bible studies led by the Holy Spirit, rejoiced in their new life in Christ and were motivated by a love of wanting to be with God's people. For them, ministry was a verb, something they participated in, something they all should do.

People who subsequently grew up in this environment were considered right with God if they believed the Assemblies' doctrines.

Many years later came a new generation, who were considered right with God if they obeyed the religious authorities in the Assemblies. Importance was placed on the human leadership rather than what the Bible teaches. For them, Ministry was a noun, something a Preacher was and did for them as they sat, listened, and obeyed.

Young people who grow up with committed parents can simply parrot good behavior to get good fruit, like successful marriages, but not ever develop an intimate relationship with Christ. The older people are satisfied with the young people who obey time honored standards of conduct. But the young people can grow up to be Pharisees. They are outwardly moral, but lack mercy, humility, and compassion, finding solace in their own purity and success in following the dictates, and getting the approval of, their human leaders. The new arrivals, judging themselves by the conscience of others, are chicken to challenge old dogma's built around the charisma and judgment calls of past leaders from long ago, long after time changed past circumstances.

After leaving, love became a primary motivator again, instead of fear. Love is stronger than fear. There is recovery. God is greater than mind control. The Lord in Christians is greater than being crushed by cultic tactics to control. From what they had been told by others who had gone through similar situations, the healing could go on for several years.

Now there was mercy and grace instead of legalistic robotic rule following. Micah in chapter 6 said, "What does the Lord require of you but to love mercy, to do rightly, and walk humbly with your God?"

It is tempting to believe that leaders who have great speaking ability, who deeply understand the Bible and have great faith that penetrates all areas of their lives, who make great personal self-sacrificing efforts to help poor people, are also godly leaders who should be followed. But they can lack love, and their efforts be considered nothing in the eyes of God. There are ten thousand instructors of Christ, but not many fathers. Most teachers have a heart of an instructor, but few have the loving heart of a father.

When Stephen was stoned by religious people who were filled with self-righteous indignation, he prayed for God to be merciful, and not judge those men for the evil they inflicted.

It is easy to self-promote when evil is seen in others, and become proud and condemning in newfound knowledge. But it is wrong to be rude and self-serving. Love doesn't lash back in anger or think evil of others. To have Grace is to have undeserved goodness towards others who have wronged us. Christians shouldn't let bitterness, hate and anger take a foothold, speaking evil of those who have wronged them. It is a device and snare of Satan to not forgive.

Christians should rather walk in mercy, compassion, and love. What is love? Love is patient, love is kind, love is gentle. True Christian love is being sad with the sin in others, and glad when others see the truth. Love never fails.

I waited patiently for the Lord
And He inclined to me
And heard my cry
He also brought me up out of a horrible pit
Out of the miry clay
And set my feet upon a rock
And established my steps
He has put a new song in my mouth —
Praise to our God
Many will see it and fear
And will trust in the Lord

- King David in Psalms 40 -

22·

O Lord my God, if I have done this
If there is iniquity in my hands
If I have repaid evil to him who was at peace with me
Or have plundered my enemy without cause
Let the enemy pursue me and overtake me
Yes, let him trample my life to the earth
And lay my honor in the dust

David in Psalms 7, when he heard what Cush said

The Mark

People who had gotten marked over his lifetime had always caused a lot of problems, as far as Rhett knew.

Some of them created mayhem for years, stirring up the Assemblies by being very contentious, promoting disputed doctrine, or being immoral.

There were a lot of imprinted feelings with the markings. People were marked, and if they did come back to an Assembly meeting they were asked to sit in back and leave right afterwards. Nobody was really supposed to shake their hand, although some did. The default was to assume they were wrong and the marking proper.

Usually the marked people just left with their families and were never contacted again. They just disappeared, mostly. Jar was an exception. Rhett sometimes heard of them from time to time and was vaguely interested. The marked men, and sometimes women, were usually spoken poorly of in the rumors associated with them. Rhett never really knew if they were true, and nobody could follow up with them since the people were marked.

The feeling was, since they were marked it didn't really matter what was said of them. The very fact they had left made them wrong, and it had to be justified that those who were marked really were bad. It made the survivors all feel better about themselves. Some who were marked really did have obvious moral sin or were very argumentive. But many did not, just being marked for a contention with the leaders over a doctrine, or for not agreeing to go along with somebody else's marking.

The fear of being marked weighed heavily. He expected to be marked after he sent his First Appeal. He was very careful of the wording, getting counsel and critique from many others to not give any basis for a marking. He knew Deo Trophy and his followers could latch onto one or two items, blow it out of proportion, or simply claim he said many false statements, paint Rhett with the broad brush of divisiveness, and dismiss him as a heretic.

Rhett was just thankful he hadn't wound up as some older men and women who were being held hostage by their relationships with their grown and married children. There is nothing like parents having grown kids permanently damaged by a dishonest leader to convince them of the problem.

His own wife and children were well down the road of recovery, forming new friendships and renewing old ones. No longer were the peaceful meadows of their relationships subject to a bulldozing by disapproving leaders, and asphalted over by Orderly Following.

If Deo was able to pull off marking several ministers who opposed him, then Rhett knew he wouldn't pose much of a problem. The same fate that befell them would fall on him. It was just a matter of time. But there was no marking after Rhett's First Appeal, or after his Second Appeal, or even after his Third Appeal which contained two witness statements confirming Deo's dishonesty.

Rhett began to feel a little superhuman; maybe Cary Murdock and Julian Petros wouldn't mark him. The feeling was short-lived.

During a quiet winter evening in November of 2009, nine months after he left, Rhett was playing a game of chess with his twelve year old son when the phone rang. It was Cary Murdock. He said he was on a speaker-phone at his home with Julian Petros and George Taylor. Cary said they wanted to sit down with Rhett in person to answer his questions and address his concerns. There was no wanting to discuss it to see what the truth was or work it out, no humility, but just to convince Rhett they were right.

Rhett began to pray, earnestly asking the Lord to help him answer questions and ask questions over the next few hours. Sabrina was praying also. Rhett felt the Lord's presence and help in the emotionally riddled debate, keeping his voice clear and controlled. Sabrina felt he came across too strong once, briefly.

Cary accused Rhett of his "sneaky recording" of their January 2009 local leadership meeting.

Rhett reminded Cary of what happened: Tim Mervin said publicly in his area, Southern California, that a leader in Virginia, not saying any names, had said in January, 2009, "It was said in Virginia that Peter Waters, Bach Jude and I have sinned. They say you all, and you younger couples, are no longer accountable to us and it relieves you to follow us. If anybody doesn't want to be here you are free to leave."

Cary called Tim and had said it wasn't true, no leader in Virginia had said that, even though it was Cary who had been the one. Tim asked Cary if Cary had mentioned any of the California ministers by name publicly, but Cary was silent. So a few people in Tim's area who were loyal to Deo were spreading it around that Tim wasn't telling the truth, since Cary had proved Tim to be wrong. Cary wanted Tim to apologize for his inaccurate report.

Rhett was thoroughly irritated when he heard of this, and produced a twenty minute segment in full context to prove that Cary had not told the truth to Tim. The recording proved Cary had said people should not be following Tim in his own area, and Cary had said their names multiple times, and also publicly.

Rhett had e-mailed the recording of the meeting to two people since Tim had a hard time using computers, and it cleared up who had told the truth. The e-mail attachment with the recording was passed around afterwards. People wanted to hear it for themselves.

Rhett pointed out three people confirmed Cary had said, "somebody secretly recorded one of our local leadership meetings and passed it all over the place. It caused a lot of damage and was taken out of context."

"Cary," said Rhett, "what you conveyed to them was a lot different than the truth, and that recording *was* in full context!"

Before Rhett left in March of 2009, Cary insisted nobody else could be at any meeting with Rhett except the three leaders in Richmond Leadership. Cary now offered to also have three of Rhett's neighbors at the requested meeting, including Mark Shifflett. Rhett had reason to believe they had been thoroughly convinced over the last several months that Rhett was wrong.

Rhett declined, stating if they released the recording of the November 2008 Texas Leadership meeting in which they had all agreed to put James back in ministry in the near future, and lift the markings on the California leaders, then this would show an effort on their part to want to fix things and work together.

Cary declined. Maybe it was because Deo Trophy had apologized in the Texas meeting to James Stark, something most people knew nothing of in Virginia. Rhett said he would be glad to consider anything they sent him in writing but he did not want to have a meeting. George Taylor informed Rhett, "This is your first admonishment."

They didn't ever send him anything in writing.

That December Calvin Hobkins rented a large beach house near Nags Head with several families who had left the Assemblies. The time was spent in quiet reflection, beach walks, visiting, rehashing old pains, and establishing new friendships. As Rhett and Sabrina traveled the four hour trip home, they both agreed this was the best December retreat ever, and felt the presence of the Holy Spirit working in their little group. It was a time of rejuvenation and refreshment, and very peaceful.

Justin Ranger, Sabrina's brother who had moved out to Virginia in 2000, came with his family. Justin told Rhett that Julian Petros talked to him the week before.

"What did you guys talk about?" asked Rhett.

"You mainly. Julian talked a few hours about you," said Justin.

"I assume it wasn't favorable to me," said Rhett.

"You're right," replied Justin.

"It doesn't surprise me. When Julian spent all those hours running down James Stark and those other leaders, I knew he would do it to me later on. And, I'll bet he'll do it to you too if you leave the Charlottesville Assembly," said Rhett.

"He said he's seen your little rabbit tracks around."

"Better then leaving wolf tracks," said Rhett, "if he said he saw my wolf tracks around then that would bother me."

The next few months were uneventful, except for a warning that a marking letter was coming his way.

The marking letter finally came in the middle of March of 2010, sent by Julian Petros. It was signed by almost every man in the Richmond Assembly, including Rhett's previously close and personal friends. Even Mark Shifflett and Toby Tait signed it. There were only three people who didn't sign, one of them being Albert Murdock, Cary Murdock's father. All of the accusations were mostly true: Rhett had said Julian lied, he sent out statements showing Deo Trophy was dishonest, and Rhett did send a man an e-mail, after he inquired several times why Rhett had left, that Cary made some untrue public statements, and had 'trashed' the California ministers publicly.

Rhett had said these things, but thought he had been careful about saying Julian lied, even though Julian admitted to what was said. The letter said, "You should have allowed Julian to correct your mind." The marking letter accused him of telling falsehoods, and was read in at least one other Assembly besides Richmond.

Rhett poured twenty hours over the next three days into a three page document with detailed proof he had told the truth, and e-mailed it out to a few hundred friends. He entreated them for a response, if he had said something inappropriate about Julian he wanted to apologize for it.

They never responded.

The best defense is a good offense, and the truth tends to work with you rather than against you over time, thought Rhett.

Rhett complained to his dad about it, "Why did they mark me a year after I had left, and months after my last e-mail in which I stated it was my last attempt?"

Mycroft said, "Remember the plane that was mysteriously destroyed over the Atlantic after leaving New York in 1996? The FBI investigation was shut down sixteen months afterwards. Most people didn't question the vague investigation, they forgot about flight 800 due to other things happening in their lives. Nobody will ever know if the Navy was involved in a missile test or not. The memory of most people lasts about one year."

"Deo said they closed that investigation for a reason."

Randy and Rosie Greens came out to Charlottesville to visit shortly after Rhett's marking. Rosie, Rhett's younger sister, was allowed to come over with her kids while Rhett was at work so the cousins could play, and the kids thoroughly enjoyed it. Rosie was one of Sabrina's best friends from childhood, and Sabrina was anxious their relationship could be severed over this.

When Rosie was little, Rhett would gently pull her curls to see them spring back into shape. They were really pretty. Rosie didn't mind, she had a really easy going personality.

Rosie's blond springing curls had grown into long brown hair as she got older, and her faith grew too, drawing strength from the Lord as she regularly read her Bible.

Randy visited Julian Petros and Hobbs Madison, Jarvo's younger thirty-three year old brother. Randy didn't want to see Rhett since he was marked.

Hobbs had his own concerns and had stopped going to the Charlottesville Assembly with his family. He was also spending time with his father, Jar, again.

Randy hoped to encourage Hobbs and others during the visit. Randy was having his own concerns about Orderly Following, and had talked to Byron and Deo about it before his trip.

Hobbs was worried he might do something to terminate his relationship with Randy, and pondered whether to have his wife and daughters wear pants while Randy and Rosie were out visiting. It was cold, very cold, and the wind chill on their hill next to Jar's house made pants practical, but then Randy might be offended. Hobbs wanted to avoid a conflict.

Hobbs prayed, *Lord, help me to do your will and not be an offense to Randy when he is out visiting.*

Randy needed to go to his brother's home a mile away, so Hobbs offered to drive Randy over in his four wheel drive SUV with chains. It was cold and gusty that afternoon.

As they briefly drove on the main road, sloughing through the snow flurries, there was Wilma, Hobb's neighbor, out on the road. She kept one hand down to keep the wind from whipping up her knee-length pink skirt. Wilma had nothing to do with the Assemblies, she didn't even know about them.

Hobbs rolled to a stop and rolled down the window on Randy's side. A blast of cold air blew in. Wilma stood looking in at them, a picture of misery.

"Wilma, you need some help?" asked Hobbs.

"Well, yes, my car is stuck," said Wilma, dejectedly looking down at the snow, eyes tearing.

"Let me get a chain on it and I'll get you unstuck. You doing okay?" asked Hobbs.

Wilma looked up, and after a glance at Randy told Hobbs, "Well, actually I'm not okay! I'm driving to work and I get stuck and I need to work out in this cold today making deliveries. I'm going to this church in Richmond where they will shun me if I don't wear a skirt, so I'm looking for another church but if I leave that church now I'll lose my friends because they will all shun me when I leave. My husband left me, and my son is doing drugs, so I need my friends. So, honestly, to answer your question, I'm not doing okay!"

Randy sat watching, intent on her words, deep in his own thoughts.

"You could come over to our house some evening and just hang out with my family," said Hobbs.

"Well, thanks for the offer," said Wilma.

After Randy got back to California he began to see through the abusive authority even more as he made questioning phone calls, following up on what was told him, and his eyes were opened. Within a few months he was back in contact with Rhett, much to Rhett's relief.

It was so nice having his two brother-in-laws back with him!

It was Mars Thomas from Northern Virginia whose two sons had married Calvin Hobkins' daughters. He had been politically run out of his own church as a minister long ago, and this helped him see through Deo's politics. He was able to get out of the Assemblies with two of his three sons, the two who married Calvin's daughters.

He sent this e-mail:

Rhett Stuart,

The Bible teaches that God created and ordained the family. The family is the building block for every nation, destroy the family and the nation will fall as well.

The family is also the building block of the Church, the Body of Christ; destroy the family and you destroy the Church. It is Satan's desire to destroy that which God has ordained; it is the spirit of antichrist that seeks to destroy the foundation of godly influence and structure in God's plan for His people. The Bible tells us the spirit of antichrist was alive and well during the time of the apostles and we know it is even stronger now as we approach the end time.

Don't think it strange that there are ministers crept in unawares, who are influenced by this spirit of destruction and division. They have taught a false doctrine of "markings" that have perverted the scripture, by taking the teaching farther than the scriptures intended. They have embraced the apostate teaching of "excommunication." This doctrine sets fear in the lives of family members, a fear that gives control to the leadership, fear of being excommunicated if you don't agree or submit to leadership. Those who have been marked in this way have been separated from their loved ones and families have been destroyed and divided just as Satan intended. This is the antichrist teaching that destroys families and divides the Church which is Christ's body.

Any preacher that embraces and practices this teaching is the enemy of Jesus Christ and His Church. They are antichrist, the only way they can maintain their power is to have followers that yield to their teaching, take away the followers and their power is gone. This is what we have done in our family by separating from this ungodly leadership; we take away their power over us.

I believe if many in the assembly knew they could escape with their families intact, many more would leave the oppressive leadership and be free from the enslavement of the antichrist belief system.

If you have been marked "excommunicated" from the assembly count yourself happy if you left with your family intact. You are not alone, many have been persecuted for standing against the unscrupulous religious leaders of their generation and God became a father to them as they came out from among them and were separated either voluntarily or involuntarily. May we be the leaders of our home as Christ intended. The leadership of the Body of Christ is to build up the home not tear it apart as these do.

No matter of E-mails or writings will change the minds of people who are willing to follow these leaders to their own destruction, it will take divine deliverance for some to escape from this snare, it has always been the remnant, the few who have followed Christ no matter what the cost and Christ knows who they are. You have not been marked but delivered from evil men. Thank God for your deliverance and you are welcome in our fellowship anytime. Stand strong and firm in Christ.

Your brother in Christ, Mars Thomas

After Rhett's marking, he felted released. The fear of it no longer hung over his head, wondering when it would come. Markings, as the Assemblies did them, had a lot of deep seated fear loaded into them due to the totality of the shunning. This fear kept people in line and from questioning leadership.

The Pharisees kept people in line like this by threatening to cast any Jews out of the Temple who confessed Jesus. The Jews were their own isolated group, shut off from the outside world. They didn't even talk to the Samaritans, treasured social standing and relationships would be lost if they were cast out. There was nowhere else to go. The cast out Jews couldn't associate much with the Gentiles, or even the Samaritans. Some of their friends likely retained some discretionary contact, but there was probably widespread contempt, just as there was contempt for anybody marked by leaders of the Assemblies. The contempt was driven by fears of losing social status for both men and women.

Some leaders have reputations for tearing apart and severing relationships, and some leaders earn a good name in helping to heal and build relationships. The wise woman from Tekoa told King David —

"We will eventually die like water spilled on the ground, which can't be put back in the jar. Yet, God does not take away a life; but He devises ways so His banished ones are not separated from Him."

Mercy triumphs over justice.

Rhett and Sabrina were almost completely disconnected from their past life and friends. There were many in California they could visit but they were in California, 2700 miles away. Laura, Rhett's sister, introduced them to the home school co-op in Charlottesville, providing some much needed local friends. Slowly and surely they met new people, made new friends, and the Lord gave them peace as the Holy Spirit comforted them.

As their family slowly healed they got their sense of humor back. Rhett's daughter wrote a paper as part of her school work after her fifteenth birthday:

Fifteen means I'll be learning how to drive in six months. That will scare every member of our family, including me! It's also predicted that by the time it's over we'll all have very unhealthy hearts, on account of skipping so many beats. That's only one of our organs under hazard!

Rhett hadn't realized what a wallop his headship had taken, sitting under two lectures a week, sings, and visiting late after meetings. It was disruptive to a normal family life; it had been all about what the leaders wanted. The leaders publicly dictated what they should do and everybody willingly did it. Now Rhett was truly leading his family, asking the Lord for help and guidance. There was the Bible, friends, and godly older people in California to get counsel from. Those who biblically teach and set a good example should be respected, and share in the fruit of our lives as we grow in Christ. But no longer was there a forced system of rules and regulations. Rule keeping leads to more and more rules, "The person who keeps rules continues to live by them."

Deo's leaders still denied there was such a system, and that was part of the hypocrisy. Regardless if these leaders denied their existence, the rules were in place. Unwritten rules, with consequences for not following them.

It had all started with the leaders preaching public judgment calls on specific clothing and lifestyle choices based on Biblical applications. The 1960's and 1970's had presented some serious challenges for the American Christian family, and there was preaching that rose up to meet those challenges.

But over time this type of preaching, combined with peer pressure among followers wanting the leader's approval, and fear of indirect or direct public rebuke from the leaders for not conforming, morphed into a system of rules that was regarded with the same importance as scripture. Judgment calls by leaders for good reasons which produced good fruit, evolved from standards into rigid rules with consequences for disobedience. But the circumstances that instigated the original preaching had changed.

Ministers originally tried to help by pointing out the bad consequences of some activities that could turn Christians away from the Lord and create problems for their families. But these warnings evolved into a system of rules that easily turned Christians away from the Lord as the leaders attempted to mediate with God for them, and it created lots of problems for families.

Doing the right thing to please the Lord evolved into doing things to please the leaders. The parents let their rights to decide things for their own families slowly dwindle away until it was actually regarded as a bad thing.

Galatians teaches us to not get caught up with rules and regulations that so easily morph into scripture. The Jews had the best system of rules the world has ever seen, designed by God. God doesn't need a system of rules anymore as a tutor to bring us to Christ; we are right with God by faith. Living by rules is weak and inferior to living by faith; it's bondage.

Those who intentionally try to create rules for us to live by are trying to look good to others, and they don't want to be persecuted for Christ. They lack the courage to have a personal relationship based on simple faith in God. Sometimes they use flattery and manipulation, but their motives are wicked when they want to point Christians away from God's undeserved goodness, His Grace, and herd Christians toward themselves. They want to feel good and boast about all the people they control, those who obey them! But this is loathsome to our jealous God!

There are always false teachers with charisma trying to impersonate the Holy Spirit by creating rules and systems of their own making, fabricated by their own understanding.   Having unbiblical control over others makes these 'ministers of self righteousness' feel important, as they get their approval from men, rather than God. The Pharisees wanted this same approval, and it motivated them to crucify Jesus. Since Jesus threatened their position and approval from the people, they took Him out with false accusations and political pressure. The Pharisees claimed God was backing them up and they had the authority to push through the Son of God's crucifixion.

It's easy to adapt a system of rules and then claim we are right with God when we follow them. But it just doesn't work that way! And it doesn't matter if a leader claims otherwise. It's wrong to be motivated by the conscience of others, what really matters is what God thinks!

The only thing Christians have to boast of is Jesus Christ. Nothing we do comes anywhere close to that! It isn't what we Christians are doing but what God is doing! And God is creating completely new lives in His Christians! This is the Rock we need to build on!

He is the one who died for the sins of the world, and we become totally new by having faith in Him. The old nature was crucified when Christ is accepted, so Christians have a new life to live, and it's the Holy Spirit who teaches us how! We can't get a good relationship with God by keeping rules, but by having faith. God wants a personal relationship with us, through Christ! We need to deeply and intimately embrace what God really wants for us, and seek His will in how we conduct our lives.

It is resisting God to be Worldly by living a life of rule keeping, and also resisting God to be Worldly by living a life of selfish pleasure. Some sin is the filthiness of the flesh, like the prodigal son, and the sin is obvious from the outside. And others so subtly sin inside, in their attitude and pride, by allowing the filthiness of the spirit to motivate them. Like the older son who stayed home and did what was right but lacked mercy and forgiveness. Jesus told the story of the prodigal son to the Pharisees, and His main point was the attitude of the older brother towards his prodigal brother. The Pharisees were like the older son who was unmerciful and lacked grace. Their spirits were filthy with self-righteousness.

Self-righteously disputing over rules by running others down who don't obey leads to Christian cannibalism. Living for the Lord in freedom, motivated by the Holy Spirit, helps Christians avoid this. God is not fooled; He knows when Christians are just robotically following rules of human origin, and worshiping a human created system to get God's approval.

Some become suspicious about not living by a system of rules. It sounds so liberal, like Christians can do anything they want? No rules to go by, outside of God's word? Christians shouldn't use their freedom as an excuse to do whatever they want, but to seek the will of the Lord. Those who follow their own desires hurt their own personal relationship with the Lord because the Holy Spirit is then being resisted.

There are always those who need help with their lives, marriage and family; they need the company of those who have stable marriages and families. Older respectable people who lead by the example set with their own personal lives are very helpful for younger Christians needing guidance. And some of these are pastors and teachers who help prepare other Christians to minister and help others to be strong in their faith, so they won't stumble over the trickery of false doctrine, and cunning craftiness of deceitful scheming.

It's God who allows Christians to grow and have fruit, to minister and help others. God just wants us to walk with Him in a heart-to-heart relationship. The ministry of helping others starts with those we are closest to. All Christians should truly, and only, boast of Christ and what God is doing.

It is so pleasant to have a renewed deep personal relationship with Jesus Christ, and the peace it brings as we walk with Him and do his will.

The fear of the Lord is clean, enduring forever
The judgments of the Lord are true and righteous altogether
More to be desired are they than gold
Yes, than much fine gold

Sweeter also than honey and the honeycomb
Moreover by them Your servant is warned
And in keeping them there is great reward

Who can understand his errors?
Cleanse me from secret faults

Keep back Your servant also from presumptuous sins
Let them not have dominion over me
Then I shall be blameless
And I shall be innocent of great transgression

Let the words of my mouth and the meditation of my heart
Be acceptable in Your sight
O Lord, my strength and my Redeemer

- King David in Psalms 19 -

References

Chapter 3: Quotes from Maurice Johnson from mauricejohnsonarchives.com

Chapter 12: Combatting Cult Mind Control by Steve Hassan (Vermont, Park Street Press, 1990)

Chapter 12: Snapping by Flo Conway and Jim Siegelman (New York, Stillpoint Press, Inc ,2005)

Chapter 12: The Future of Immortality and Other Essays for a Nuclear Age by Robert J Lifton (New York , Basic Books, 1987)

Pages 147, 195: The Prince by Niccolo Machiavelli, paraphrasing by Rhett Stuart.

Holy Bible, KVJ, NKJV (Thomas Nelson Inc), paraphrasing by Rhett Stuart

Chapter 17: *Some of the Sociopath traits are based on the psychopathy checklists of Dr. Hervey M. Cleckley and Dr. Robert Hare. The Hare Psychopathy Checklist-Revised (PCL) is a psycho-diagnostic tool devised by Robert Hare to assess the main characteristics of psychopathic behavior, based in part on Dr. Cleckley's work.

Recommended Reading

The Pilgrim Church by E.H. Broadbent
Obedience to Authority by Stanley Milgram
Crisis of Conscience by Raymond Franz
The Bible (of course!)

CPSIA information can be obtained
at www.ICGtesting.com
Printed in the USA
LVHW092139270321
682694LV00017B/131

9 780982 954706